THE SAUSAGE REBELLION

Map of Mexico City, c. 1910. Drawn by the author.

CHORIZOS Y CHORIZONES

"Chorizos y Chorizones" (Chorizos and big weenies). El Pinche (literally, the scullery, but also a derogatory slang term) and the Mexican pueblo hold a string of sausages representing the military, foreigners, bankers, temperance (in the form of an old woman), the clergy, and elite politicians. Ironically, for a nationalist cartoon, the pinche wields a menacing knife while sporting a French chef's toque. From *El Pinche*, June 9, 1904. Courtesy of the Benson Latin American Collection, University of Texas at Austin.

THE SAUSAGE REBELLION

Public Health, Private Enterprise,
and Meat in Mexico City,
1890–1917

JEFFREY M. PILCHER

University of New Mexico Press
ALBUQUERQUE

PRINTED IN THE UNITED STATES OF AMERICA

YEAR   PRINTING
10 09 08 07 06   1 2 3 4 5

ISBN-13: 978-0-8263-3796-2 (pbk.)
ISBN-10: 0-8263-3796-1 (pbk.)

Library of Congress Cataloging-in-Publication Data

Pilcher, Jeffrey M., 1965–
  The sausage rebellion : public health, private enterprise, and meat in
Mexico City, 1890–1917 / Jeffrey M. Pilcher.
      p. cm.
  Includes bibliographical references and index.
  ISBN 0-8263-3796-1 (pbk. : alk. paper)
    1. Meat industry and trade—Mexico—Mexico City—History.
  2. Meat industry and trade—Political aspects—Mexico—Mexico City.
  3. Meat industry and trade—Mexico—Mexico City—State supervision.
  4. Meat industry and trade—Government policy—Mexico—Mexico City.
  I. Title.
  HD9424.M6M496 2006
  338.1'76'009725309041—dc22
                              2005022340

Book design and composition by Damien Shay
Body type is Columbus 10.5/14
Display is Caslon Antique

TO
FREDERICK AND
KIM PILCHER

CONTENTS

LIST OF ILLUSTRATIONS

PREFACE

Counting sheep has a long and honorable lineage in Mexican historiography, dating back to the renowned traveler Alexander von Humboldt and to the hacienda studies of François Chevalier. The heroic generation of social historians refined the science of sheep counting in the 1970s, most notably, through the works of Charles Harris and the seminar on the hacienda directed by Enrique Semo at the Instituto Nacional de Antropología e Historia. More recently, innovative studies by Elinor Melville and Richard Salvucci have situated sheep in the emerging fields of environmental history and the new economic history, so it was only a matter of time before cultural historians began to inquire into the consumption of mutton. In this book I hope to show that consumer preferences had a critical role in the political, economic, and social history of the Porfirian meatpacking industry. Moreover, for those who felt that I may have romanticized Mexican popular cuisine in an earlier work, the present study offers a glimpse of the dark underside of urban provisioning.

As always, I have relied on the kindness of archivists and librarians. In Mexico, I am deeply grateful to Victor Nava, who shared his vast culinary library, and to Filiberto Hernández, who gave me a tour of the old slaughterhouse at Azcapotzalco. Meat inspectors Javier Arzate and Laura Varinia Muñoz Huerta patiently explained their work and allowed me access to valuable documents. My greatest archival debt is to the staff of the Archivo Histórico de la Ciudad de México, and particularly to Francisco Arias, who cheerfully brought me dusty volumes for ten years. I would also like to thank the staff of the Biblioteca Miguel Lerdo de Tejada, the Hemeroteca Nacional, the Archivo Porfirio Díaz, the Centro de Estudios de Historia de México, Condumex, the Archivo General de Notarias del D.F., the Archivo General de la Nación, and El Colegio de Michoacán. In the United States, I took great pleasure in working at the National Archives and Record Administration in Suitland, Maryland, the Latin American Collection at Tulane University, the Rockefeller Foundation archives, the Bancroft Library at the University of California, Berkeley, the Special Collections at the University of Texas, El Paso, and particularly Daniels Library at The Citadel. The Citadel Foundation generously supported the research by providing ten years of annual travel grants and a year-long sabbatical to write up the results. I also benefited from travel grants from the Rockefeller Archives and from the Andrew Mellon Foundation to work at Tulane University.

Although I cannot record everyone who contributed to my work, I do want to single out a few exceptional colleagues and friends. This book, like so much else, grew out of a dissertation directed by Bill Beezley, and his influence is apparent on every page. John Hart served as a model of archival thoroughness and sage advising. Mark Wasserman shared archival materials on the Terrazas clan, offered valuable suggestions for the manuscript, and wrote a much appreciated letter at a critical moment. My coauthors of an article, Sydney Watts and Roger Horowitz, worked for more than three years to sharpen my understanding of the butcher trades; who knows how much better this book would have been if the article had dragged on even longer? Allen Wells, Steven Topik, and the anonymous reader for the University of New Mexico Press also offered many thoughtful suggestions for improving the manuscript. A number of fellow researchers in Mexico offered support, guidance, and friendship, especially Linda Arnold, Rob Buffington, Steven Bunker, Barry Carr, Linda Curcio-Nagy, Matt Esposito, James Garza, Martín González de la Vara, Arturo Grunstein, Glen Kuecker, Victor Macías, John Mraz, Ariel Rodríguez Kuri, Ray Sadler, and Drew Wood. My friends and colleagues in Charleston have made the past decade extremely rewarding, and I salute them one last time. In particular, Sensei Alan Jackson insightfully reconstructed Porfirian blueprints and taught me many valuable lessons for life. David Holtby, Lyman Johnson, and the skilled staff of the University of New Mexico Press performed, yet again, the miracle of turning a disjointed manuscript into an attractive volume.

Finally, I thank Donna Gabaccia, who was probably happy to keep this project at a distance for all those years. She helped me to find a voice at a difficult moment in an otherwise wonderful year in Cambridge. Now that the commute is finally ending, she can tuck the butchers away on the shelf alongside the monkey and assorted other beasts.

INTRODUCTION

The Original "Fresh Mex"

"Meat fresh-killed this morning?" shouts the meat man.
"If not, I don't want it," says Concha to the butcher.
"Do you question the freshness and fatness of my meat?" banters the butcher.
"Question?" grunts Concha. "Why should I question one
whose tricks I know by experience?"
"Oh come, come, my Red Rose," chuckles the butcher, "do you not receive
from my shop chickens that melt in the pan they are so tender?
Steaks that cannot—"
"Cannot be chewed," Concha finishes the sentence.[1]

———

This lively exchange between the housekeeper Concha and her local butcher could seemingly have taken place anywhere at any time. Both the flirtatious sales pitch of the vendor and the sharp replies of the customer have been repeated in countless marketplaces, probably since the Neolithic era. The merchant naturally sought to maximize the return on his highly perishable stock of meat, while the shopper worried that she might get swindled into paying for an old and unwholesome cut. Their adversarial or perhaps mutually respectful relationship constitutes a crucial link in the cycle of urban provisioning, but like so much of the ephemera of everyday life, it usually leaves little record for the social historian. Nevertheless, this particular conversation, recorded in Mexico in 1946, holds a key to understanding the history of the country's meat supply. The cultural preference for freshly slaughtered meat expressed by Concha and other Mexicans diametrically opposed the industrial technology of refrigerated meatpacking, which was developed in Chicago in the final third of the nineteenth century and introduced to Mexico a few decades later. Advocates of capitalism tout the success of corporations in satisfying consumer desires, but the sausage rebellion was,

1

in part, a struggle of Mexican shoppers, who wished to preserve their access to freshly slaughtered meat against foreign businessmen seeking to change those tastes to conform to the new technology.

Individual shoppers like Concha generally have little overt influence on economic structures, but the rise of centralized meatpacking in Mexico also faced militant opposition from her anonymous butcher and his fellow tradesmen. The process of industrialization incited fierce resistance from craftsmen such as the Luddites, who smashed textile mills in nineteenth-century England. These struggles did not stop the advance of mechanization but did allow labor to negotiate the terms of change, a conflict dramatized by Upton Sinclair's classic 1906 novel, *The Jungle*, about Chicago packinghouse workers.[2] Giant meatpacking corporations in the United States used the cost advantage of refrigerated railroad shipping to drive independent butchers out of business, transforming them into factory workers, or at best distributors of products manufactured centrally. Refrigerated technology arrived in Mexico in the carpetbag of businessman John W. DeKay, whose shady past in Chicago's packinghouses was matched only by the balance-sheet fictions of his Canadian banker, George I. Ham. Although usually a divisive lot, Mexican slaughterhouse workers, livestock merchants, and retail butchers set aside their internal rivalries during the sausage rebellion in order to confront the meatpacking machinations of Ham and DeKay.

The government of Porfirio Díaz (1876–1911) played a crucial but far from consistent role in mediating conflicts between shoppers, butchers, and meatpackers. During the colonial period, municipal officials had operated with a clear mandate to regulate the sale of meat based on medieval Catholic beliefs about the sinfulness of humanity and the religious principle of a moral economy. Nineteenth-century liberal ideology challenged this tradition of state oversight by viewing the pursuit of self-interest not as a threat to society but rather as the source of material abundance. Of course, the physical reality of putrid meat could quickly silence abstract claims about property rights and market efficiency. Nevertheless, translating such concerns into an effective regulatory regime proved difficult. In Mexico City, wealthy livestock merchants preserved their autonomy by taking advantage of jurisdictional and political conflicts between the elected city council and the Federal District government. Moreover, the uneven development of scientific knowledge only gradually allowed medical officials to reclaim authority over the market-place in the interests of public health. Indeed, the medical profession still struggled to assert its disinterested expertise at the end of the nineteenth century, despite the faith in modern technology expressed by the Porfirian administrative elite, who were known as *científicos* (scientific ones). Political conflicts between rival elite factions and the favor given to imported capital further compromised the actions of the Mexican state during this era of incipient industrialization.

The sausage rebellion represented a battle by local officials, butchers, and consumers to retain control over the Mexico City meat supply against the foreign meatpacker DeKay and his patrons within the Porfirian regime. During the first decade of the century, the Díaz dictatorship had steadily concentrated power in the federal government and in the hands of provincial allies such as the Terrazas-Creel clan of Chihuahua. The Mexico City slaughterhouse thus became one of the patronage favors handed out first to the Terrazas, powerful cattle barons in their own right, and then to DeKay. Confronted with these threats, proletarian slaughter-house workers, petty bourgeois retailers, and wealthy livestock merchants forged a cross-class alliance that also counted on the tacit support of consumers, whose preferences were ignored by the new company, and of elected city officials, who had lost power to Porfirian centralization. In the waning days of the Díaz dictatorship, the butchers waged a war against the meatpackers, carrying out strikes, industrial sabotage, and even shop floor attempts on the lives of the foreign managers. As the Porfirian government collapsed in the Revolution of 1910, the butchers succeeded in defeating the foreign company and restoring their traditional craft—unfortunately including their traditional methods for cheating shoppers like Concha.

Despite being fought out against the epic backdrop of the Revolution of 1910, the sausage rebellion ultimately brought authoritarian control rather than social revolution to the Mexico City meat supply. Like many other trades during the early years of Porfirian industrialization, slaughterhouse workers and retail butchers began to assert their class interests and reject the paternalistic control of labor exerted by wealthy livestock merchants for much of the nineteenth century. The sausage rebellion diverted this incipient union movement into a nationalist crusade dominated by these powerful merchants against the common threat of foreign meatpackers. Conflicts resurfaced in the 1920s, but by that time, corrupt, state-controlled labor confederations had developed effective mechanisms for stifling union democracy. Mexican consumer movements were likewise drawn into the authoritarian, corporatist government through the creation of an elaborate welfare bureaucracy around mid-century. Yet this post-revolutionary version of moral economy, like the colonial state before it, proved graft-ridden, inefficient, and unable to assure working-class residents of regular supplies of meat. Even traditional sources of freshly slaughtered meat disappeared in the 1990s, when the neoliberal government closed down the Mexico City slaughterhouse as an efficiency measure. Thus, although Mexican historians continue to debate the broader nature of the great social movement begun in 1910, there was no revolution at the stockyards.

Nevertheless, the sausage rebellion does provide a significant example of local labor and business triumphing over foreign capital, and as a result it offers insights on the nature of economic nationalism in the late Porfirian and early revolutionary eras. Admittedly, the Mexican butchers' struggles formed only an isolated urban episode within a much larger revolutionary movement that was centered primarily in the countryside. Moreover, the success of the sausage rebellion owed much to the weakness of foreign capital in this case. Unlike the huge financial reserves of U.S. firms such as Armour and Swift, DeKay was distracted by the constant search for investment capital. Still, the Mexican butchers demonstrated an often-overlooked cosmopolitanism within the working classes. They learned from the experience of North American counterparts who suffered from the effects of proletarianization, and used that knowledge to resist a similar fate. The sausage rebellion thus counts as a significant victory for local labor and business against foreign capital and provides an example that is still pertinent in an age of globalization.

The sausage rebellion comprises many stories, the first of which is a social history of the Mexico City slaughterhouse. The distinctive racial hierarchy of the Mexican butcher trade offers significant contrasts with European guilds, made up of apprentices, journeymen, and masters, ranked by different levels of skill and capital, but united by a common training in all aspects of the business, from selecting livestock to cutting meat. The Mexican meat trades, by contrast, were divided along functional lines into livestock merchants, retail butchers, and slaughterhouse workers, each of which came from different social strata. Writing of hog butchers in particular, Juan Arias elaborated on this division of labor in the mid-nineteenth century. "The first is a speculator on a large scale, the proprietor of the establishment...whose theoretical and practical knowledge is employed solely in the purchase of live flesh in order to sell it dead." This was distinct from the bacon salesman, "who possesses the artistic part of the trade, the culinary professor, the maker of chorizos and blood sausages, *putifarras*, head cheese, wienies and pigs feet and *salchichones* (big sausages)." Arias opposed these two, largely Hispanic, professions with Aztec imagery of the third, the "sacrificer of pigs, a man whose constitution would have made him best suited to the role of priest in the times of cannibalism."[3]

Although their relatively small numbers have caused them to be overlooked in studies of Mexican guilds, butchers formed an important part of the larger workforce. In Europe, butchers had a long reputation as one of the most militant of guilds, and their skill with knives made them particularly feared by officials and citizens alike. Constant surveillance by the government, combined with the social divisions of the Mexican guild structure, made it difficult for meat cutters to assert their workplace autonomy. Nevertheless, the sausage rebellion demonstrates the success of a developing country labor movement in defying the power of an early multinational corporation. At the same time, attempts by the Porfirian regime to instill questionable foreign health standards drove many butchers into the criminal underworld. Meat shortages had always encouraged such gray-market trade, particularly at the end of both the eighteenth and the nineteenth centuries, when cycles of economic growth drew large numbers of rural migrants to Mexico City. These newcomers brought with them traditional methods for raising and butchering livestock, blurring the geographical boundaries between city and countryside. An examination of the production and consumption of meat can thereby contribute to the study of the Porfirian criminalization of urban society.[4]

Second, the sausage rebellion provides a business history of the meat sector that throws light on the process of industrialization during the Porfirian era. Mexico, like many other Latin American countries at the turn of the century, attempted to balance two different approaches to development, a classical liberal model based on raw material exports and a more interventionist approach seeking to build domestic markets. Following the work of Alfred Chandler Jr. on business organization, Stephen Haber has provided a particularly insightful discussion of the political and economic structures that shaped Mexican development. Local businessmen hoped to shortcut the century-long process of industrialization by importing technology from Western Europe and the United States. Factories designed for continental markets proved excessive for an agrarian country such as Mexico, where consumer demand was limited to a handful of cities. Equipment therefore operated well below capacity, making it difficult to pay interest on the imported capital, and encouraging monopolistic control of markets. The problem of low productivity was compounded by Mexican labor, which had not yet submitted to the new rhythms required for mass production and worked instead at the self-made pace of agriculture. As a result, Mexican manufacturers came to depend on monopolizing protected markets to assure profits given the lack of effective consumer demand.[5]

The history of the Mexico City meat supply offers a unique case study in the difficulties that businessmen and government officials faced in balancing the potentially contradictory imperatives of building export revenue and developing internal markets as well as fitting imported technology to domestic industry. The jealously guarded privacy of family held corporations combines with the closed-door negotiations of government officials to make Mexican business history extremely difficult to document. Even Haber acknowledged that his sources of public accounting records were doubtless misstated, but he argued that if Mexican accountants lied in roughly the same way, then a consistent overall picture of industrial profitability would emerge. Unlike the case of strictly private corporations, municipal oversight provides rare insights into business practices at the slaughterhouse. In particular, the Porfirian trust in imported technology is revealed as misguided and the cause of a succession of troubles, which were often compounded by the bad faith of foreign contractors. The competition between raw material exports and domestic consumption also appears as a source of nationalist conflict. John DeKay originally sought his packinghouse concession primarily to feed the British export market, but the Porfirian government negotiated a hard bargain over the terms of who would profit and who would pay for this enterprise.

As negotiations between DeKay and the Mexican government show, the business history of the sausage rebellion entails a third, political, history of state power and regulation. The Porfirian dictatorship exerted authority over historically independent regions by playing off rival elite factions to ensure that President Díaz served as an indispensable political arbitrator. Economic privileges and monopolies, such as the Mexico City slaughterhouse concession, provided an important source of patronage within this system. Yet by handing control of municipal services to outsiders, first to the northern Mexican cattle barons and then to foreigners, Díaz alienated important local constituencies. DeKay recognized the necessity of cultivating the Porfirian elite, but as a cultural outsider, his efforts to gain favor often proved misguided. Moreover, Díaz's need at least to balance the interests of the meatpackers with those of politically powerful traditional livestock merchants limited the support that DeKay received during the course of the sausage rebellion.

Political struggles for control of the meat supply also had important implications for public health and the police powers of the Mexican state. Definitions of public health (*salubridad*) have shifted subtly over time from an early modern concept encompassing urban order to one focusing on disease and the individual. Colonial meat inspectors performed their duties in much the same way as their modern counterparts, by examining animals before slaughter to evaluate their health and by assuring the clean handling and prompt sale of their meat. Nevertheless, a large part of the colonial inspector's job would now be considered police functions such as limiting the sale of meat to designated markets and preventing livestock from running loose in the city. Colonial guilds shared the regulatory burden by setting standards for the trade, and they used this knowledge to contest nineteenth-century attempts by medical professionals to increase state power. Nor was the objectivity of science entirely clear in the conflict between differing standards of wholesome meat, as Mexicans insisted on totally fresh meat while U.S. suppliers asserted the benefits of products aged under refrigeration. Moreover, meat became an important element of the discourse of national health at the turn of the century, as intellectuals worried that shortages would impede industrial development and lead to excessive consumption of *pulque*, the intoxicating and nutritious drink of the masses, with consequent threats to public order.[6]

The intersection between political authority and medical professionalism also provides a useful perspective for engaging debates on the sociology of the state and the rise of liberalism. The current ascendancy of

Anglo-American economic conservatism, with its emphasis on balanced budgets and limited government, has prompted renewed scholarly interest in the historical relationship between the state and the marketplace. In an important theoretical work, Margaret Somers traced what she calls the "fear and loathing of the public sphere" to John Locke and his narrative of Manichaean struggle between the state and the individual. By imagining a state of nature in which private property existed prior to the state, he defined the private as the only location of true freedom.[7] Although neoliberal governments in contemporary Latin America have rushed to embrace this program of privatization, their nineteenth-century predecessors were open to alternate narratives of state development, including the works of Montesquieu, Rousseau, and Tocqueville, as well as the ideology of the French revolutions of 1789, 1830, and 1848. Moreover, the experience of industrialization does not lend conclusive support to the Anglo-American model, for scholars have shown that on a per capita basis, France maintained parity with British manufacturing throughout the nineteenth century.[8]

Studies of Mexican liberalism have emphasized the pragmatism with which early republican leaders applied European ideas to Latin American situations. The basic economic issue of the nineteenth century, the question of industrial protection versus free trade, grew out of a late colonial desire to escape from Spanish trade restrictions, and anyway had little direct concern to the purveyors of fresh meat. Nevertheless, livestock merchants stayed abreast of debates in which a conservative intellectual, Lucas Alamán, freely adopted the ideas of liberal European economists in his campaign to stimulate domestic industry. Steven Topik demonstrated the similarly eclectic approach used by the Porfirian government to foment Mexican industry at the end of the nineteenth century.[9]

In contrast to elite-centered studies of political economy, scholars have recently begun paying closer attention to the participation of the masses in nation building as well as their understanding of the economy. The present work uses the butcher trades to examine the construction of liberal ideals in Mexico. Despite their great wealth and political influence, livestock merchants remained on the fringes of the elite because of the social stigma of their bloody profession. Liberal property rights thus represented not a fashionable European doctrine for them, but a convenient business tool in asserting their autonomy from municipal regulators. At the same time, the economic discourse of supply and demand allowed them to counter popular beliefs about their monopoly power. Disputes that arose in the meat supply therefore offer an invaluable transcript at the intersection of elite and popular mentalities. Moreover, the struggles of the sausage rebellion help to connect the nature of Porfirian industrialization with the revolutionary ideology of 1910.

Fourth, and finally, the sausage rebellion provides a cultural history of the practices of meat consumption in Mexico and how they helped to shape the political arena. Because of their lack of organization, consumers have traditionally had relatively little power in the marketplace. In particular circumstances, such as the eighteenth-century English grain riots described by E. P. Thompson, consumers gained genuine political power through collective action based on moral outrage.[10] Yet meat seldom inspired such riots, in Mexico as elsewhere, because it remained a luxury good, and in times of crisis, the urban poor fell back on the staple grain, maize. Rural dwellers fared worse, rarely having access to meat except during a few religious festivals each year. Even within the cities, social class divided consumers and dissipated the possibilities for collective action. Although foreigners immediately think of fajitas, the colonial elite consumed mutton and scorned beef as a lower-class meat. Over the course of the nineteenth century, the Spanish taste for mutton was replaced by a northern European preference for beef, but the quality and quantity of meat still divided rich from poor.

Despite the adoption of foreign fashions, the Mexican elite retained distinctive methods of preparing meat, as numerous foreign travelers inadvertently testified. The aptly named William Bullock, an Englishman who visited the country shortly after independence, heaped scorn on the meat served by his Mexican hosts. "The sheep here are rather handsome in appearance whilst living," he observed, but "the mutton [is] lean and tasteless to those accustomed to the fine English breeds." His chauvinistic pride swelled further in discussing the English national dish. "The beef is in general hard and dry, but this may probably arise from the slovenly and injudicious manner in which the butchers perform their office, as well as from their mode of cooking. I have only once or twice met with good roast or boiled beef, and that at the tables of English or American residents."[11] Writing in 1895, John G. Bourke concurred: "The Mexican butcher is generally a fraud, a delusion, and a snare. He worries himself very little about questions of roasts, joints, and chops, but boldly cuts his meat in a manner to suit himself."[12] Such ethnocentric comments fail to account for the development of a distinctively Mexican national cuisine.[13]

Those who visit a Mexican market to observe a butcher at work will immediately realize they are not in the meat department of a U.S. supermarket. Instead of thick, neatly cut steaks of well-aged beef, wrapped in clear plastic, they find butterflied strips of meat, corresponding to no known part of a cow, sawed with ragged edges but remarkable thinness, and hung on hooks and rods. The thick cuts of meat called *suadero* might be steak except for the checkerboards carved across the front. The butchers will also no doubt have scattered odd chunks of *retazo* about the stall in a baroque display of craftsmanship. Although these meats would be of little use in making Anglo-American roasts or steaks, they are ideal for *carne asada* (grilled meat) and *mole de olla* (chile pepper stew). Indeed, fajitas, the Tex-Mex specialty of skirt steak pounded thin and marinated, seared quickly on a hot fire, and served with salsa and fresh tortillas, are nothing more than a fancy version of the standard method of cooking and eating beef in Mexico.

Of course, nobody wants to eat rotten meat, but those familiar with supermarket meats in the United States or aged Omaha steaks may not realize just how different freshly slaughtered meat can taste. The human sense of taste is extremely complex—based on smell and texture as well as flavor—and it differs widely across cultures. Much of the appeal of U.S. steak comes from the tenderness made possible by the marbling of fat interlaced among the muscle. Dry-aging under refrigeration increases the tenderness even more through the release of enzymes that break down the connective tissue of the muscle. Such meats lend themselves to the high heat of the grill or the oven, which browns and caramelizes the exterior while leaving thick layers of juicy tissue inside. Without access to feedlot-fattened cattle, Mexicans focused instead on the rich taste of freshly slaughtered meat, and developed alternative cooking methods for making it tender. A Mexican perspective on refrigerated meat was recorded in a newspaper advertisement by local butchers when confronted with meat from DeKay's packinghouse. They described the changes that take place in meat while aging under refrigeration: "It loses its juice, it becomes discolored, it is insipid and acquires a rare tenderness, due, perhaps, to the beginning of decomposition."[14] A migrant worker from Guanajuato, living in Los Angeles in the 1920s, likewise explained: "I don't like the meat, that is to say, the meat here [in the United States], because it is not fresh."[15]

Consumers in the United States reacted in much the same way, at first; only an overwhelming cost advantage assured the transition to refrigerated supply, and tastes gradually adjusted. Modern trends have actually gone back toward Mexican preferences in some ways. Supermarkets rarely devote commercial space to the refrigerators needed for dry-aging meat, and as a result, most meat is sold relatively fresh, from four to ten days after slaughter. Moreover, the desire for leaner, less-marbled meat has led many modern cooks away from roasting and grilling back to braising and stewing. Even those skeptical of cultural relativism can surely concede, in matters of taste, that the tenderness prized by U.S. consumers was considered to be a sign of unwholesomeness by Mexicans.[16]

The personal relationship between Mexican consumers and the butchers who selected and prepared individualized portions made ordinary residents of Mexico City into participants in the sausage rebellion against foreign meatpackers. DeKay's plan for improving industrial efficiency meant eliminating these middlemen and selling directly to consumers in company-owned retail shops. By insisting on the superiority of Anglo-American methods of preparation, however, he alienated the very people on whom his plans depended. One could use this case study as evidence that culture impeded Mexican economic development, but such an argument risks exaggerating the dichotomy between a pre-modern "moral" economy based on personal ties and a modern "political" economy supposedly ruled by inexorable laws of supply and demand. In fact, a paternalistic "moral" economy reemerged in the United States, as well, with a new, more health-oriented outlook, as part of Progressive-era outrage against the Chicago meat trust.[17]

The industrialization of meat in the United States has inspired a monumental historiography, considering virtually every aspect of production and consumption. Upton Sinclair was only the most prominent of many Progressive-era writers to decry the machinations of the meat trust, while apologists for Armour and Swift told Horatio Alger stories of these capitalists' rise to prominence.[18] Labor historians have approached the packinghouse "jungle" from many different angles, ranging from classical studies of unionization to more recent examinations of community, gender, and racial integration within the meatpacking workforce.[19] The challenge posed by the meatpacking oligopoly to political and social ideals of free competition has been examined in a thoughtful study of business history.[20] Historians of science, technology, and medicine have likewise turned their attention to the health concerns raised by the progressive movement.[21] The ecological imperialism of the refrigerated meatpacking industry has been discussed in an important work of environmental history.[22] Even the culture of consumption has been addressed in an insightful recent analysis of the role of ordinary cooks in shaping technological change in the U.S. meat industry from colonial times to the present.[23]

In contrast to the supposed success story of industrialization in Chicago, the failure of meatpacking in Mexico has led it to be ignored within the historiography. Considerable research has focused on livestock in the first wave of the Columbian Exchange and on the late-colonial meat monopoly.[24] The collapse of colonial institutions in the early republican era has left little information on the meat supply in the nineteenth century.[25] An excellent study of regional industrialization in Porfirian Michoacán by José Napoleón Guzmán Avila has outlined the history of John DeKay's Mexican National Packing Co. By focusing on production, however, it lacks context on the Mexico City meat supply, particularly on local consumption patterns.[26] The current volume thus fills a large gap in the historiography of Porfirian and revolutionary Mexico.

The book begins by outlining the origins of the Porfirian meat trades in the colonial era and during the liberal reforms of the nineteenth century. This chapter examines each of the four major actors that struggled to control the meat supply: livestock merchants, meat cutters, city officials, and consumers. A number of conflicts emerged during this long formative period and continued to disrupt the meat supply during the Porfirian era. The first of these struggles arose out of the peculiar organization of the guilds, as colonial inheritances continued to shape the structure of the industry. Second, the perennial troubles of supplying sufficient quantities of meat to Mexico City demanded attention from the Porfirian state. Third, the ideals of liberalism, arising first in opposition to colonial monopolies, were used by canny livestock merchants to stymie government attempts to change their business. These efforts were counterbalanced by a fourth trend, the efforts of city officials to use medical knowledge to gain regulatory control over meat supplies.

"The Porfirian Jungle," chapter 2, examines the city government's ill-fated first attempt to modernize the meat supply by replacing the old municipal slaughterhouse. Porfirian officials had to choose between two alternative models, the public abattoirs of Paris and the private packing-houses of Chicago. These two designs reflected radically different approaches to livestock production and meat marketing, but the decision was ultimately based on price alone. Although officials signed the first contract in 1891, problems with a succession of builders delayed the opening until 1897. Even then, a combination of design flaws and industrial accidents caused the facility to be closed within a month. Because of its short life and poor implementation, this first experiment did not provide an adequate test of the North American refrigerated model under Mexican conditions. This episode is significant primarily because of the way it mobilized capital, labor, consumers, and regulators, thereby influencing future ideas about this new technology.

City officials, having wasted large sums of money, learned from the experience that they had no interest in entering the meat business and instead turned the slaughterhouse over to private contractors. Chapter 3 examines subsequent attempts by the Terrazas-Creel clan to reconstruct the facility as part of a larger plan of establishing a national meatpacking trust. Local butchers protested vehemently that the new management would not take sufficient consideration of their interests. Indeed, when the plant reopened in 1905, the management had streamlined production, putting rival merchants at a serious disadvantage. Nevertheless, the northern cattle barons failed in their attempt to monopolize the meat supply of Mexico City. The most powerful of the capital's livestock merchants responded by using political connections to force the Terrazas to negotiate market-sharing agreements. Less influential merchants meanwhile resorted to clandestine slaughter, thereby becoming part of the Porfirian underworld.

Ultimately, the greatest threat to the Terrazas interests came not from illicit butchers but rather from the competition of foreign businessmen. Chapter 4 recounts the history of the Mexican National Packing Co., which, despite its name, was founded by John DeKay with the support of Chicago meatpacking interests. In 1908, the company opened a modern packing plant at Uruapan, Michoacán, in the cattle country of western Mexico. DeKay created an elaborate marketing plan combining heavy advertising with strategically located retail shops to educate Mexicans, both elite and common, about the benefits of U.S.-style meats. In the hopes of building customer loyalty, all products bore the label "El Popo," after the lofty volcano Popocatépetl, for nostalgic appeal to Mexicans and because "DeKay Meat" made a poor brand name. But rather than compete head on with the foreigners, the wily Terrazas used political connections to force the foreign company to buy out their interest in the Mexico City slaughterhouse. DeKay paid a high price for the merger, but in doing so he won the backing of the científico elite for his plans to revolutionize the Mexican meat industry.

The final chapter narrates the sausage rebellion of local meat trades against the Mexican National Packing Co. Merchants and workers tried to sabotage the company's modernization program at every turn, resorting to union actions, attacks on retail shops, even attempts to murder the foreign plant managers. John DeKay's troubles were compounded in early 1910 with the failure of George Ham's United States Banking Co., which had financed the purchase of the slaughterhouse. In these trying times, government support was indispensable for the company's continued operations, and this seeming favoritism toward the foreigners prompted livestock merchants to reverse a century of liberal demands that the government respect private property. Instead, they insisted on intervention to assure the public well-being, thereby providing an important example of how attitudes toward the state changed as a result of political and economic conditions. The merchants' requests were answered when the Revolution of 1910 installed a reform-minded municipal government that was determined to investigate the Mexican National's business practices. Ultimately, the butchers were incorporated into the unions and chambers of commerce fomented by the revolutionary state, thus bringing an end to the sausage rebellion.

The Mexico City meat supply stands at the intersection of important historical themes: production and consumption, political and moral economy, business and labor, and the marketplace and the state. By examining a crucial episode in the development of meat provisioning, this book attempts to illuminate the inherent tension between public health and private enterprise in the broader supply of food. Economists may decry the loss of efficiency and the reduced supply resulting from the sausage rebellion and the failure of El Popo to modernize production, but they do so only by ignoring the taste preference for fresh meat among Mexican consumers like Concha.

CHAPTER ONE

The Butcher Trades

I n the 1890s, at the dawn of the modern, industrial era in Mexico, the nation's capital still depended for its meat supply on an unsettled and unsettling combination of colonial and nineteenth-century institutions. The lynchpin of the system, the municipal slaughterhouse of San Lucas, maintained an antiquated practice of "conducting 250 or 300 cattle into a closed perimeter inside of which the butchers, with great danger to themselves, killed the animals in crowds, here and there, causing confusion and terror through the bloody spectacle. The butchers, with cold blood, notable valor, and at times a ferocious pleasure similar to that of the bullfighter, released from misery, in a few moments, their numerous victims."[1] Elsewhere in the city, clandestine butchers enacted similar bloody scenes on an individual basis beyond the control of municipal health inspectors. Although such illicit sources of meat were essential for impoverished consumers, wealthy Mexicans dined on lavish banquets prepared according to the dictates of French haute cuisine. Meanwhile, a cartel of wholesale merchants controlled this dualistic market using the techniques of a monopolistic supply system inherited from medieval Spain. These powerful businessmen skillfully exploited the overlapping jurisdictions between municipal and federal health officials, who struggled to establish their medical authority while coping with the laissez-faire legacy of a mid-nineteenth-century liberal regime.

With tradition and modernity juxtaposed at every step in the supply chain, Porfirian institutions must be viewed from a broad historical context. This chapter introduces each of the four participants in the marketplace—consumers, butchers, livestock merchants, and government officials—as they pursued their separate, often antagonistic interests. In theory, paternalistic relationships unified these diverse actors, but in practice, numerous conflicts arose between them. City officials maintained a distant, at times authoritarian stance toward the consumers whose health they were charged to protect, and attempted to restrict any efforts by private individuals to secure meat outside of regular supply channels. Livestock merchants likewise assumed a paternalistic attitude in representing the well being of workers, at least to the extent that they coincided with their own goal of maintaining an exclusive cartel. When those interests clashed, however, labor relations became tense at the municipal slaughterhouse and in retail butcher shops. Perhaps the greatest area of conflict lay between government officials and powerful merchants, who struggled for control of the meat supply throughout the nineteenth century.

Porfirian historians looked back to three great revolutions in their nation's past, each of which had a profound effect on the meat supply as well. The first great transformation came with the Spanish conquest and the introduction of European livestock. Pre-Hispanic civilizations possessed only a few domesticated animals, turkeys and small dogs, and a basically vegetarian diet has remained the norm in rural areas of Mexico up to the present. The one possible exception to that rule was the generation immediately following the conquest, when European livestock expanded out over the landscape at the same time that plagues decimated the Native American population. By the late eighteenth century, however, the demographic trends of the early colonial era had reversed and meat became scarce even in Hispanic cities. The second revolution came with the wars of independence (1810–1821) and the abolition of the hated colonial meat monopoly. The coming of free trade in meat swung the pendulum of state authority too far; the chaos of the early republic led to the complete collapse of regulatory control and the privatization of the municipal slaughterhouse. The third social transformation came with the Liberal Reform, which reached its apogee with the Constitution of 1857 but more broadly encompassed the work of an entire generation from 1850 to 1880. Although ostensibly committed to laissez faire economics, the liberal regime faced the painstaking task of reasserting police power over Mexico City meat markets. The first step in this campaign came with a new regulatory code, promulgated in 1850, which reestablished a municipal abattoir for cattle, although sheep and hogs continued to be butchered in private facilities scattered across the city. The complete centralization of slaughter came only two decades later, about 1870, as the result of another lengthy battle between city officials and wealthy merchants.

During these periods of upheaval, buyers and sellers in the capital's meat markets engaged in three fundamental and ongoing conflicts. The first of these, and perhaps the most fundamental, was simply the struggle to assure adequate supplies. Basic ecological limitations arose from the balance between human and animal populations, as livestock grazing lands competed with grain production. Because cattle and sheep, unlike maize and wheat, can carry themselves to market, ranching operations were displaced to distant provinces in the far north and along the coasts. The large urban demand for meat within the central highlands prompted the creation of integrated livestock markets extending throughout New Spain. Nevertheless, the colonial monopoly on urban meat supplies, which was intended to ensure the stability of provisioning, contributed to shortages by restricting local competition. Although nineteenth-century reforms sought to provide more reliable access to meat, the livestock cartel survived and combined with poor transportation and political instability to block improvements. The Porfirian government made progress in improving economic infrastructure, but population growth steadily eroded productivity gains. As a result, meat supplies remained just as precarious in the 1890s as they had been a century earlier.

A second major area of conflict arose from the ideological struggles between liberalism and conservatism. Mexican liberalism was founded in large part on eighteenth-century Enlightenment ideas, which included attacks on the meat monopoly and the butchers' guild. After the abolition of these privileges, merchant butchers adopted the ideology of liberalism, particularly the emphasis on laissez faire, to assure their freedom from government regulation. The common people had likewise supported free trade, but as a remedy against the colonial monopoly. For them, government action was still needed to guarantee adequate supplies of meat in times of dearth. Both liberal and conservative politicians recognized the dangers to public health and order posed by unregulated meat markets and urban slaughterhouses, but their agreement over goals did little to provide institutional continuity during this unsettled period. Even when the Porfirian dictatorship restored a measure of stability, considerable uncertainty remained in the administration of meat markets because of the government's pragmatic interpretation of liberalism.

The científico elite put their faith in the progress of science and in particular the rise of medical authority, but the third basic conflict, over regulatory control, offered no easy answers to the dilemmas of urban meat supply. Veterinary medicine made important advances during the nineteenth century, and Mexicans were at the forefront of this international movement. The diagnostic technology of the microscope allowed health professionals to screen livestock for dangerous diseases such as trichinosis, which Mexican experts discovered independently of their European colleagues.[2] But fully utilizing this scientific knowledge depended on the active collaboration of workers. Butchers' guilds had long been accustomed to acting as the primary assurance of quality through their skills in selecting livestock and preparing meat, and conflicts naturally arose as health inspectors sought to supplant their authority. As the final step in the supply chain, domestic knowledge was equally important in assuring the health of consumers. Particularly in Mexico, where the boundaries between rural and urban life were so permeable, countless hogs were raised on kitchen scraps within the city limits. These animals, slaughtered without the approval of health authorities, nevertheless provided an important contribution to the diet of the urban poor, who could not always depend on regular supply channels. Just who was best qualified to regulate the meat supply therefore remained an open question at the end of the nineteenth century.

A CARNIVOROUS CULTURE

The conspicuous consumption of meat has been a hallmark of nobility in many societies, but foreign travelers have seldom been prepared for the carnivorous appetites of the Mexican elite. Moctezuma's grand banquets astonished the Spanish conquistadors, who ate with special caution for fear of encountering human body parts. Writing about 1840, Fanny Calderón de la Barca observed that wealthy Mexicans ate meat for virtually every meal and in extraordinary quantities—more, she believed, than in any other country in the world.[3] These noble feasts seemed all the more exceptional given the poverty of ordinary Native Americans, who subsisted on a basically vegetarian diet of corn tortillas, beans, and chiles under both the Aztec Empire and the Mexican Republic. Although consumption patterns in Porfirian Mexico City were differentiated by class, gender, and ethnicity, the Mexican preference for meat, like the national cuisine in general, arose largely from plebeian tastes.

The Catholic calendar regulated patterns of meat consumption in colonial Mexico according to cycles of feast and fast, which in turn mirrored pre-Hispanic religious practices. Church doctrine varied through the centuries, but strict observance required abstaining from meat on Wednesdays,

Fridays, and Saturdays, major saint's days, and all of Lent except for Sundays. The balance of Christmas feasts and Lenten fasts matched the agricultural cycle in Europe, where it was customary to slaughter a hog in November as the onset of winter made foraging difficult. In Mexico, frosts posed less of a danger to livestock, but meat consumption likewise peaked in the dry winter months when grass became scarce. Rural dwellers usually consumed meat only at religious celebrations and family festivals. For example, a cow might be butchered for the village's patron saint or a turkey at weddings. By contrast, the greater population and wealth of Hispanic cities allowed the daily slaughter of livestock. For those who could afford it, meat was available even during religious fasts because of the Bula de la Cruzada, a papal decree exempting medieval Spanish knights from Catholic dietary restrictions, which was also extended to New Spain. Moreover, the archbishop of Mexico City offered regular dispensations from Lenten fasts. Wealthy Mexicans thus gained exemption from the dietary restrictions of both piety and poverty.[4]

The types of meat available to shoppers varied according to class, but both aristocrats and plebeians alike demanded the freshest possible products. The colonial elite retained a Hispanic preference for mutton that was acquired during the *convivencia*, the long collaboration between Christians, Jews, and Muslims in medieval Iberia. Beef was considered a working-class food and sold for a fraction of the price of mutton in Mexico City butcher shops. This was in sharp contrast to the relative price of beef in northern Europe, particularly France, where mutton was considered a middle-class item at best, with more status than pork but still inferior to beef. And whereas French law prohibited the sale of meat on the day it was slaughtered, Mexicans insisted on meat slaughtered the very same day and denounced butchers who sold leftovers. A rare exception to that rule appeared in an eighteenth-century cookbook by Dominga de Guzmán, which specified an aged *carnero* for mutton stew, although with the revealing description "bien manido" (well rotted).[5] Admittedly, preserved beef, known as *tasajo* and *cecina* in the south and *carne seca* along the northern frontier, became an important rural industry that had markets even in Mexico City. Nevertheless, the taste for fresh meat was predominant not only in Mexico but also in Spanish colonies as distant as Argentina and the Philippines, thus frustrating environmental determinists who might attempt to explain this cultural preference based on the Iberian or Mexican climate.[6]

19

The hog butchers' art (*tocinería*) exemplified the distinctive cuisine that emerged in colonial Mexico through the blending of Native American and Spanish traditions. Although rendered pork fat was a lower-class food throughout much of Europe, a nineteenth-century Mexican author called it the "soul of the kitchen."[7] A visitor from the United States described Mexican lard as "beautifully white and sweet"—nothing like industrial versions found in modern supermarkets.[8] Pork fat also provided the ideal medium for cooking spicy chile dishes, far superior to Spanish olive oil, and Native Americans even mixed it into tamales (corn dumplings) to give them a light and airy texture. Another essential component of this national cuisine, chile peppers, likewise suffused Mexican tocinería, from traditionally spicy Spanish chorizos to the milder *longaniza* sausages and at times to *morongas* and *morcillas* (blood sausages). Even the preparation of humble *chicharrones* (cracklings) became an art form in New Spain, with the skin boiled twice in fat, once at a low temperature and the second time much hotter, to ensure the proper puffy texture.

Over the course of the nineteenth century, wealthy Mexicans gradually shifted their preference from Hispanic mutton to French beef, ostensibly following the fashions of Europe, but nevertheless helping to establish a national cuisine common to both elite and commoners alike. One indication of this change in taste can be seen in annual statistics for livestock slaughtered in Mexico City (see figure 1.1). Although incomplete, these figures demonstrate a long-term decline in mutton that was reversed in absolute numbers only with the tremendous urban growth at the end of the nineteenth century, and even then continued to fall in per capita terms.[9] Cookbooks provide another source for following this transition beginning in 1831, when the first published volumes appeared. The *Novísimo arte de cocina* (Newest art of cooking) listed dozens of mutton and pork dishes, but only a handful for beef, including one for dried beef, a roast of beef or veal, a tripe stew, and three preparations for tongue. Far more comprehensive was *El cocinero mexicano* (The Mexican chef), which displayed a thorough knowledge of European cuisine and even compared English and French approaches to *bistec* (beefsteak); yet the majority of the beef recipes were not for steaks or roasts but rather organ meats. Just two decades later, however, the *Manual del cocinero y cocinera* (Manual of the chef and cook) provided upwards of seventy-five recipes for beef and veal, more than for either mutton or pork. Recipes

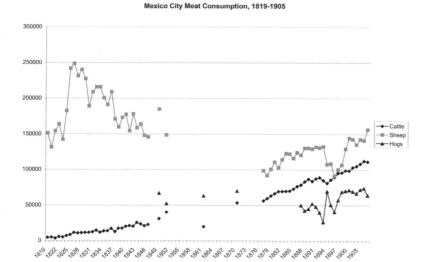

1.1 Mexico City meat consumption, 1819–1905. Sources: AHCM, vol. 3768, exp. 7; *Anuario estadístico de la República mexicana*: 1906 (Mexico City: Secretaría de Fomento, 1910), 37–39.

included English *rosbif,* French veal stew, and perhaps the first Mexican version of *milanesa*, an Italian breaded veal scallop that has become a popular favorite in modern Mexico.[10]

For those who could afford it, the obsession with European cookery reached a peak during the Porfirian belle époque, but even the most fashionable restaurants and cookbooks retained a distinctively Mexican taste. Middle-class housewives put their female kitchen assistants to work preparing dishes many could not even pronounce: *veal blanquette, beef à la mode,* and *bistec à la Maître d'hôtel.* Nevertheless, cookbook authors such as Vicenta Torres de Rubio remained aware of their audience's preferences. In a recipe for English rosbif, she explained the necessity of hanging the meat to age—two days in the summer and up to eight in the winter—and after giving a roasting time of two and a half hours, she warned: "This is *a la inglesa.* But as not all tastes correspond to the English point of doneness, I will indicate another procedure more adequate to our inclinations and customs."[11] The most sophisticated realized that the French foods in Mexico City restaurants bore little resemblance to Parisian fare, but this mainly gave them the opportunity to disparage their less-traveled countrymen.

Antonio García Cubas gave the following commentary upon finding the
French term *rôtis* misspelled on a Mexican menu as "*Rots*. Free translation
'ragged ones' (rotos), allusion of our street people (léperos) to the frock
coat crowd, but translated by the cognoscenti (instruidos) as roast."[12]

While the Mexican elite explored the delicacies of continental cuisine, the urban masses struggled simply to put food on the table. Total
meat consumption probably followed a gradual but steadily increasing tra-
jectory over the course of the nineteenth century because the greater
weight of cattle offset the more numerous but declining supply of sheep.
Yet population was increasing even more rapidly and per capita meat consumption may well have fallen by as much as 40 percent during the same
period. Unfortunately, the scarcity of data, together with the abundance
of clandestine slaughter, frustrates any solid conclusions about nineteenth-century standards of living.[13] A Porfirian journalist calculated that
working-class families devoted 60 percent of their budget to food, with
10 percent spent on meat and another 5 percent for cooking fat. A map of
Mexico City meat outlets in 1894 (see figure 1.2) shows butcher shops
evenly distributed throughout the city, including in proletarian neighborhoods. Retail butchers often extended credit for day-to-day purchases,
which also helped ensure customer loyalty. Nevertheless, given the high
percentage of working-class budgets devoted to staples, even small rises in
the price of meat could make the difference between *mole con carne* (beef
in chile sauce) and *puros frijoles* (nothing but beans).[14]

The urban poor therefore retained the rural habit of consuming
much of their meat during public celebrations such as the saint's days of
the various barrios as well as the national saint, the Virgin of Guadalupe.
The latter festival, held on December 12, featured a goat dish known as
chito consisting of organ meats fried in rendered fat. The traditional
accompaniment was *salsa borracha* (drunken sauce) made with *pulque*, the
fermented juice of the *agave* (century) plant, which is also distilled to
make tequila. The presence of alcohol at such festivals alarmed Mexican
police, but medical authorities were also concerned by the makeshift
cooking facilities used by the thousands of people who descended on the
capital from outlying, often indigenous communities. This clash between
popular culture and public health authorities was particularly sharp in
1848, the year that ended the U.S.-Mexican War and that began a new
regime of meat inspection, just a few months before the Virgin's Day. As

Mexico City
Meat Shops,
c. 1894

1.2 Map of Mexico City carnicerías, 1894. Source: *El Municipio Libre*, May 15, 1894.
Drawn by the author.

the first celebration of the national saint since Yankee invaders had
departed, it was a particularly joyous occasion, and any official action
that might have been interpreted as an attempt to suppress the festival
would surely have aroused strong resistance. The details of this distur-
bance remain obscure, and one can only imagine inspectors attempting to
enforce the new health code by rounding up hundreds of goats brought
into the city by rustic villagers who hoped to make a little cash during
the celebration. In any event, the city council found it necessary to clarify the new regulations at its next meeting, on December 15, by affirm-
ing the legality of chito sales in public places during religious festivals,
but limiting the preparation to corrals in the suburbs and requiring previous notification so the inspector could ensure the health of the animals.
To avoid similar confrontations, on October 20 of the following year, the
city posted a broad sheet reminding the public of the new regulations.[15]

Another aspect of rural consumption that survived in the city was the
widespread raising and slaughter of livestock. In the countryside, there

was no strict division between butchering an animal and cooking it. Even cookbooks for the wealthy, such as the eighteenth-century manuscript of doña Dominga de Guzmán, included recipes for large quantities of sausage, and from there it was a small step to selling it in the streets. A municipal ordinance of December 22, 1756, wryly noted "the total disorder that exists in the sale of meat and other pork products and the pernicious abuses that are experienced in their marketing, as they are sold year round in the streets, plazas, convents, inns, and other locations...(and at a voice that could be from Toluca)."[16] Merchants' complaints about competition from unlicensed slaughter continued well into the Porfirian era. Nor was the sale of food in the streets limited to unprepared foods. Outdoor kitchens were a necessity for the poor because of the fire hazards of cooking in the crowded and run-down tenement houses of the capital. Workers often purchased bowls of chile pepper stew or *carnitas*, bits of fried meat, from women who set up small braziers on street corners and public plazas throughout the city.[17]

For poor and rich alike, the consumption of meat was sharply divided according to gender. The cultural dichotomy between carnivorous men and vegetarian women appeared already in the Bible and has continued down to the present. European associations between meat and masculinity were transferred to Mexico in the belief among colonial authorities that only a steady diet of meat allowed hard work in the silver mines, despite the ubiquity of Native American porters carrying tremendous loads while eating little more than tortillas and chiles. In the countryside, gendered consumption patterns were reinforced by the division of labor during village festivals, the only time that meat was generally available. Consigned to the kitchen, women expressed power through the act of apportioning meat rather than by consuming it. Despite this apparent discrimination, they could nevertheless pick out choice portions of meat while tasting a dish, which was an essential part of the work of cooking. Meanwhile, a similar example was set for the Mexican elite through state banquets, which followed the European practice of separating the sexes. During an 1891 dinner in honor of Porfirio Díaz's birthday, for instance, the president and his cabinet consumed course after course of French food and wine while their wives looked on from a balcony. Such customs filtered down through the ranks of the middle classes by way of etiquette manuals that circulated widely among the *gente decente* (polite society). These works emphasized that women should eat small portions with delicacy and issued warnings such as "a plate served to excess would be a true insult."[18]

Despite divisions of class, gender, and ethnicity in the access to meat, late-nineteenth-century Mexicans shared a number of food habits, particularly the desire for freshly slaughtered beef. Although Porfirian nabobs might have imagined themselves tucking into a *bifstec à la Chateaubriand* in a fashionable Parisian bistro, to a foreigner such a recipe looks more like fajitas with French fries.[19] To satisfy this common desire for fresh meat, consumers in the capital were drawn into a conflictive collaboration with merchants, butchers, and regulators. The following section examines the businessmen who worked to assure steady supplies of livestock for the city while at the same time excluding competition that might lower prices for consumers.

THE MAKING OF A CARTEL

A cartel of livestock merchants known as importers (introductores), with antecedents dating back to the colonial era, dominated the meat business of Porfirian Mexico City. Their title derived from the colonial *alcabala*, an import duty paid at the city gates, and like the Victorian jobbers of London's Smithfield market, Mexican importers purchased cattle and sheep wholesale from drovers, supervised the slaughter in municipal abattoirs, and sold the sides of beef and mutton to retail meat cutters throughout the city.[20] The importers considered themselves to be champions of liberalism and free trade, although the ideology of laissez-faire was also a convenient tool to defend their trade against municipal regulation. Nevertheless, the livestock merchants genuinely feared a monopoly by rivals within the trade. As usual in the case of cartels that depended on informal arrangements rather than legally enforceable contracts to limit competition, Porfirian meat merchants were plagued by jealousy and suspicion. And although politically powerful, they often sought to diversify their fortunes into more socially acceptable occupations, leading to considerable turnover from one generation to the next.

The Porfirian importers were heirs to a colonial tradition of monopolistic economic power. Following medieval Iberian practices, the Mexico City council had contracted the *abasto de carne* (meat supply) to a private individual, who guaranteed abundant quantities of beef and mutton at a fixed and fair price for one or more years. As the contractor's title of *obligado* implied, supplying the monopoly was considered to be a public service obligation of wealthy citizens, an example set by the conquistador Fernando (Hernán) Cortés, who fulfilled the Mexico City abasto from his personal estates in 1526.[21] This arrangement of a single contractor monopolizing the sale of meat survived in Puebla, Guadalajara, and most other Hispanic cities until virtually the end of the colonial period, at least in those years that municipal leaders could find an individual willing to undertake the financial risk.[22] In Mexico City, by contrast, the system became increasingly commercialized during the eighteenth century. The council still auctioned the abasto to determine the price of meat and held the obligado responsible for adequate supplies, especially of beef, which was consumed by the lower classes. Nevertheless, with several prominent nobles vying for a share of the lucrative trade in mutton, the contractor was obliged to divide the city's retail markets in return for an annual rent plus slaughter fees. Already by the end of the colonial period, the abasto functioned as a cartel of wealthy merchants and stockmen, excluding outsiders and allowing preferential access to urban markets for the members, although they were nevertheless forced to supplement their own herds with livestock purchased from throughout New Spain.[23]

Private investment had also become extensive in the physical plant of the late colonial abasto system. Although the municipal slaughterhouse, located on the southern edge of the city at San Antonio Abad, remained the only location to butcher cattle legally in the city, the supply of sheep was divided among no fewer than twenty-four private *casas de matanza* (slaughterhouses). Six of these belonged to members of the abasto clique—the counts of Valparaíso, Bassoco, and Pérez Gálvez, the marquises of Aguayo and Jaral, and a Spanish stockman, Angel de Puyade—and were clustered in the neighborhood of San Antonio de Abad. The other eighteen were spread around the city on the grounds of assorted religious cloisters and hospitals that had obtained the right to butcher livestock tax free and often supplemented their income by selling meat illicitly out the back door. Legitimate sales of meat took place either at the municipal slaughterhouse or in one of twelve authorized *carnicerías* (meat shops), distributed in a great circle around the city, outside the affluent central district, but for the most part still within the grid of Spanish residences (see figure 1.3).[24]

By the end of the colonial period, the responsibilities of the abasto had come to outweigh the privileges, and the merchant elite joined

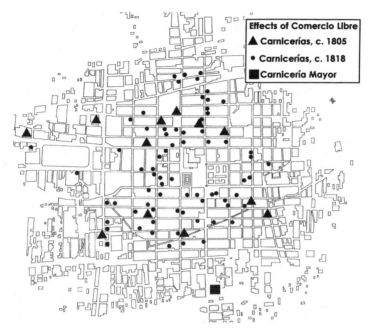

Effects of Comercio Libre
▲ Carnicerías, c. 1805
• Carnicerías, c. 1818
■ Carnicería Mayor

1.3 Map of Mexico City meat supply at independence. Sources: AGN, Abasto, vol. 5, exp. 13, fo. 376; AHCM, vol. 8, exp. 256, 267. Drawn by the author.

ordinary shoppers in opposing the monopoly system. Livestock production declined throughout New Spain during the eighteenth century as population growth diverted land from cattle raising to cereal production. The added shock of droughts and Apache raids in the 1780s and 1790s made it difficult for merchants to fulfill their contractual obligations.[25] In the summer of 1805, angry crowds formed outside several carnicerías with empty meat hooks. Mexico City officials fined the abasto holder, Gabriel de Yermo, who promptly challenged the penalty in court. After demonstrating that he had actually imported more livestock than his predecessors, the Basque merchant protested a system that held him responsible for the actions of rival suppliers who had failed to anticipate demand. In subsequent years, individuals simply refused to accept the burden, forcing the city council to form a collective Junta de Abasto (supply committee).[26] Outside the capital, the monopoly system also came under attack by reform-minded officials, who followed the doctrines of the French physiocrats and attributed

Spain's economic decadence to the burden of antiquated commercial practices. About 1800, Intendant Manuel de Flon temporarily abolished the meat monopoly in the city of Puebla in the hopes of encouraging local agriculture. Nor was *comercio libre* (free trade) just an abstract doctrine of Enlightenment intellectuals; it had entered the wider currency of popular discourse in opposition to the privileges of wealthy merchants. As Ward Barrett has shown in a study of the provincial town of Cuernavaca, recurrent meat shortages had prompted widespread popular dissatisfaction with the local abasto.[27]

A decade of war for independence dealt a final blow to the meat monopoly as urban supplies fell victim to insurgents and royalist forces alike. In 1811, for example, General Félix Calleja requisitioned a herd of sixteen thousand sheep from San Luis Potosí to feed his troops on campaign. Under such conditions, merchants refused to risk long-distance trade, and meat prices doubled over the already high rates of 1808. After various experiments with limited free trade, on March 1, 1813, Viceroy Francisco Javier Venegas declared a permanent comercio libre on beef and mutton, while simultaneously abolishing import duties and sales taxes. As can be seen from the previous map (figure 1.3), this reform led to a dramatic increase in the number of carnicerías from thirteen to more than a hundred by 1818, although they were still clustered within the Hispanic city center, indicating that poor Native Americans living in peripheral barrios remained only occasional customers. The grandees of the abasto clique abandoned the retail trade to local stock raisers, many of whom were probably unlicensed street vendors of previous years. Hog butchers, in attempting to defend their own guild, painted a fly-by-night image of individuals slaughtering cattle in every public thoroughfare and "selling the meat by the by."[28]

The business continued in an unsettled pattern through the general instability of the early national period (1821–1848), as the city government allowed the municipal slaughterhouse, the lynchpin of the colonial regulatory system, to be privatized out of existence. The council first rented out the facility as a fund raising measure in 1816, but neglected to enforce regulations prohibiting the slaughter of cattle in private rival corrals. As a result, the unprofitable abattoir passed through a succession of contractors and subcontractors, including Pedro Prieto, the city's garbage collector, until 1833, when Colonel Mariano Barrera took over the property and converted it into a gunpowder factory. The Mexico City council thus granted de facto recognition to the various private slaughterhouses operating more or less openly. An official later recalled that "they slaughtered cattle in a corral on the side of the granary [recogidas], facing south, in another at the Cacahuatal [Street of the Peanut Field], in those [two] on the Garrapata [Street of the Tick, appropriately], and in all of the hidden ones of the city, without order, many without paying taxes, neither the alcabala, nor the municipal [duties], and without any policing."[29]

In the case of mutton, free trade legitimized public sales of mutton from the private slaughterhouses established in the colonial period by noble families and religious cloisters. At least a few survivors of the abasto clique, the former Conde de Pérez Gálvez and the Puyade family, maintained their great estates and casas de matanza throughout the first half of the nineteenth century. These merchants continued to refer to the abasto by name despite the formal abolition of the monopoly. Nevertheless, more specialized importers gradually acquired ownership of the roughly twenty sheep slaughterhouses in the city or else rented them from ecclesiastical institutions.[30]

After the chaos of the early republic, a group of shrewd livestock importers reformed the late-colonial cartel in response to challenges that arose during the mid-century liberal reform period. Led by Rafael Villegas, Ramón Ocaranza, and Antonio Escandón (not to be confused with the railroad developer of the same name), this generation of importers maintained their grip on the business through control over the slaughter of livestock, both sheep in private casas de matanza and cattle at the municipal abattoir. When the city first refurbished the slaughterhouse at San Lucas, about 1850, the importers quickly asserted their influence over labor and even municipal officials through political stratagems described later in this chapter. These powerful merchants also found a handy tool for maintaining their autonomy from city regulation in the guarantees of individual property rights contained within the liberal Constitution of 1857. The Lerdo Law abolishing corporate property-holding, the centerpiece of liberal reform, posed both challenges and opportunities. Deprived of free access to the Mexico City commons, formerly used to graze livestock prior to slaughter, the importers purchased these newly privatized lands along with casas de matanza from religious orders. The

shift in consumption from mutton to beef, a trend that had been underway for decades, offered another test for mid-century importers.
Merchants prospered if they could assure regular supplies of both cattle
and sheep during the turmoil of the wars of the Reform (1858–1861) and
of the French Intervention (1862–1867). Such flexibility also proved vital
during political negotiations, around 1870, when the return of peace
allowed city officials to launch a new campaign against private casas de
matanza. Once again this generation of importers demonstrated their
political skills, before finally retiring in the next decade and leaving their
successors to supply the rapidly growing population of Porfirian cities.

As in the colonial era, consumers in late-nineteenth-century Mexico
City had privileged access to meat compared to the rest of the country.
Researchers at the Colegio de México have estimated a nationwide annual slaughter of approximately 800,000 cattle in the 1880s, and more than
a tenth of that total, some 85,000 head a year, went to feed the capital,
even though its inhabitants accounted for less than 3 percent of the
national population. Yet even with forty cities of more than 10,000 people in the central plateau, poor internal transportation guaranteed that
much of the country's beef cattle was sold in foreign markets.[31]

According to a 1902 livestock census, more than 45 percent of the ten
million cattle in Mexico were located in the arid northern and Pacific
northern regions (see figure 1.4). Although sheep from Coahuila and
Nuevo León had been driven profitably to Mexico City in the colonial era,
the relatively low price of beef did not justify such long-distance trade,
and ranchers often slaughtered cattle for their hides and tallow, leaving
the carcasses to rot. Railroads opened the possibility of more economical
transport in the late nineteenth century, but by that time, northern stockmen found it more profitable to ship the animals across the border to feedlots in the United States. Only haciendas in the lowest tier of northern
states, Zacatecas, San Luis Potosí, and southern Tamaulipas regularly supplied cattle to markets in Central Mexico.[32]

The Porfirian era also brought important changes to the livestock raising regions in the piedmont along the Gulf and Pacific coasts, which traditionally supplied the bulk of the cattle for Mexico City. About 10
percent of Mexican cattle were raised in the Gulf Coast states of
Veracruz, Campeche, Tabasco, and Yucatán, although the irregular geog-
raphy of Mexican ranching limits the usefulness of statewide census

1.4 Map of livestock regions in Porfirian Mexico. Source: Diego López Rosado, *Historia y pensamiento económico de México*, 6 vols. (Mexico City: UNAM, 1968), 1:116–17. Drawn by the author.

aggregates. The Huasteca Potosina, a region encompassing southern Tamaulipas, eastern San Luis Potosí and northern Hidalgo and Veracruz, offered the country's finest grazing land, with summer rains and winter dews providing lush pastures throughout the year. The Sotavento Coast of southern Veracruz and Tabasco likewise became an important cattle raising area with exports to Cuba, whose livestock industry had been devastated in the Ten Years' War (1866–1876), and to the Yucatán, where former cattle pastures were planted with the lucrative cash crop henequen.[33]

The Pacific Coast had a less favorable climate and required considerable maintenance to assure adequate waterholes through the dry winters. Although the southern coastal states of Chiapas, Oaxaca, and Guerrero had another 10 percent of Mexican cattle, commercial ranching remained limited, because of both the lack of export markets and the success of indigenous communities in preserving their village lands against Spanish incursions. Haciendas in the Mixtec Alta of Oaxaca and around Arcelia,

Guerrero, produced livestock for urban markets, but small farmers used the bulk of the cattle in these states as draft animals. The central region made up the remaining third of the nation's cattle, with more than 1,750,000 animals in Jalisco and Michoacán alone. In these Pacific Coast states, cattle were often raised by smallholding *rancheros* instead of great hacendados. The growth and spread of this class through colonization expanded the scope of Porfirian cattle raising to new regions such as Coalcomán, in the Southern Sierra Madre.[34]

Elaborate networks of cattle trails and grazing pastures, at times dating back to the colonial era, connected these widespread haciendas and ranchos with livestock importers in Mexico City. Thus, at least some young cattle from Chiapas were sold to ranchers in the Sotavento, where they matured on the lush grass and were then driven to central Mexico for slaughter. During the colonial era, this trade was formalized through livestock fairs held each autumn in Tlaxcala, Puebla, and Toluca. Smaller towns such as Teziutlán in northern Puebla also specialized in fattening and reselling cattle in the nineteenth century. By the 1890s, large landowners in the Huasteca had begun to modernize their operations by planting improved forage such as guinea grass. These incipient feedlots often proved highly profitable by transferring the risks to small producers, since cattle were most vulnerable in their first year.[35] Common pasture lands were therefore prime targets for privatization during the reform era, especially by Mexico City importers. Rafael Villegas, for example, purchased three fields from the commons of San Juan Tenochtitlán to graze livestock before going to slaughter. Unlike butchers in New York City, who by common consent waited for drovers to arrive at the livestock market located near the Bull's Head Tavern, Mexico City importers sent agents out to purchase livestock in towns throughout the states of Mexico and Puebla, thereby heightening competition within the cartel.[36]

The expansion of the railroad network during the Porfirian era gradually improved the marketing of livestock. In the United States, cattle cars were already carrying large numbers of animals from western plains to eastern cities by the late 1850s. The first railroad line in Mexico, built in the 1860s from Veracruz to Mexico City, likewise offered livestock shipping rates, but cattle were not shipped in significant numbers until the 1890s. Perhaps the most important railroad line was the Mexican Central, which brought cattle from San Luis Potosí, Aguascalientes, Guanajuato, and Jalisco to the capital. Nevertheless, livestock still had to be driven considerable distances overland to reach the rail heads. The Huasteca region, in particular, lacked rail communications, and so existing trails remained essential for delivering livestock at least as far as Pachuca. Railroads had also just begun to extend into the cattle raising territory in central Michoacán at the turn of the twentieth century. Moreover, railroad shipping entailed considerable wastage among livestock crowded together in cattle cars. Nevertheless, with the growth of railroad shipping, Mexico City importers gained important political connections to powerful railroad interests within the nation's industrial establishment.[37]

Serapión Fernández, the leading Porfirian importer, looked the part of the fin-de-siècle tycoon, dressed for his portrait in a frock coat and starched collar with a neatly-trimmed beard (see figure 1.5). Yet his enormous, meaty hands, which seemed to swallow up a fashionable cane, betrayed the hard, physical labor that had brought Fernández to his position. In 1882, after more than a decade in the business, he operated a carnicería on prime real estate across the street from the National Cathedral and a second a few blocks north. By 1884, he had gained a seat in Congress as deputy from Michoacán, having reputedly paid large bribes for this ceremonial position. To further cement his social status, he built a neoclassical mansion in the fashionable suburbs west of the city center. Fernández's prominence made him a natural spokesman for the cartel, but it assured no special deference from other members. The González brothers, Manuel and Hernando, actually had a larger business importing cattle into the city.[38]

Mexican consumers accused the importers of monopolizing the meat supply, but measuring the degree of concentration within an industry remains an inexact science, even among modern economists. A few surviving volumes of the daily slaughterhouse accounts, preserved at the Biblioteca Nacional de Antropología e Historia, indicate that a core group of importers made up the bulk of sales, but many others brought in smaller numbers of livestock. Samples containing several consecutive months from 1871 and 1885 allow some tentative observations about the importers' business practices. In the former year, twelve importers accounted for 90 percent of the livestock butchered, while fourteen did so a decade and a half later. Merchants tended to concentrate sales in blocks, with twenty or thirty animals slaughtered each day for a week followed by a lull while

1.5 Serapión Fernández, cattle merchant and congressman from Michoacán. From John W. DeKay, *The Men of Mexico and the Land They Love* (Syracuse, NY: Mason-Henry Press, 1906).

waiting for new deliveries from the countryside. As a result, only about eight or ten importers slaughtered on any given day.[39]

Popular complaints notwithstanding, such concentration probably afforded the importers little power to set prices at artificially high levels. Established merchants may well have used intimidation to keep outsiders from slaughtering livestock at San Lucas. Enforcing market-sharing agreements among the core members of the cartel, however, would have been far more difficult because of the prohibition against monopolies contained in the Constitution of 1857. Without legally binding contracts specifying production levels, jealousy and suspicion no doubt worked to frustrate attempts to raise prices by restricting supply. Even when confronted with an outside threat, the importers found it difficult to agree on collective action. In 1844, for example, when a Mexico City lawyer, allegedly acting on behalf of foreign interests, submitted a plan to build a municipal abattoir, the bulk of the importers joined together to petition authorities to reject the plan as a monopoly. Nevertheless, two politically connected merchants, Juan Pérez Gálvez and Carlos Sánchez Navarro, broke ranks and sought to highjack the proposal for their own personal gain. The high meat prices paid by consumers probably resulted more from the cost of rural livestock and inefficient production rather than any overt manipulation, for nineteenth-century importers never regained the legal monopoly held by abasto merchants of the colonial period.[40]

"THE GREAT SPECULATORS"

Porfirian hog importers likewise operated a cartel that dated back in theory to the colonial era but had nevertheless undergone significant changes over the course of the nineteenth century. As a formal guild, colonial *tocineros* (hog butchers) had enjoyed legal protection against competition from grocery stores and other unauthorized pork vendors. About fifty shops divided the market at the end of the eighteenth century, in contrast to the handful of nobles controlling the abasto. Because of the diverse nature of the tocinero's art, the city council maintained a schedule of prices for ham, sausage, fresh meat, and pork fat, unlike the bidding used to set a flat rate for mutton and beef. The moral economy was therefore maintained by an annual procedure known as the *experiencia de cerdo* (pork experiment), overseen by the municipal president, involving the slaughter and dismemberment of three sample hogs, in order to adjust prices and account for changes in the cost of rural hogs and feed.[41] John Kicza's study of business in late colonial Mexico City found tocinerías to be precarious undertakings with heavy mortgages. Contrary to European guild practices, the owners generally entered the business from other forms of retail commerce and left the administration to experienced craftsmen, who were the closest approximation to master butchers in New Spain. Both owners and managers were invariably European by ethnicity and often by birth, but not of high social standing.[42]

The coming of free trade had far less impact on tocineros than on abasto merchants, and business practices changed little through the early republic. Already in 1792, Viceroy Revillagigedo had broken the butchers' monopoly by revoking the ban on sales outside of licensed shops, thereby exposing them to competition from the skilled tocineros of Puebla, Toluca, and Apam. Nevertheless, during the wars of independence, attorneys successfully argued for the preservation of guild rules on production to avoid public disturbances, since pigs regularly escaped from poorly maintained pens, not to mention the fire hazards from making lard and soap in unlicensed locations.[43] As a result, tocinerías remained scattered around the outskirts of the city at mid-century in roughly the same locations as during the colonial era. Notary records indicate that business practices had changed little from the late colonial enterprises, with heavily indebted shops, little concentration of ownership, and frequent turnover. The total number of tocinerías had dropped to thirty-one in 1854, but only three individuals owned two shops each, although family networks such as the Martínez brothers and the Montes de Oca clan increased the concentration somewhat.[44] Tocineros thus paralleled the general experience of tradesmen, who used informal communities to preserve their customs for decades after the liberal Constitution of Cádiz abolished the guilds in 1812.[45]

Hog importers purchased local livestock far more easily than did importers of cattle and sheep, whose range was restricted to distant provinces. Swine were raised on small farms throughout central Mexico, and even in many urban homes using kitchen scraps, which led to considerable illicit competition for licensed butchers. Kicza found virtually no vertical integration among colonial tocineros, who lacked rural estates for raising hogs and instead purchased them from producers in the present-day states of Puebla and Mexico. This organization began to change gradually after independence; Margaret Chowning has described a landowner from Michoacán purchasing a slaughterhouse in the capital as an outlet for his hogs, while at least one prosperous Mexico City tocinero raised animals on a ranch near Otumba. As urban consumption grew toward the end of the nineteenth century, hog importers pioneered the use of railroad transport to extend their source of supply into the Bajío. In the 1880s, hogs constituted 70 percent of the livestock carried on the Mexican Central Railroad, although cattle subsequently eclipsed their numbers.[46]

A turning point in the hog business came around 1870, when the Mexico City council ordered the closing of pigpens within city limits, which constituted a major nuisance for urban residents. The tocineros retained the services of attorney Manuel Romero Rubio, a prominent liberal politician, to demand compensation for their property, which they valued at more than $300,000. Failure to do so threatened to undermine the foundations of Mexican law, Romero warned, and no property owner could ever live in peace. "The most alluring projects for betterment and welfare would be converted into threats and the most cruel of sarcasm, the *public good*."[47] Lacking the funds to indemnify the tocineros, the council responded with a lengthy justification based on eighteenth- and nineteenth-century decrees. The tocineros, however, maintained copies of these same decrees, which allowed their attorneys to refute the city's legal case. The case dragged on for two years, as the council simultaneously fought to close the private casas de matanza of sheep importers, but eventually the demands of sanitation won out, forcing the tocineros to accept the new ordinances, without indemnification. As their petitions had predicted, the expense of relocating the pens outside the city forced a number of tradesmen to leave the business, concentrating production in the hands of the wealthiest merchants.[48]

The most prominent of these hog importers, Pedro Serrano, came to dominate the industry by the Porfirian era. Born in 1826 in the town of Calimaya, Mexico State, his father had worked as a tocinero in Mexico City and may have rented a shop from an ecclesiastical institution in the late colonial period. The youth did not inherit the business, but he did maintain connections with the informal guild of the early republic. His mentor, Francisco Chavolla, owner of the Tocinería "El Chivato" (The Big Goat), probably helped him get started in the business in the 1850s. If this guild background had served him well, Serrano also learned to use the liberal regime to his advantage, particularly the Lerdo Law disentailing Church property. On September 23, 1856, just three months after the passage of the law, he successfully filed suit to purchase his first shop from the Mercedarian Colegio de Belén. He rented another shop about the same time, and by 1870, he was a leader in the campaign demanding indemnification for the pigpens. Nevertheless, the loss of the pigpens served him equally well by allowing him to rent additional shops from butchers unwilling or unable to adapt to the changing profession. Even Serrano faced recurring problems; for example, in 1873 a fire broke out in a shop he rented on the Puente de Fierro. Another of his shops was closed down in 1880 by sanitary inspectors for failing to meet codes. Undeterred, he made the necessary repairs to prevent sewage from contaminating the water supply and gained permission to reopen within three months. In 1887, he purchased the hacienda of Quiringüicharo in La Piedad, the hog district of Michoacán, in order to supply his expanding business.[49]

By the early 1880s, a decade after the removal of the pens, Serrano operated eight separate factories and many more retail outlets, making him the leading tocinero in Mexico City. An industrial census of 1879 counted thirty factories with an average of ten employees in each, but a city guide published three years later listed only seventeen, nearly half of which belonged to Serrano. Moreover, Vicente Montes de Oca and Antonio García, the patriarchs of two other prominent tocinero families, owned two factories each, giving the three of them control of nearly three-quarters of the industry. The guidebook may have provided an incomplete listing, but an alternate explanation for the conflict between the two sources was suggested by Manuel Navarette. This aspiring importer complained in 1877 that "the great speculators" Serrano and Montes de Oca possessed almost all the outlets for hogs in the capital and even paid rent on ones that were closed in order to limit the competition. "Those men corner the market on almost all of the livestock that arrives in the city, making illusory almost all of the importers' profits, obliging them through an immoral and unconscionable coercion to sell all their hogs to those men at prices they set."[50]

Although Serrano dominated the market, a dozen or so merchants regularly imported smaller numbers of hogs into the city, and the city accommodated their needs when constructing a new centralized slaughterhouse for hogs at San Antonio Abad. The regulations of 1870 had improved sanitation by restricting the animals from living in the city, but they still had to be driven through the streets each morning, creating a nuisance for residents. City officials first drew up the proposal for the new slaughterhouse in 1879, anticipating a daily capacity of six hundred animals, but the final, less ambitious project did not open until around 1886. Located on the south side of the canal from the cattle and sheep abattoir of San Lucas, the sturdy brick building contained a central patio for butchering hogs, which opened onto a series of chambers for salting hams, rendering lard, making soap, and storing raw materials. Notwithstanding these shared facilities, San Antonio Abad did not represent the advent of modern meatpacking, and a separate wing contained a dozen individual chambers for importers to perform their work. Sanitation and inspection, rather than economies of scale, motivated the construction of the new abattoir. Indeed, Serrano had already made plans to relocate his business to a private slaughterhouse elsewhere in the city in order to circumvent the restrictions of a communal workspace.[51]

Both cattle and hog importers maintained cartels controlling Mexico City meat markets in 1890, although the degree of concentration within the two industries had shifted over the course of the nineteenth century. The legal monopoly of the abasto had allowed a handful of powerful nobles to dominate sales of meat and mutton in the late colonial era, but independence threw open the trade in a particularly free-wheeling fashion. A measure of order had returned to the trade by mid-century, and the resulting arrangement left more than a dozen wealthy merchants competing for the market. Hog butchering institutions had remained more stable because of the larger capital investments in tocinería shops, but by the end of the century, production had been even more tightly concentrated. The concentration of power within the merchant elite also had important effects on workers within these industries.

"THE NATURAL BORN ENEMY OF THE PIG"

Butchers have labored under a nefarious reputation that dates back at least to the ancient Romans. In medieval Italian cities they were considered the most militant of guilds, and the French Enlightenment author Diderot described them as "men whose faces bear a ferocious and bloodthirsty stamp."[52] A Mexican satirist of the mid-nineteenth century called the butcher "the natural born enemy of the pig. A person accustomed since childhood to sustain himself on chicharrones."[53] Master butchers in European guilds often possessed considerable wealth to compensate for their social stigma, but in colonial Mexico, the meat trades were stratified by race as well as by wealth. Spanish grandees controlled the abasto monopoly, middling Creoles and mestizos sold meat at retail, and poor Native Americans worked in slaughterhouses with virtually no opportunity for advancement. The municipal reorganization of the industry in 1850 transformed labor relations, but the patriarchal structure of the trade remained in place, with importers using their power and credit to control both slaughterhouse workers and retail meat cutters. Nevertheless, the importers relied on the meat cutters not only for their labor, but also as allies in their struggles with city health officials, and this gave the working butchers a latent source of power that later fueled union activism.

Tocineros operated one of the most highly skilled and capital-intensive guilds in all of New Spain. Modern images of corner butcher shops cannot convey the full magnitude of these colonial factories, which included living quarters, work areas, and pigpens in addition to the store-front. The slaughter was performed in a central patio, which also contained a variety of cauldrons for rending choice strips of fat into lard, frying the skin into chicharrones, and transforming the remaining scraps into soap. Hams, bacon, and sausages were prepared in a salting and drying room, then left to hang until ready for sale. The typical colonial tocinería employed five workers, including butchers, soap makers, and general servants. More details of the division of labor and status within the trade can be gleaned from an account drawn up in 1811 for a relatively prosperous shop, worth nearly $20,000, owned by one Manuel Fernández de Peredo. The managing partner, Francisco Sánchez, listed small cash advances to a *mayordomo*, Ignacio Hernández, the drover, Marco Ramírez, the *matador*, Miguel, and a soap maker who apparently did not even merit recording a first name. Juan Arias's mid-nineteenth-century literary description of tocineros—classifying them into three categories, shop owners, sausage vendors, and pig slaughterers—implied that the mayordomo, Ignacio Hernández, rather than the matador, Miguel, probably performed the culinary jobs of preparing hams and sausages. Sánchez's inventory also included a water-carrier, Francisco, who made daily rounds through the neighborhood, and two individuals, Domingo and Eusebio, who probably cared for the pigs.[54]

Ethnic and trade specialization likewise prevailed among abasto workers, although to a lesser degree than among tocineros. Retail butchers selling mutton and beef were known as *tablajeros* for the "tables" or chopping blocks on which they cut meat in the various carnicerías around the city. According to municipal regulations, only clean and well-dressed Spaniards could perform this important public service, although census data indicates that a number of mixed-race castes as well as Native Americans also undertook this commerce. Municipal regulations attempted to separate retail sales from the wholesale contractor, but by the eighteenth century, high annual rents insured that only nobles and wealthy merchants could afford an outlet, and so tablajeros worked as employees for the abasto cartel in a patron-client relationship that undermined the paternalist intentions of the legislation. Master butchers in eighteenth-century France developed an elaborate hierarchy of cuts, reserving tenderloins for noble houses while selling less refined meats to bourgeois families and offal to the poor. In Mexico City, however, officials prohibited differential pricing; all beef had to be sold at the same fixed price and so meat cutters had little incentive to develop such specialized systems of cuts until the nineteenth century.[55]

Slaughterhouse workers had the lowest status within the meat trade, yet they nevertheless developed a collective identity based on their essential skills. The colonial abattoir at San Lucas consisted of a large pen with small and large compartments for butchering cattle and sheep individually, an enclosed patio that served as a meat market, and corrals for holding livestock before the slaughter. The floor was made of *tezontle*, a red volcanic rock commonly used for construction, but a porous one that tended to absorb the filthy waters, making it difficult to clean the slaughterhouse. The facility operated with around twenty-five employees, including a handful of officials such as the inspector of weights. The rest appeared on abasto inventories as simple *peones*, but despite the contractors' indifference, this cadre of butchers took pride in their work and considered themselves apart from the retail meat cutters as the *común de carniceros* (community of slaughterhouse workers). In an 1813 petition to the city council, they recalled "for extensive years having always slaughtered bulls for the meat supply of this city, on the site called the *rastro* [abattoir]; they taught their sons this same trade ... and thus from one [generation] to the next they have inherited this destiny."[56]

This incipient trade union, already threatened by the rise of private slaughterhouses for sheep in the late colonial period, was decimated in the chaos of the early republic. The abasto merchants who maintained these casas de matanza employed smaller teams, averaging about six workers per location, and did not hire members of the carnicero collective. One can only speculate on the rivalries between these different groups of laborers, but the colonial livestock merchants certainly had little sympathy for the city butchers they depended on for slaughtering cattle. When workers from the común sought day jobs in private slaughterhouses during the upheavals of independence, the contractors "made things very difficult for us (nos dificulta mucho)."[57] The privatization of cattle butchering in the early republic may well have destroyed the solidarity of the colonial común, and a new organization had developed by the mid-nineteenth century, when documentary information is once again available.

The ordinance of 1850 helped to formalize labor relations at the San Lucas slaughterhouse into a contractual arrangement that was mutually beneficial and yet plagued by suspicion between importers and so-called butcher "captains." These formidable captains retained great control over operations on the killing floor. They recruited their own teams of peons to assist them in herding the cattle into the corral and dragging out the carcasses for dressing and sale. Their practice of cutting meat to their own specifications likewise demonstrated their independence, as did the elaborate brands they carved in the hides, to the chagrin of the importers. The butcher captains took their pay directly in the form of viscera, which they resold to female ambulant vendors for a tidy sum, and they may also have received cash wages of as much as two pesos a head by 1870. The ordinance of 1850 specifically required the importers to pay the municipal taxes, perhaps to prevent them from using competition between rival captains as a way of driving down their wages.[58]

Despite their independence within the workplace, the butcher captains remained subordinate to the importers in significant ways. One demonstration of this patriarchal labor relationship can be seen in the way that butcher captains assisted the importers in their goal of monopolizing the meat supply. The slaughter captains depended on cattle importers for work, and were often accused of helping limit competition by refusing to slaughter livestock for independent suppliers. In 1870, for example, during a struggle with the city council over private casas de matanza, the municipal government attempted to assume the task of supplying the city, but the captains walked off the job in support of their employers. City officials even accused the butchers of resorting to violence in support of the importers' monopoly. In turn, the merchants stood by their faithful workers, denying that they had rioted or rebelled: "Their conduct has been, on the contrary, dignified and measured, as it should correspond to the laboring citizens."[59] At the end of the century, *El Economista Mexicano* concluded that the Mexico City meat monopoly dated to about 1850, when the butcher captains assumed their formal organization.[60]

The city's retail merchants likewise remained subservient to the importers, as they had since the colonial period. This dependency resulted first from the general scarcity of credit facilities in Mexico, which meant that small shopkeepers relied on their wholesale suppliers to bankroll their daily operations. The unequal relationship was also maintained by the organization of the industry in which large numbers of independent tablajeros held little bargaining power against the handful of wealthy importers. The first count of retail operations, taken in 1849, listed ninety-four carnicerías specializing in mutton and beef and nineteen vendors of tocinería. There were also sixty-four *casillas mixtas* (mixed stalls) selling beef, mutton, and pork, indicating the gradual decline of colonial trade specialization. Two decades later, the number of small shopkeepers had grown to more than 250 outlets. In addition to these fixed locations in storefronts and market stalls, ambulatory vendors selling all manner of meats and other foods were common on the streets and in the *costumbrista* paintings of everyday life in mid-century Mexico City. These scenes depicted portable carniceros who fixed sides of meat on the backs of mules and went door-to-door cutting slices off by request. With so many retailers, competition served primarily to reduce the already-low profit margins of small vendors without affecting the wealthy importers.[61]

Despite its masculine associations, the butcher trade included many women, although they tended toward the least prestigious end of the profession. Colonial women had sold tripe and offal in the streets while male tablajeros maintained formal shops for higher status meats. Women also operated most of the unlicensed butcher shops, called *trapiches*, on the margins of the cities such as Puebla and Guadalajara. The very term *carnicera* was an insult for women, similar perhaps to the modern usage of "butch." As late as 1904, a sanitary inspector in Xochimilco found that male butchers had wooden tables to display their meats at the same time that women prepared tripe while sitting on the ground. Women also operated considerable numbers of regular meat outlets in the Porfirian era, but they appeared predominantly in urban markets, where capital requirements were low, rather than as independent shopkeepers.[62]

Yet male slaughterhouse workers and retail merchants were likewise considered untrustworthy and violent by the larger society. During the colonial era, Mexico City cloisters rejected the daughters of slaughterhouse workers who wished to become nuns. One Pedro de Artecona was denied admission to a lay brotherhood in 1753 because his "profession of tocinero is by nature scarcely decent and not at all corresponding to...the Holy office...but only to selling fresh pork meat, fat of the same, sausage, weenies, and ham."[63] Even more serious was the case of a tocinera from Querétaro named Ana de Pineda, who was denounced to the Mexican Inquisition for hanging bacon and hams from two crucifixes in her shop. The Holy Office concluded, "without doubt she must be a Jew"—notwithstanding kosher laws forbidding the handling of pork.[64] In the nineteenth century, regulations at San Lucas took the precaution of ordering all knives and hatchets to be locked up at the slaughterhouse to prevent their use for violent crimes. The government also attempted to raise the moral standards of workers by prohibiting gambling and swearing, although enforcement of these codes remained problematic.[65]

The meat trades of New Spain never achieved the European guild ideal of a community of apprentices, journeymen, and masters, bound together to control quality and regulate prices. Even the collective identities that had formed among workers during the colonial era were fragmented in the early republican era. The system of butcher captains that arose in the mid-nineteenth-century slaughterhouse proved particularly well adapted to facilitate a patriarchal control of the industry by importers. In turn, these patron-client relations extended down to the teams of peons recruited and paid by the captains. Retailers likewise depended for credit and supplies on the wholesale importers. Only by acting collectively could the more numerous slaughterhouse workers and retail meat cutters challenge the power of the merchant cartel. In doing so, however, they received little support from government inspectors, who maintained a paternalistic attitude consigning consumers and workers alike to a dependent status, as will be discussed in the following section.

LIBERALISM AND REGULATION

The concurrent development of liberal ideology and medical science in the nineteenth century led to a fundamental reevaluation of the question of who was best suited to guarantee the quality of meat sold in markets. In early modern Europe, the technical skills of master craftsmen had given the guilds considerable authority over production techniques, although Catholic beliefs about the sinfulness of humanity had nevertheless justified government supervision of markets. Enlightenment philosophers however challenged this Scholastic conception of human nature by considering the pursuit of self-interest not as a threat to society but rather as a source of material abundance. The balance between public health and private enterprise tipped particularly far toward the latter in nineteenth-century Mexico City as a result of a general atmosphere of government instability. Overlapping jurisdictions of municipal and federal authorities likewise undermined the police powers of the city. The replacement of political appointees by medical professionals began to redress this balance in the second half of the nineteenth century. Officials within the Board of Health (Consejo Superior de Salubridad) used their scientific training to assert an image of impartiality and thereby counter the arguments formerly made by businessmen that inspectors would violate the principles of free trade. As in Europe and the United States, the rise of medical science allowed the Mexican state to reassert public health regulation, but only gradually and in the face of considerable opposition.[66]

Overseeing the meat trade was a vital concern for municipal authorities in colonial Mexico City. Although responsibility for supply was contracted out through the abasto system, a special tribunal called the *fiel ejecutoria* supervised public abattoirs and meat markets. Public health and pollution remained constant concerns, especially in the early years when the market was located in the Zócalo, the central plaza of the city. In 1543, clergymen and other prominent residents finally prevailed on the city council "to remove the slaughterhouse from the public square, because it is not in a proper place and there is much stink."[67] Once the abattoir had been relocated to the south side of the city, deputies of the fiel ejecutoria stood watch to ensure that livestock was well-fed and free of disease, although judging by the regular complaints of consumers, that ideal may rarely have been attained. The city also appointed inspectors of weights (fiel repesador) in each carniceria so that patrons could have their meat weighed independently if they suspected fraud. In a study of eighteenth-century criminality, Gabriel Haslip-Viera has identified more than a hundred cases of butchers being prosecuted for consumer fraud. The bulk of these charges involved simple short-weighting of customers, but one late colonial official testified that in some months between two and three hundred steers were carried into the city "dead and completely rotten."[68] When livestock shortages became acute, as in the summer of 1805, the *alcalde* (mayor) personally toured the markets as a paternalistic demonstration of the government's concern for the meat supply. Authority over the meat supply theoretically fell to the city council, but jurisdictional disputes had already surfaced in the colonial period; indeed, successful bids for the abasto contract required bribes to the viceroy, his secretary, and other officials.[69]

The declaration of free trade and the instability of government institutions led to a virtual collapse of regulatory authority in the early republican era, briefly replacing the paternalistic state with a market-place governed by supply and demand. With municipal revenues invariably depleted and palace revolutions constantly looming, authorities concentrated the enforcement of "orden y buena policia" (order and good policing) on the worst offenders against health and sanitation. In 1822, the cabildo denounced the "completely pernicious tolerance of vagabond pigs in the streets," and ordered the apprehension and slaughter of all such animals, although a decade later, the council found it necessary to reissue the ban.[70] The proliferation of slaughterhouses posed even worse problems, polluting the city while facilitating the sale of unwholesome meat. In 1839, General Ramón Rayón drew particular attention to "the unbearable foulness, the putrefaction of blood, the inadequate disposal of manure" in a corral on Cacahuatal Street.[71] The paternalist instinct thus remained for government officials to protect residents from pollution as well as from contamination. Nevertheless, a municipal commission convened a few years later admitted the "grave danger to public health" posed by the illicit sale of corrupt meat by *capoteros*, who operated clandestine slaughterhouses in the suburbs. "It seems incredible that a city like Mexico has neglected for such a long time the important matter of the meat supply," the report concluded.[72]

Already by 1830, officials had discussed the possibility of reestablishing the colonial abasto, but the importers fiercely resisted all such attempts using the language of liberalism. In 1844, they published a lengthy petition in the liberal journal *El Siglo XIX* denouncing a private proposal to construct a municipal abattoir as a "genuine assault on our fortunes according to both ancient and modern laws that guarantee property." The importers even denied the need for a municipal meat inspector, claiming that such an official would merely serve the interests of a slaughterhouse contractor. In response to the allegations of unwholesome meat being sold, they argued that their own knowledge and honor provided the best protection for consumers against unwholesome meat. "The multiplication of slaughterhouses allows that sick animals could be sold. But this never happens. We are honorable." The importers blamed any cases of fraud that had occurred on dishonest proprietors of small retail stalls, thus showing the mutual distrust that underlay labor relations. To conclude their petition, the importers returned to the principles of liberalism and denounced the proposed slaughterhouse as a monopoly "according to the doctrines of

Jovellanos and Say"—two of the leading continental interpreters of the free-trade advocate Adam Smith. The editors of *El Mosquito Mexicano* also took up the importer's cause, calling the project an "odious speculation" intended to monopolize the meat supply.[73]

The city council declined the proposal, continuing its policy of neglect and teaching the butchers an important lesson about the effectiveness of liberal discourse, particularly the supremacy of property rights, in defending their autonomy from both potential competitors and municipal control. The irony here was that cattle and sheep merchants were asserting their right to regulate themselves based largely on the qualifications of a guild structure that had never really existed. Liberal language was thus not taken straight from European philosophies, but rather mixed with local experiences to form a distinctively Mexican ideology.

The city finally imposed a new regulatory regime in the aftermath of the disastrous U.S.-Mexican War (1846–1848), but the new inspector, Francisco Carbajal y Espinosa, faced an uphill battle in asserting his authority over the importers. Upon taking his post in the summer of 1848, the former National Guard lieutenant colonel was confronted by a genuine insurrection of livestock merchants who refused to pay newly imposed city taxes. The most prominent tax rebel, Rafael Villegas, owned one of the two main slaughterhouses for cattle, and Carbajal promptly took advantage of the incident by closing the facility. Rather than join in solidarity, the rival slaughterhouse owner, Manuel Arellano, announced his opposition to Villegas in a declaration resembling the political *pronunciamientos* of contemporary caudillos (warlords). Arellano may have expected to be rewarded for his loyalty to the government with a monopoly on the cattle business, but he was soon disappointed when Carbajal ordered livestock to be driven from the private Garrapata Street abattoir to the old municipal corral at San Lucas. Outraged at the duplicitous meat inspector, Arellano used cronies on the city council to delay the opening of San Lucas and filed a complaint with the Federal District governor claiming that the municipality had deprived him of property rights to the Garrapata slaughterhouse, which was precisely the opposite of the position he had taken earlier in his pronouncement against Villegas. The city council agreed that after decades of neglect, San Lucas was unfit for slaughter, awarding a temporary victory to Arellano, but the inspector proceeded to renovate the old facility over the winter, and had it ready for reopening in April 1849.[74] A bitter legal battle ensued, in which Arellano protested the inspector's "despotic and most dangerous proceedings against my property." Carbajal meanwhile responded by accusing the merchant of defrauding the municipal treasury.[75]

The council ultimately resolved the dispute through a negotiated settlement in which the prominent merchant relinquished the Garrapata slaughterhouse for a generous indemnification. The city's regulatory powers were consolidated with the publication of a new federal ordinance, dated April 1, 1850, which declared San Lucas to be the sole legal slaughterhouse for cattle in the city. The twenty-four existing casas de matanza for sheep and thirty tocinería shops were allowed to remain open provisionally, perhaps for fear of additional indemnity claims that city finances could ill afford. [76]

Although the regulatory regime had been established in law, implementation relied on the inspector's authority, which was soon undermined when Arrellano followed through on his vendetta against Carbajal. In January 1851, the powerful merchant won election to the city council along with Manuel Morales Puente, son of another prominent livestock dealer. Meanwhile, their allies within the syndicate of importers and slaughterhouse owners engineered a vote demanding Carbajal's removal from office. When the cabildo took up the matter, the presence of Arrellano and Morales tipped the balance against the inspector. Carbajal's supporters in the meat trade circulated a petition in his favor, which garnered large numbers of signatures, including some who had formerly supported Arellano in his battle to keep the Garrapata slaughterhouse open. Nevertheless, the Federal District governor rejected an appeal, concluding that the council vote was legally binding. Even after a replacement had been chosen, Carbajal refused to hand over his office, and his final words in the city register, recorded on July 3, 1851, survive as an archival epitaph: "Until the last moment I have complied with my duties."[77]

Carbajal's downfall had important implications for the regulation of meat in Mexico City. By demonstrating their power to bring down the inspector, Arellano and his cronies had set a precedent and encouraged future challenges to the 1850 ordinances. Indeed, Carbajal's replacement, Ignacio Muñoz Campuzano, served for less than two years before being replaced on a temporary basis by Miguel Buenrostro, a prominent liberal attorney and former council secretary. When a permanent inspector,

Bonifacio Tosta, was named in June 1853, he promptly attacked the attorney's record, and within another two years Tosta had also been removed from office and replaced by Buenrostro once again. The musical chairs undermined the inspectors' effectiveness in office, and even the basic registration of slaughterhouses quickly became a dead letter. Without some degree of permanence, officials had little chance of gaining the knowledge needed to regulate the trade, not to mention acquiring the respect of merchants and workers. The constant turnover in political office during the early republic, which was so deleterious to national progress, thereby filtered down to basic police powers.[78]

Two decades of civil strife followed before the municipal government finally acted to remove pig pens and sheep slaughterhouses from the city. In the mid-1860s, the French-imposed empire of Maximilian had taken an important first step by providing space at San Lucas for capoteros, who had formerly butchered sheep in clandestine locations in the suburbs for lack of an authorized casa de matanza. This reform both legitimized the work of the informal trade and imposed greater competition on the more prominent merchants who controlled the private slaughterhouses.[79] In 1869, a few years after the legitimate government of Benito Juárez returned to power, the city council revoked the licenses of all such private casas as well as of the tocinero's pig pens. Mutton sales had been declining for decades and a number of slaughterhouses had long been abandoned, but the remaining owners refused to relinquish their property without prior indemnification. When the city council rejected their petition, Antonio Escandón and Ramón Ocaranza appealed directly to Secretary of the Interior Manuel Saavedra. The merchants complained about the wretched conditions at the municipal abattoir and the infringement on their constitutional guarantees of private property, then argued that the city lacked the legislative authority to close the casas because they had been authorized by federal law in 1850. The tocineros challenged the council on similar grounds, likewise demanding indemnification for their property.[80]

The slaughterhouse battle continued for another two years, eventually encompassing lawsuits, public letters, appeals to federal authorities, and even physical violence. The council naturally recognized the inadequate conditions at San Lucas, which could scarcely accommodate the current demand for beef, let alone mutton. They even considered using forced prison labor to clean up the slaughterhouse. City officials would not relent, however, in their insistence on asserting police powers, and in December 1870 they decided to hold the livestock merchants responsible for abattoir improvements by raising slaughter fees for cattle and by imposing new taxes on sheep. The importers then registered their protest by refusing to slaughter, prompting the council to begin purchasing livestock with municipal funds. The imperial government had used such a ploy in 1866, after merchants refused to accept price controls intended to gain relief from wartime shortages. "The success of this measure corresponded to the hopes of those who conceived of it," wrote the council, noting that prices had fallen in the city as the supply of cattle rose. Finally, in a swipe at the liberal doctrines invoked by the butchers, the city officials concluded: "deeds, which speak more loudly than theories, have come to justify the good judgment of this decision."[81]

Four years later, however, slaughterhouse workers walked off the job in solidarity with the merchants. Municipal officials depicted this as a veritable uprising; in a report to Interior Secretary Saavedra, they denounced the butchers for "resorting, as they have, to a riot (motín), impeding with threats the slaughter of cattle, as is their custom. Such acts merit the most severe reprisals."[82] The council insisted nevertheless that the city remained well supplied with meat, although this optimistic claim was refuted a few days later by the press, which reported with alarm the "exorbitant price" for meat.[83]

The importers demonstrated their political skills once again by outmaneuvering the city council with a novel legal strategy seeking to redefine the taxes as a form of rent, thereby binding the city to a contractual relationship of providing adequate services at San Lucas. In a personal letter to President Juárez, Ramón Ocaranza offered, in essence, to give up the casas de matanza, which were anyway simple corrals with little capital invested, in return for improvements at San Lucas, where the importers now made most of their money on cattle. This appeal to the chief executive apparently caught the council off guard, for the secretary responded by simply rehashing the argument for a public slaughterhouse: "The most sacred object of municipal administration is without doubt the care of health and public hygiene, because the lives of the inhabitants depend upon it." The abattoir's "importance is so evident that in no pueblo, however insignificant, in which there is a town council, does it fail to exist, and only in Mexico, in the Capital of the Republic there is no slaughter-house, and even more, they try to call into doubt the right of the Municipality to establish it, which they classify as a monopoly, when even in the most free countries on earth it is legitimately authorized."[84]

While accepting the council's argument in principle, Juárez awarded victory to the importers in his arbitration decree of January 12, 1871. He ruled first that the city council had to renovate the slaughterhouse within six months—before closing the casas de matanza. Moreover, he ordered a reduction in slaughter fees and insisted that the money go directly to upkeep at San Lucas and could not be used to help balance the municipal treasury. The city council dragged its feet in complying with the federal order, perhaps fearing that even the modest fee increases would be abolished, as the importers had requested, when the works were concluded. The president did not go that far, however, and the renovations were completed by November 1874, more than five years after the struggle had begun.[85]

Despite this political victory for the importers, the balance of power had already begun to shift toward an increasingly professional corps of medical authorities. Modern veterinary medicine had emerged in Enlightenment France, where the first schools were established in the 1760s in response to widespread cattle epidemics, and by the 1850s, European doctors had uncovered anthrax and other contagious animal diseases. Inspired by French advances, in 1856 the Mexican government created a veterinary school within the recently founded National School of Agriculture. The curriculum was established by a Mexican doctor with European training, Leopoldo Río de la Loza, with the assistance of Eugene Bergère, a French military veterinarian resident in Mexico. The first class of five students, including José de la Luz Gómez and Manuel Aragón, graduated in 1862, allowing the government of Maximilian to appoint for the first time a trained veterinarian to serve as meat inspector. Scientists thereby replaced retired military officers and lawyers, who had previously supervised the trade, although civil war continued to impede progress in health reform until the end of the decade.[86]

Dr. Manuel Aragón, confirmed in the post of meat inspector by the liberal regime in 1870, had a powerful tool in the microscope he used for carrying out his duties. Perhaps the first demonstration of the scientists' authority came when the Federal District governor, Tiburcio Montiel, once again issued an order to close the city's pigpens in 1871. Unlike the primitive corrals for sheep, the tocinerías had been maintained at great expense and their owners were determined to defend them. To do so, however, the tocineros found themselves forced to respond in the unfamiliar language of medical science. In a petition to President Juárez, Miguel Fuentes and Higinio Gutiérrez began by admitting the inconvenience of maintaining pens in the city, but pointed out that many other aspects of modern life such as the railroads also brought discomforts along with benefits. They then argued: "In effect, the disposition [closing the pens] follows from the assumption that the pens are unhealthy, a concept that has never been supported by the governor and that appears to us false in every aspect. We confess that we are not competent in scientific questions, and since neither is the governor, we judge it appropriate to consult first with the Board of Health." Their novel proposal involved a study of tocinería workers to determine if they were any less healthy on average than other inhabitants of the city. Where before merchants had adopted the language of liberalism, they now attempted to harness the scientific method, but their plan was doomed since Mexican medical authority, embodied in the Board of Health, had advised against the pens in the first place. The tocineros were therefore forced to accept the new ordinances, without indemnification.[87]

Another important step in the assertion of police power through medical authorities came with the reorganization of the Health Board in 1872. The Consejo Superior de Salubridad had been founded by Antonio López de Santa Anna in 1841 as an extension of the *Protomedicato*, the colonial era regulatory body for physicians. The liberal government dramatically expanded the board's purview to include market and slaughterhouse inspections, along with vaccination programs, civil registrations, and even the inspection of prostitutes. The reorganization also brought a regular annual budget and new laboratory space, first in the School of Mines and later in the old customs house on the Plaza of Santo Domingo. Although the inspectors were now federal employees of the Health Board, the municipal government retained ownership of the San Lucas slaughterhouse and also maintained its own overseers and tax collectors, thereby establishing the potential for continued conflicts of jurisdiction. The appointment of Dr. Eduardo Licéaga as head of the board in 1886 further expanded the prestige and influence of federal sanitary authorities. A close friend and personal physician to President Díaz,

Licéaga immediately began work on an ambitious health code, approved in 1891, which extended the board's jurisdiction outside the Federal District to include territories, ports, and border crossings. This trend toward centralization likewise extended to the regulation of the meat industry as the Porfirian era progressed.[88]

Meat merchants and health officials struggled throughout the nineteenth century to define the boundaries of government authority in the marketplace. The collapse of the colonial regime and the civil wars of the early republic hamstrung the city's police powers, allowing the temporary ascendancy of the importers. A lack of continuity between liberal and conservative administrations delayed the reestablishment of a stable regulatory regime, even though officials on both sides of the ideological divide shared the common goal of preventing abuses in meat markets and limiting urban pollution. The rise of medical professionalism began to shift the balance of power in favor of regulators, but politically powerful importers resisted this trend at every step. Moreover, institutional inertia and a shortage of funds often stymied attempts to improve the meat supply; for example, the crowding of cattle in the slaughter pens at San Lucas made it virtually impossible to carry out adequate veterinary inspections. The delivery of meat to retail shops constituted another problem, and in December 1886, the city council ordered the use of covered cars rather than mules, but when summer rains flooded the city a few years later, meat merchants petitioned for a return to the unhygienic transportation methods of the past. Even more worrying was the rapid urbanization, which threatened to overwhelm every improvement in public health and meat supply that the government achieved.[89]

THE MEAT SUPPLY ON
THE BRINK OF MODERNITY

The Porfirian shopper confronted a seemingly Hobbesian struggle of all against all just to put meat in the *cazuela* (cooking pot). Popular beliefs depicted the meat cartel as a rapacious monopoly of importers who fattened themselves like hogs on the backs of the starving masses. These images also bore aristocratic overtones, although the colonial nobility had in fact abandoned the meat trade at the time of independence. Retail butchers, meanwhile, were viewed as knife-wielding petty merchants who passed off unwholesome cuts of meat and short-weighted customers at every opportunity. Meat inspectors, far from being impartial guardians of the marketplace, appeared as lackeys of the meat monopoly and as enemies of poor residents who tried to supplement the family budget by raising piglets on kitchen scraps.[90]

These popular images were clearly exaggerated; in fact, consumers often developed personal relationships with the butchers who extended them credit on a daily basis. Meanwhile, meat importers could only dream of having the power to determine prices arbitrarily that the popular sectors attributed to them. Nevertheless, the attempts of municipal authorities to regulate the industry did in fact facilitate increasing concentration within the industry. And although it is difficult to define precisely the moral economy of meat consumption—who ate how much and what kind of meat—the fundamental inequality of the provisioning system remains clear. While the Porfirian elite and the emerging middle class indulged in refined European haute cuisine, prepared with a Mexican accent of course, the working classes struggled to add scraps of meat to the staple diet of tortillas and beans.

The nineteenth-century experience with liberalism points to the difficulty of establishing a legal framework to ensure the proper functioning of markets. The principles of free commerce and private property actually provided Mexico City meat importers the weapons to subvert such a regime. The case of the meat supply thus supports the recent thesis of José Antonio Aguilar Rivera that the instability of early republican government in Mexico derived not from any Hispanic incompatibility with liberalism but rather from the inherent fragility of the liberal constitutional model itself. Appalled by the constant revolutions plaguing the nation in the decades after independence, statesman José María Luis Mora complained that Mexicans were too timid in adopting the liberal institutions of the United States and Western Europe. Aguilar's comparative study demonstrated, to the contrary, that an overly doctrinaire adherence to the principle of limited power left the government vulnerable to, and even encouraged, pronunciamientos by opportunistic politicians. The U.S. federal government had reacted to similar threats, from Shay's Rebellion to the Civil War, by temporarily assuming extraordinary, at times dictatorial, powers that were denied to their Mexican counterparts. Health authorities were likewise hindered for much of the nineteenth century in their efforts to impose a regulatory regime in Mexico City.[91]

Notwithstanding their impressive victories, the importers faced a daunting prospect in their long-term struggle to control the meat industry. Even while insisting on their property rights, butchers had used the language of public service to resist municipal efforts to regulate their establishments. At times, the interests of merchants and the state coincided, when the sanitary goals of health officials seeking to eradicate clandestine slaughter matched the commercial desire of the butchers to limit competition. When interests conflicted, the butchers asserted that their professional experience best guaranteed the well-being of consumers, particularly the poor. This argument proved largely successful in confrontations with political appointees such as Francisco Carbajal, but their reputation gradually faded before the consolidation of medical authority. The butchers tried valiantly to adopt a patina of scientific respectability, to the point of advocating public health studies, but in this early knowledge economy, the Health Board held the upper hand. Thus the liberal dream of democratic capitalism succumbed to authoritarianism in Mexico, even as the power of private property gave way to scientific administration.

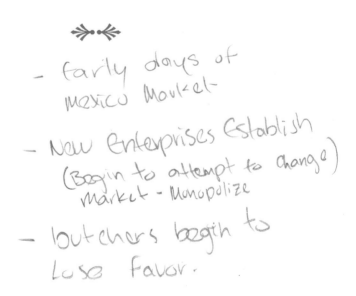

- Early days of Mexico Market

- New Enterprises establish (Begin to attempt to change) Market - Monopolize

- butchers begin to Lose Favor.

CHAPTER TWO

The Porfirian Jungle

As administrator of the San Lucas slaughterhouse, José de la Luz Gómez bore a grave responsibility for ensuring the health of consumers in the capital. His qualifications for the position were impeccable, including the very first diploma in veterinary medicine granted by the National School of Agriculture and, by 1890, nearly three decades of experience in the field of bacteriology. This slim man with rounded shoulders and oval spectacles risked his own safety each morning while carrying out livestock inspections within the chaotic slaughter pens at San Lucas. In addition to his daily workload as a member of the Health Board, Gómez also devoted his energies to planning the modernization of the nation's meat supply. The construction of a new slaughterhouse offered a potentially dramatic showcase for the Porfirian development project, but it could also ruin his personal reputation if the design did not live up to expectations. Slaughterhouse workers faced even greater hazards when the imported technology threatened to create a Mexican version of the Chicago packinghouse "jungle."

Dreaming of modernity while standing in manure, Gómez epitomized the lower ranks of the Porfirian technocratic elite. The científico clique came to power in the final decade of the nineteenth century as the Porfirio Díaz administration underwent a transition from liberal to positivist government. "Effective suffrage and no re-election," the revolutionary battle cry that won Díaz the presidency in 1876, had grown increasingly awkward as he engineered his own re-election in 1884 and every four years thereafter. While introducing technocrats into the government, he therefore substituted another slogan, "plenty of administration and not too much politics."[1] Mexico's chronic budget deficit had long impeded effective administration, but the Dublán Accords of 1888 refinanced the foreign debt, making European and U.S. investment capital available on a large scale. This in turn allowed Mexico to import technical expertise from abroad, for notwithstanding their name, the científicos were bankers more often than engineers. The combination of foreign capital and skills achieved some of the great triumphs of the Porfirian age, including the completion of a drainage canal to prevent the recurrent flooding of Mexico City and a massive expansion of the national railroad network.[2]

Nevertheless, the Porfirian development project also required the inculcation of factory discipline among Mexican laborers to match the productivity of industrial countries. Britain's hundred-year head start to industrialization entailed advantages not only in technology, but also in training workers to handle these new machines efficiently. The Mexican workforce consisted largely of rural migrants who were accustomed to the demanding yet self-made pace of agriculture. By contrast, industrial mass production required different work rhythms, timed to the clock, and failure to keep pace with this machine-filled environment could bring not only disapproval from overseers but even disabling injury or death. Certainly at the San Lucas slaughterhouse, butcher captains continued to perform their work using traditional methods and with little interference from either importers or city officials. Attempts to increase efficiency in North American packinghouses had magnified the hazards to workers, who were forced to wield their knives at ever greater speeds. Under the best of circumstances, therefore, transferring industrial meat processing techniques promised to impose similar demands and dangers on Mexican workers. At the same time, the creation of a new slaughterhouse compromised a delicate balance of power that existed between butchers and their employers.

The struggle for modernization was not just a question of social engineering but also a political battle between rival elites seeking to bolster their economic power. Unable to match the productivity of foreign capital, Mexican manufacturers competed instead for political favor to gain protected markets. The import duties and tax exemptions that could make an inefficient factory profitable formed part of a political arrangement designed to reward loyalty to President Díaz. By encouraging rivalries within the elite, don Porfirio sought to protect himself against the palace coups that had long bedeviled Mexico. He brought young científicos such as Treasury Secretary José Yves Limantour into the government not only to utilize their financial expertise, but also as a counterbalance to the old guard of liberal *caciques*, generals who still held power at the state level. To complicate further the political calculations, Díaz toned down the anticlerical policies of the liberals to establish a working relationship with the Catholic opposition. The deft hand needed to balance these competing interests helped ensure Díaz's position as the indispensable man of Mexico. Yet contrary to the científicos' positivist belief that "order and progress" went hand in hand, the spoils system intended to promote political stability often stymied economic policies.

This chapter examines the first attempt to construct a modern slaughterhouse in Mexico City in the final decade of the nineteenth century. The United States and France offered two competing technological models, and Mexican officials' failure to appreciate the differences augured poorly for the future success of the project. Moreover, construction delays continued for seven years, and when the slaughterhouse finally seemed ready for service, officials rushed to open it without having resolved all technical difficulties. The resulting crisis left shoppers virtually unable to find meat, inspiring recriminations between merchants, butchers, officials, and consumers. As a result, the slaughterhouse opening offers unique historical insights on the market culture of Porfirian Mexico.

COMPETING DESIGNS

The second half of the nineteenth century was a time of upheaval in the supply of meat throughout the North Atlantic world. Advances in medical science had prompted widespread concern about unwholesome slaughterhouse practices that in many cases had changed little since the Middle Ages. Reformers agreed on the general need for improvements, but debated the institutional framework in which the meat industry should function. Generally speaking, continental Europe favored public abattoirs that were open to all merchants, while Britain and the United States opted instead for private slaughterhouses, which ultimately formed the basis for an industrial revolution in meat supply.[3] Porfirian modernizers were aware of these two competing models, but the choice of an appropriate technology for Mexico City was not at all clear.

By contrast, the problems with the existing system were obvious to anyone familiar with the San Lucas slaughterhouse. An architect's drawing from the end of the nineteenth century (see figure 2.1) illustrates the maze of departments and rooms that had been built haphazardly around the original eighteenth-century corrals. The sheep pens zigzagging along the west side of the facility had a ramshackle appearance but nevertheless proved satisfactory given the relatively stable demand for mutton. The existence of twelve separate chambers allowed regular merchants to maintain their animals apart from those of their rivals, while the butchers worked in a common central patio from which porters carried the meat to an adjacent market. A similar arrangement for cattle, however, could not keep pace with the steady growth in consumption. The corral had been built for an average daily slaughter of 150 steers, but by 1890, workers crowded together more than twice that number inside, making it difficult for the butcher captains and their teams to perform their duties. The chaos of slaughter under such jam-packed conditions also allowed thieves to make off with considerable quantities of meat. The location of San Lucas, formerly on the outskirts of town, had become another serious problem as a populous working-class neighborhood had grown up around the slaughterhouse. Moreover, decades of service without sufficient water for cleaning had left San Lucas with a "constant bad odor perceptible at a great distance, owing to the violent putrefaction of blood and other organic materials."[4]

Around 1880, government officials prepared two ambitious projects for replacing the slaughterhouse. The first, drawn up by José de la Luz Gómez, envisioned a grandiose new facility measuring 42,000 square meters with marble floors and tile walls—"ornate and in good taste"—for the meat market. An alternate project, developed a few years later by the Department of the Interior, called for a radial design with a central slaughter chamber from which livestock pens emerged like the spokes of a wheel. This latter model was perhaps inspired more by prison reformers than by actual slaughterhouses in Europe or the United States. In any event, the city's persistent financial instability precluded for another decade the construction of a new abattoir.[5]

These rather whimsical plans notwithstanding, two competing designs had taken shape simultaneously in the mid-1860s at the La Villette abattoir in Paris and the Union Stockyards of Chicago. The former, conceived by Baron Haussmann as part of his monumental reconstruction of Paris, exemplified a rational approach to urban design. The centerpiece of La Villette was a great iron and glass hall with sufficient space to house all the cattle consumed in the French metropolis, while providing each animal with an individual stall. By contrast, the Union Stockyards grew haphazardly, as *Scientific American* reported, into a "true labyrinth of sheds and

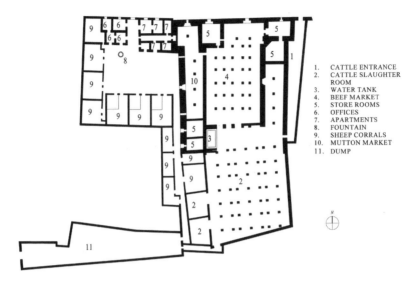

1. CATTLE ENTRANCE
2. CATTLE SLAUGHTER ROOM
3. WATER TANK
4. BEEF MARKET
5. STORE ROOMS
6. OFFICES
7. APARTMENTS
8. FOUNTAIN
9. SHEEP CORRALS
10. MUTTON MARKET
11. DUMP

2.1 Site plan of San Lucas slaughterhouse after Engineer Jesús Galindo y Villa. Source: AHCM, vol. 3764, exp. 39, Galindo report, September 30, 1900. Redrawn by Alan Jackson.

enormous halls that communicate in various ways by passages, staircases, and suspension bridges."[6] This ungainly tribute to Yankee tinkering, built in haste without an overall plan, nevertheless represented the advent of a radical new approach to industrial supply based on private packinghouses, while La Villette remained an old-fashioned municipal slaughterhouse, however meticulously engineered.

Siegfried Giedion has shown that these distinct provisioning methods grew out of fundamentally different agricultural traditions. The French meat supply ultimately depended on small-scale production by countless family farms, "where each cow [had] its own name" and received meticulous care. This individual attention extended to the slaughter as well, which was conducted by handicraft methods in separate booths. Meanwhile, in the United States, the ranchers' practice of turning cattle loose to graze on the Great Plains, then rounding them up to be driven to market, lent itself to mass-production techniques. The division of labor had already transformed pork packinghouses in Cincinnati by 1850, so that with each trained workman performing a separate cut, hogs were slaughtered and dressed completely in less than a minute. Chicago meatpackers Gustavus F. Swift and Philip D. Armour took the next important step in centralizing production in the 1870s by developing refrigerated railroad cars to transport meat to eastern cities. By shipping dressed carcasses rather than livestock, Swift and Armour halved their transportation costs while also avoiding wastage, which could amount to a loss of 10 percent of an animal's weight in transit. Despite the resistance of railroad companies and local butchers, this price advantage proved decisive, allowing the Chicago packers to dominate eastern markets by the mid-1880s. Most independent meat merchants were either driven out of business or reduced into mere salesmen of meat from the refrigerated branch houses that served as distribution points for the meatpacking giants.[7]

Once they had consolidated their hold on the domestic market, the Big Four packers began to look abroad for further expansion, and Mexico offered a natural entry into Latin American markets. In 1890, the Mexico City council agreed to rent one stall at the hog slaughterhouse of San Antonio Abad to Swift representative W. E. Lewis. Nothing came of this venture, whether from Swift's distaste for Mexican conditions or from local opposition to foreign interlopers. Sometime later, but before 1898, unnamed U.S. interests built a small packinghouse on Nonoalco Street, on the northwest side of the city, adjacent to the railroad station. Once again, the attempt to gain a foothold in the Mexican market proved a complete failure. The meatpacking technology developed in Chicago therefore remained virtually untested in Mexico as the city council undertook the construction of a new slaughterhouse.[8]

THE PERALVILLO SLAUGHTERHOUSE

The Mexico City council issued a call for bids to construct a new slaughterhouse in 1888, the year that the Dublán Accords made it possible to undertake such a significant public works project, thereby indicating the importance of the project to the Porfirian establishment. City officials carefully considered both the location and the specifications of the new facility with the twin goals of improving municipal sanitation and ending the threat of monopoly by established importers. Nevertheless, the political nature of Porfirian enterprise soon undermined the project, to the embarrassment of both the contractor and the council alike.

The choice of a suitable location for the new slaughterhouse required a balance of city planning with real estate prices. Urban growth around San Lucas had created serious health hazards, and the abattoir had to be far enough away to ensure adequate sanitation, yet close enough to allow transportation of meat to the city. The marshes surrounding Lake Texcoco made an eastern location unsuitable, while property values to the west had risen with the creation of affluent suburbs along the Paseo de la Reforma leading to the presidential residence at Chapultepec Castle. The slaughterhouse had traditionally been on the south side of the city, away from the predominant winds, but the railroad switching yards, increasingly important for transporting livestock, congregated in the north. Planners also took careful consideration of access to water supplies since recurring shortages had rendered San Lucas virtually impossible to keep clean. They ultimately decided on a property four kilometers northeast of the city, along the Grand Canal and near the Peralvillo racetrack. The neighborhood had gained notoriety as the site of a crime spree by Francisco Guerrero, known as "El Chalequero," a butcher by trade, who raped, robbed, and murdered a number of women beginning in the early 1880s. After his arrest in 1888, Guerrero was compared to Jack the Ripper, and perhaps the sensational headlines from his trial led city officials to consider Peralvillo an appropriate location for the new slaughterhouse. In any event, they paid $24,693 for two separate lots, totaling just under 100,000 square meters, on the former hacienda of Aragón.[9]

The city received bids modeled after both the Parisian La Villette and Chicago's Union Stockyards, yet municipal officials seemed unaware of the broader implications of these design choices and made their decision based on cost alone. The most celebrated architect in Mexico, the Parisian-trained Antonio Rivas Mercado, submitted an imposing design for a municipal slaughterhouse worthy of Haussmann himself. A rival plan, by José Collazo, promised to incorporate the latest technology from Chicago for the price of $900,000. A third serious bid came from Juan Llamedo, but whether he followed a French or U.S. model remains unknown because he withdrew the project from consideration in February 1890, shortly before the city assigned the contract. The winning contractor, Francisco R. Blanco, did not prepare a proposal at all; rather, he took over the Collazo plans through a deal that remains vague, although the price rose to $1,100,000 in the process. Mexico City officials considered Rivas Mercado's French-inspired design as too expensive, and after Llamedo withdrew, they awarded the contract to Blanco in March 1890, establishing a minimum daily capacity of 800 cattle, 1,200 sheep, and 500 hogs, and stipulating that he finish the project in two years or pay a fine of $500 for each day he fell late.[10]

Priscilla Connolly, in her study of Porfirian public works, observed that the government contracted out major projects both as a legacy of colonial administrative practices and for the modern expedient of attracting foreign capital and technology. She distinguished concessions that transferred exclusive state privileges to private hands, such as railroad right-of-ways and port authorities, on the one hand, from public goods such as defense, education, and health, on the other.[11] Yet this typology does not lend itself to the slaughterhouse contract, which more closely resembled the hybrid nature of the eighteenth-century abasto. Blanco received the right both to construct and administer Peralvillo, but as a result he assumed the obligation of supplying livestock in case of shortages. This arrangement lasted only until the city had amortized the building costs, but if the council decided to contract out the administration again at that point, Blanco retained the right of first refusal. The contract did not constitute a simple monopoly on meat like the sixteenth-century abasto; it explicitly called for a municipal slaughterhouse in which any individual would be free to slaughter livestock, thereby benefiting the lower classes by undercutting the existing monopoly of the importers. Nevertheless, with the Chicago packinghouse approach, city officials had unwittingly chosen a design intended to lower cost not by assuring free trade but rather by maximizing industrial efficiency.

The firm of Francisco R. Blanco & Cia. had well-established credentials with the construction of neighborhood markets at Loreto and San Juan, and had also recently completed renovations to the city's principal market, La Merced. Work began promptly on May 1, 1890, with the opening of an office by Nicolás de Teresa y Miranda, the superintendent of construction, and half a dozen assistants, including one Federico Pombo. Building materials began arriving at customs in August, since virtually the entire plant and equipment had been ordered from the United States. The heart of the assembly line process lay in the aerial rails used to convey animals from one cutting station to the next, and specialized motors, refrigerators, pumps, and steam generators were also needed. Blanco invited President Díaz to plant the ceremonial first stone on September 21, 1890. The city government assigned oversight of the construction to one of the foremost architects in Mexican public service, Antonio Torres

Torrija, who had designed the new penitentiary, then under construction at San Lázaro. Although he had already proven his skills in constructing the hog slaughterhouse at San Antonio Abad, Torres Torrija undertook a tour of packinghouses in the United States in order to familiarize himself with the latest technology.[12]

Following his return, Torres Torrija insisted on seeing detailed construction plans, which caused a power struggle on the building site that suspended all work beginning on March 5, 1891. Blanco had submitted general blueprints, as required by the contract, but Torres Torrija demanded more thorough specifications, since the cabildo would ultimately have to pay any cost overruns. The general contractor thereupon went back to engineer Rafael M. de Arozarena, who had drawn up the plans, but the latter insisted on the need for more time. Finally in July, after the building site had been abandoned for more than four months, Arozarena informed Blanco brusquely: "I believe that, even though you're not an engineer, you should well understand that in an installation of this nature there are details of machinery and connections that can only be made according to the advance of the project."[13] One can only speculate about what Torres Torrija witnessed during his tour of the United States, but in fact even the most carefully designed building projects, right down to the present, leave all sorts of technical details to be worked out at the end.

Regardless of who was at fault, Blanco struggled valiantly to retain the valuable contract. In an attempt to gain more time, he sent a missive to the council in August explaining that even though no construction had taken place at the site since the spring, engineers had continued refining their plans and therefore the company should not be considered in default. He also explained that the high cost of steel from local producers made it impossible to meet the previous goals and even implied that the city inspector was conspiring with his own engineers to undermine the project. When that failed, Blanco attempted one last, desperate measure that is extremely revealing of the political nature of Porfirian enterprise.[14]

On October 12, Francisco R. Blanco & Cia. formally ceded its interest in the Peralvillo contract to the partnership of Luis Pombo and José de Teresa y Miranda, two prominent members in the Porfirian establishment. The former was an attorney from Oaxaca and longtime associate of President Díaz, while the latter owned a leading construction company, whose credits included the Mexico City Mercantile Center, and also served on the city council. The municipal connection proved particularly uncomfortable as the council met to consider the request to transfer the contract. Indeed, one might question whether Francisco R. Blanco served merely as a front for the partnership. Two family members had worked on the project: Nicolás de Teresa y Miranda and Federico Pompo, the former as superintendent of construction. Moreover, it was later revealed that José de Teresa y Miranda had provided the money to purchase the land at Peralvillo. This apparent conflict of interest may have been particularly galling to the municipal president, Manuel María Contreras, himself a leading engineer, who had only just ascended to his post the year before and who hoped to use his tenure as mayor to ensure the success of the numerous public works projects currently underway. After several meetings attempting to clarify the legal questions, the council denied permission to transfer the contract and concluded that Blanco had forfeited the concession.[15]

Fearful of losing the nearly $300,000 already invested in the project, Teresa and Pombo appealed the matter to President Porfirio Díaz, an arbitrator the city council could scarcely protest. The conflicts of interest between prominent businessmen and politicians, together with the importance of the project, made the issue particularly sensitive, and Díaz consulted his personal legal advisor, Alfredo Chavero. The final decree, issued on June 28, 1892, found both parties at fault and voided the original concession. Moreover, Díaz ordered the council to reimburse Teresa and Pombo for $168,000, or 60 percent of the construction costs incurred. Torres Torrija and Pombo squabbled over the final inventory, and both Contreras and Teresa lost their seats on the city council the following year, leaving others to deal with the problem of the municipal meat supply.[16]

THE WORKS RESUMED

The city council had been burned by the first contractor, but still had a pressing need to replace San Lucas, and therefore issued a second call for bids to complete the project. Attempting to learn from the unfortunate first experience, officials scaled back the magnitude of the project to include just cattle and sheep, leaving hogs at the public slaughterhouse of San Antonio Abad and at Pedro Serrano's private facility of San Lázaro. Moreover, the city altered the terms of the contract to make it strictly a construction job with no franchise for operating the slaughterhouse once completed. Finally, they chose a foreign company experienced in this line of work, the Pauly Jail Bldg. & Mfg. Co. of St. Louis, Missouri. This new approach seemed at first to combine for a winning formula, but difficulties continued to plague the works at Peralvillo.

Immediately after the president had issued his arbitration decree, in the summer of 1892, the city solicited another round of bids, which drew a more satisfying response than the first call. Once again, a number of proposals were rejected outright, such as Samuel Lederer's offer to finish the project for $1.2 million, a figure greater than the original contract without even considering payments already made to Teresa and Pombo. José Martínez Arnaldo even more brazenly requested the privilege of administering the new slaughterhouse without bothering to submit plans for its completion. Nevertheless, by the spring of 1893, city officials had also received three serious proposals from reputable builders. The firm of Valentín Werner and J. M Schielé requested $250,000 in Mexican silver pesos plus $450,000 in U.S. gold bonds, which was deemed "inconvenient to the municipality's credit." A second proposal, from Miguel Lebrija, promised to complete the structure for the more reasonable $462,000. Attorney Pedro S. Azcué submitted the winning bid of $380,000 on behalf of Pauly Jail. Mexico City officials signed the contract on June 20, and after the addition of a special clause regarding the arbitration of legal disputes, it received presidential approval on July 10.[17]

The contract required the company to complete the project in eighteen months and imposed significant penalties for late delivery. Project manager Edgar J. Hahn took control of the Peralvillo building site on August 10, 1893, and immediately asked for an extension on the deadline because of delays in gaining approval from the city budget office. As a local adviser, Hahn employed Rafael Arozarena, the same engineer who had drawn up the contentious blueprints for Francisco Blanco. This choice did not cause any particular friction with city officials because Torres Torrija had already resigned his position to Camilo Arriaga, who in turn was replaced by Mateo Plowes in the summer of 1894. The frequent turnover of city officials illustrated a common disadvantage that Mexican regulators faced in relation to private enterprise. Nevertheless, the contractors had their own problems as a result of bureaucratic delays at the customs houses of Laredo and Tampico. Although the contract specified that all building materials would be imported tax free, many

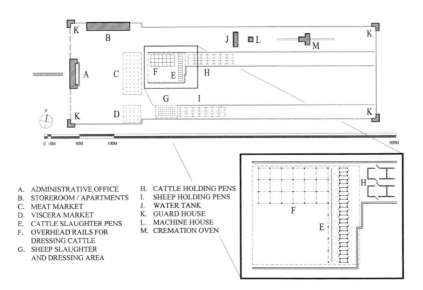

A. ADMINISTRATIVE OFFICE
B. STOREROOM / APARTMENTS
C. MEAT MARKET
D. VISCERA MARKET
E. CATTLE SLAUGHTER PENS
F. OVERHEAD RAILS FOR
   DRESSING CATTLE
G. SHEEP SLAUGHTER
   AND DRESSING AREA

H. CATTLE HOLDING PENS
I. SHEEP HOLDING PENS
J. WATER TANK
K. GUARD HOUSE
L. MACHINE HOUSE
M. CREMATION OVEN

2.2 Site plan of Peralvillo slaughterhouse after Engineer Jesús Galindo y Villa. Source: AHCM, vol. 3764, exp. 39, Galindo report, September 30, 1900. Redrawn by Alan Jackson.

shipments languished at the border for more than a month while waiting for clearance. Meanwhile, the imported refrigeration units and other machinery left behind by Francisco Blanco & Cia. appeared worthless to Hahn and he sold them for scrap. By December of 1894, with just a few months left before the deadline, city engineer Plowes found the construction site in a state of disarray. The carpentry works, subcontracted out to the firm of Grace and Alexander, had been completely abandoned for two months, while the machinery required to operate the facility had still not arrived from New York.[18]

Nevertheless, Edgar Hahn and Rafael Arozarena welcomed Mateo Plowes back, along with city public works officials Luis Labarra and Manuel Cervantes, for a final inspection at 9:30 on the morning of April 30, 1895, seven days ahead of the extended deadline. The New Peralvillo Slaughterhouse (see figure 2.2) occupied a roughly rectangular compound 434 meters long by 139 wide, with brick guardhouses at the corners, and surrounded by a metal fence on all sides except for a 150-meter length that was left unfinished on the northern perimeter. An impressive two-story brick administration building dominated the western façade, and parallel to it, across a large patio, rose the steel columns of the meat market. Just to the south, a smaller structure with the same flat roof and open sides provided a marketplace for viscera. Extending east from the markets were separate slaughter facilities for cattle and sheep, each of which was housed under slanted metal roofs. These structures, like the markets, had no outside walls, just fences to contain any runaway animals. Two parallel rows of covered corrals, each about eighty meters in length, were allocated to both sheep and cattle, although the fenced-in corridors reached all the way to the eastern edge of the slaughterhouse, allowing room for future expansion. The sheep pens bordered the southern edge of the facility, while the water tank and machine shop were located north of the cattle holding area. Underground pipes for cleaning the meat markets and slaughter chambers also ran the length of the facility.[19]

As one of the major investments in Mexican modernity, the slaughterhouse design appealed self-consciously to the científico mentality. The main floor of the administrative building comprised two great halls, one devoted to commerce as a common office for the importers, and the other to scientific progress in the form of a biology museum. Upstairs was a laboratory equipped with microscopes to protect the citizens of Mexico City from diseased meat, along with a library to ensure that health inspectors were up to date on the latest medical discoveries from Europe and the United States. With its steel girder frame and ample concrete floors, the new slaughterhouse of Peralvillo represented a clear improvement over the crowded and filthy San Lucas. The installation of the latest machinery, including aerial rails, a Westinghouse generator, Thomson dynamo, and Bigelow boilers, promised to raise Mexico's meat industry to the level of the great packinghouses in the United States.

Nevertheless, as the city officials inspected the new facility, a number of nagging doubts remained, beyond the obvious hole in the fence. The railroad approached Peralvillo from the west, stopping directly in front of the administrative office, which was flanked on either side by three small gates, spaced evenly in the fence. As a result of the architect's layout, an importer standing in the main office could presumably watch his meat being loaded from the market into carts on the main patio, then turn 180 degrees and watch it unloaded again and transferred to the Mexico City train, a study in inefficiency. Meanwhile, the connection between the slaughter rooms and the meat market, supposedly bridged by aerial rail, differed in height by a full meter, complicating the transfer of dressed car-casses. Worse still, the market's superstructure lacked horizontal stabiliz-ers—a crucial detail because of the tremors common in Mexico City—and the supporting pillars had already begun to sag under the weight of the roof. In laying the floors, on the other hand, the contractors had done their job too well, leveling the concrete completely so that waste water formed unhealthy puddles rather than draining into the gutters.

These construction defects portended considerable delays in bringing the Peralvillo facility into service. Pauly Jail's representatives promised to correct the problems immediately, starting with the most serious flaw, the meat market roof. The city engineers responded to the company's appar-ent good will by granting the new structure their tentative approval, allowing Hahn to collect the balance due on the contract in municipal bonds, which he proceeded to sell at a discount to local bankers.[20] The council agreed to the bond transfer on the assumption that it would not affect the company's liability for fixing the construction defects. To their chagrin, Hahn slipped out of the country after making a few adjustments to the meat market roof, leaving behind a long list of additional repairs. As a result, the city government undertook these works at its own expense, perhaps concluding that if it had trouble obtaining a favorable ruling from the Mexican president, there was little chance of winning a settlement against the company in U.S. courts.

Beginning in the summer of 1895, with $20,000 from the city coun-cil, Plowes began readying the Peralvillo Slaughterhouse for service. He first constructed a storehouse with four apartments for workers on the northern end of the patio between the administration building and the meat market. Having completed this task under budget, he then turned his attention to the heart of the facility, the cattle slaughtering system. There were a number of wooden booths adjacent to the first set of cor-rals, but Hahn had left without providing instructions for their use. Plowes therefore decided to reconstruct the system, removing the old booths and installing twelve new ones, each with an overhead motor to hoist the animal out of the pen after it had been stunned by a hammer blow to the head. Workers would then cut the animal's throat and leave it to bleed into a gutter before lifting it once again, this time by the rear leg, to the aerial rail for cleaning and transport to the market. On November 22, 1895, Plowes tested his handiwork using twenty cattle provided by some of the leading importers in the city. The butchers from San Lucas had some difficulty operating the new system, but with training, Plowes felt confident they would learn the new procedures, and he pronounced the system a success.[21]

Even with the new butchering machinery in place, work continued on Peralvillo through the entire year of 1896. The importers, when allowed to inspect the facility during the tests, had noticed a number of problems, the foremost being the location of the viscera market on the outside perimeter with only a fence to guard against thieves or dogs. City officials agreed with their concerns about security and added a solid wall on the southern end to protect the market. Another useful suggestion from the importers was to install wooden barriers along the cattle corrals similar to those in a bullfighting arena so that workers could seek shelter in case an animal ran loose. Plowes also replaced the concrete floors, providing the necessary decline to facilitate cleaning, and in the process noting that Pauly Jail's work had already begun to crack, even before it had been put to use. In addition, the engineer supervised the drilling of a second well to anticipate possible water shortages, a constant bane of Mexican slaughterhouses and markets. Finally, the council looked into the purchase of an incinerator for solid waste as well as to dispose of any diseased animals condemned by health inspectors. The city of Pachuca had just inaugurated a new slaughterhouse in 1894, but their incinerator produced such a vile smell that Mexico City officials decided to invest in an oven from the R. W. Albright Company in the United States.[22]

Meanwhile, health officials developed a new regulatory code to ensure that the Peralvillo slaughterhouse operated in an orderly manner consistent with the dictates of public health. Previous efforts to reform the meat trades, such as prohibitions against clandestine slaughter and the transportation of meat by mule, remained in force. Moreover, in 1894, the council had expanded the slaughterhouse veterinarians' duties to include monthly tours of retail outlets, and supplemented their efforts with an additional inspector, Juan Porras Palacio, hired specifically to guard against clandestine slaughter. The official paper, El Municipio Libre, published regular reports of these inspections along with the names of the worst offenders to reassure the public of the city's sanitary vigilance. Efficient use of the Peralvillo facility would complement these efforts by guaranteeing a supply of healthy, government-inspected meat at low cost to Mexico City consumers. While anyone was free to bring livestock to the new slaughterhouse, all had to follow the regulations scrupulously. The exact procedures were not defined clearly, since they had virtually no practical experience with the new system, but the administrator retained complete authority over when the animals entered, where they were penned, the order of their slaughter, and the methods for dressing and displaying the carcasses. All meat was inspected and graded by veterinarians, who stamped the cuts with an indelible ink seal to assure both purity and quality.

Public health officials also perceived a moral dimension to their work, and believed that only workers who behaved in a civilized fashion could produce meat fit for bourgeois families. Thus, the administrator's duties of ensuring a smooth operation included the prevention of gambling or cursing by the employees. Likewise, the sentries stood watch not only to guard against smuggling meat out of the market without inspection and quality seals, but also to prevent people from entering the market on horseback or while intoxicated. Slaughter captains in particular were warned that their men had to respect the administrator and avoid "inconvenient language, shouts, or gross jokes." Given the rough behavior of many butchers, this code of conduct may have been little more than wishful thinking. Nevertheless, the council adopted the regulations on December 1, 1896, and on the last day of the year, General Porfirio Díaz laid the final stone formally inaugurating the Peralvillo Slaughterhouse.[23]

Yet one final hurdle stood between Mexico City and its new era of public health, a reliable transportation link with Peralvillo, and that in turn depended on the speculations of one of Mexico's most powerful financiers, Pablo Macedo. A member of Díaz's inner circle of científicos, Macedo sat on the board of directors of the Compañía de Ferrocarriles del Distrito Federal de México, S.A. (Railroad Company of the Federal District of Mexico, Inc.), which had recently acquired large amounts of railroad track, including the line connecting Peralvillo to the capital. The wily lawyer had also obtained the rights to a contract, signed on December 14, 1889, by Carlos David de Ghest and the secretary of economic development, to establish one or more *colonias* (housing developments) on the east side of Mexico City. Macedo then petitioned the city council to develop this grant as the "Nueva Colonia del Rastro" (New Slaughterhouse District) in the area between the Río Consulado and the

Northern Canal. Only after the city council had authorized this real estate development, on March 5, 1897, did Macedo, along with Thomas H. MacLean, president of the Compañía de Ferrocarriles, reach an agreement with Plowes to renovate the tracks and bring the line into service. The city also ceded to the company the final stretch of track from the Northern Canal to the slaughterhouse. Delayed by these lengthy negotiations, construction of two crucial bridges across the Northern Canal did not begin, even provisionally, until the end of July, at which point Peralvillo's opening date had already been set for just a month later.[24]

THE GRAND OPENING

Cattle began filing through the front gate of the New Peralvillo Slaughterhouse early on the morning of September 1, 1897. They actually should have entered from the opposite end of the complex, but because of yet another contractor's oversight, the rear doors had never been installed, and so the cattle had a chance to preview the vast meat market. They also passed by the slaughter chamber, strung with cables and pulleys, which cast a spider's web of shadows beneath the Westinghouse arc lights. At about 4:45 in the morning, once the cattle had been secured in the holding corrals, one of their number was separated out and prodded into a tight wooden booth (see the detail in figure 2.3). It put up a fight, which caused some damage to the gates, but ended abruptly with a sledgehammer blow to the head. Workers secured a chain around the stunned animal's neck and hoisted it out of the booth. Then a knife slashed across its throat, loosing a torrent of blood into a gutter that ran the length of the concrete. The story of the Peralvillo Slaughterhouse ended here for the cattle, but for importers, workers, officials, and consumers, the struggles had only just begun.[25]

Administrator José de la Luz Gómez held high hopes that the new facility would mark a clean break with San Lucas. One problem that had constantly plagued the old slaughterhouse was interlopers and thieves, and therefore he arranged for a special watch of thirty-two gendarmes under Comandante Zea to inspect the butcher captains and their teams as they entered the facility. Gómez rightly feared disorder on the first day of operations, but all the policemen in Mexico City could not contain the problems arising from design flaws in the slaughterhouse.

After the animal had been butchered and bled, workers proceeded to cut off the lower extremity of its hind legs, and hoist it again, this time

EN EL NUEVO RASTRO

LA MATANZA DE RESES

2.3 "En el nuevo rastro: La matanza de reses" (In the new [Peralvillo] slaughterhouse: The butchering of cattle). A monument to Porfirian progress recorded by the *científico* newspaper, *El Mundo*, September 2, 1897. Courtesy of the Hemeroteca Nacional, Mexico City.

upside down (see again figure 2.3). Another worker, standing on a plank above the slaughter booth, then hooked it onto a wheeled trolley mounted on an overhead rail. Unfortunately, the track took a number of sharp turns that made it difficult for workers to push the carcasses along to the skinning station. And once there, the weight of the dangling body placed enormous tension on the hide, making it virtually impossible to remove intact. The difficulty was compounded by the three-meter height of the aerial rails, which forced craftsmen to stand on benches and ladders as they manipulated the bulky carcasses (see figure 2.4). Health officials likewise found the new conditions extremely laborious, requiring twice the number of skilled inspectors. One final impediment in the system was the gap of a full meter between the aerial rails in the slaughter hall and the meat market. While workers at San Lucas usually finished displaying the meat in the market by 9 o'clock in the morning, on the first day at Peralvillo, they had not finished slaughtering the last head of cattle until 11 o'clock, at which time no meat had yet reached the market (for an

Limpia de reses

2.4 "Limpia de reses" (Cleaning the steers). Butchers balance precariously on ladders to dress the heavy animals. From *El Mundo*, September 2, 1897. Courtesy of the Hemeroteca Nacional, Mexico City.

afternoon view, when the meat had begun to arrive, see figure 2.5). As the laborers cleaned and dressed the beef in this unfamiliar fashion, a private transport company, Express de Carnes, was waiting in the patio outside the market with eighteen special mule carts and a train of four boxcars. Nevertheless, more than a hundred meat shops throughout Mexico City had not yet received deliveries by 9 o'clock that night.

The Peralvillo Slaughterhouse contained dangerous working conditions in addition to serious bottlenecks. Two bulls had escaped on the first day, but this was a known hazard for the workers, who quickly rounded them up. The new equipment proved more difficult to master, such as the reversible corral gates, with hinges on both sides that allowed them to swing open in either direction (see figure 2.6). But if not securely fastened on one side or the other, the heavy iron doors fell flat, and during preliminary tests on August 31, such an accident severely injured a worker named Joaquín "El Frances" (Frenchy) González. A similar incident occurred that same week, on September 4, when a 22-year-old watchman, Abraham

La carne en el mercado

2.5 "La carne en el mercado" (The meat in the market). Stylishly dressed livestock importers bargain with barefoot retail butchers over sides of beef displayed by slaughterhouse workers. From *El Mundo*, September 2, 1897. Courtesy of the Hemeroteca Nacional, Mexico City.

Ortiz de la Peña, the son of a treasury employee, was crushed beneath a massive door. Another menace lay in the overhead rails, which, because of their faulty construction, could not support more than one or two carcasses without bending under the weight. Lacking a stable platform, the hangers tended to jump the track, sending sides of beef crashing to the ground. Reporters from *El Popular* observed at least ten already-skinned carcasses fall to the dirty floor, as workers went about glancing nervously in the air. On September 5, a day after the death of Abraham Ortiz, a falling cow hit another worker, José de Jesús Luna, injuring his foot and ribs. *La Patria* raged that "the new slaughterhouse has been baptized with human blood."[26]

And then came the floods. The past few years had been among the driest in the nineteenth century, which may have caused some to forget that the new slaughterhouse was located in the former bed of Lake Texcoco. Farmers had rejoiced when the summer rains returned in 1897, but as the downpour continued into fall, the situation grew serious for

Encierro del ganado

2.6 "Encierro del ganado" (Livestock pens). The poorly designed gates can be seen on the right. From *El Mundo*, September 2, 1897. Courtesy of the Hemeroteca Nacional, Mexico City.

urban inhabitants. On September 8, the *Diario del Hogar* declared the capital's streets to be navigable waterways, even as the Rio Consulado was bursting its banks to the north. At nearby Peralvillo, the deluge exposed numerous leaks in the roof; one morning the workers arrived to find the entire market inundated. The lack of outside walls posed further discomforts for the workers, as gusts of wind sprayed them repeatedly with rain. Meanwhile, the merchants resorted to umbrellas and rubber boots to conduct their business. The flooding also washed out the provisional bridges over the Northern Canal, making it impossible for the hapless Express meat cars to reach the city. Officials even resorted to pack mules in an attempt to ford the waters, but deliveries continued to arrive as late as 10:30 at night and sometimes not until the following day.[27]

The disastrous opening days at Peralvillo united the various meat sellers of Mexico City in opposition to the new slaughterhouse. On September 4, the sixteen leading livestock importers, together with nearly eighty retail merchants, sent petitions to the council complaining about the damages they had suffered as a result of their inability to supply customers with meat. But within a few days, as prices rose with the floodwaters, this solidarity began to break down. The retailers sent another commission to the mayor, Sebastián Camacho, blaming the importers for the high prices and asking for a return to San Lucas. While denying their request, Camacho resorted to an old tactic of threatening to butcher cattle at the council's expense if the importers continued to raise prices. The divisions between wholesalers and retailers grew sharper by mid-month as the latter complained that the Express Company delivered their meat in poor condition and often several kilograms short of the purchase weight. The importers responded by posting a notice next to the official scales in the Peralvillo meat market announcing that the weights were final and that the importers held no responsibility for losses in transit, a policy that virtually authorized theft by the carriers.[28]

As the importers and retailers squabbled among themselves, on September 14 the formerly silent slaughterhouse workers appeared before the council. Led by Palemón Martínez, the most respected of the butcher captains, the delegation disclaimed any reactionary intentions. "Precisely because of our humble social condition we are eager for the useful improvements that science has introduced to our trade," their petition explained. They accepted the benefits of introducing modern technology from the United States to increase their productivity by allowing them to butcher more cattle. But the Peralvillo Slaughterhouse had achieved exactly the opposite result, they insisted, slowing down their work so that many meat shops had closed for lack of merchandise, while "speculators of bad faith" raised prices in the knowledge that they faced no competition. "Panic has begun to rule among the slaughterhouse workers," the captains continued, "and we have to spend a long time convincing the operators these days, since from one moment to the next, they don't wish to continue, out of well-founded fear." Recognizing the great investment already undertaken in constructing the new facility, the butchers proposed a test, for four or five days, comparing the productivity of the old system and the new. While the city council members agreed to observe a demonstration of the slaughter methods practiced at San Lucas, they refused to abandon the new technology installed at Peralvillo.[29]

Nevertheless, the administrator, Gómez, felt pressure from public protests about the shortage of meat in the city. Following the importers' initial petition, filed on September 4, he had issued a statement refuting their arguments and demonstrating the improvements already in progress at Peralvillo. The importers complained first that wind blowing through the open facility desiccated the meat while at the same time the high roof allowed rain to enter the work areas. Gómez responded that the humidity had no effect on the quality of the meat and that simple repairs would remove the leaks. He also countered the claim that the complicated overhead rails caused meat to fall; the rails were simple, he explained, but the workers needed time to learn their operation, and indeed they had already begun to perfect the new system. The weakness of the rails did indeed pose a problem, Gómez admitted, but a request to reinforce the supports had already been submitted to the council. Finally, the lack of transportation between Peralvillo and the city was being remedied by the Express company. Yet shortages persisted in Mexico City shops, notwithstanding Gómez's assurances to the contrary. On September 25, the *Diario del Hogar* declared meat to be "in the clouds" and worried that if prices continued to rise, the poor would be forced to kill cats and dogs to feed themselves.[30]

With rising opposition on all sides, officials at Peralvillo could not afford any more accidents, but a few days later, one of the overhead rails collapsed under the weight of seven cattle, falling on the back of a worker named Fernando "El Cacarizo" (the braggart) Giles. *La Patria* reported that he "vomited blood and died" and the *Diario del Hogar* concluded that "the new slaughterhouse is now the terror of those who work in it." The secretary of the interior, an old liberal general, Manuel González Cosío, called an emergency meeting at Peralvillo with the científico mayor Camacho, the Federal District governor, Rafael Rebollar, city council treasurer, Miguel S. Macedo, don Pablo's younger brother, and a few prominent importers. Contrary to the sensational newspaper reports, Giles survived the accident, but after reviewing the situation, González Cosío ordered a suspension of work at Peralvillo until the hazards had been removed.[31]

News of the decision spread rapidly through the city as the butchers packed up their temporary camp at Peralvillo and returned to their homes around San Lucas. In the month's absence, one of the walls of the old slaughterhouse had collapsed, and bricklayers rushed to refurbish it before operations resumed on the morning of October 4, 1897. The barrio celebrated the arrival of the butchers with music and bottle rockets, while flowers and crepe paper decorated the meat hooks. Petty merchants in the neighborhood, who had suffered from the absence of their relatively well-paid customers, congratulated the butchers on their safe return. After finishing work for the day, Palemón Martínez and other captains treated their men to a splendid brunch. During the course of the slaughter, one of the bulls had escaped down the street before a pair of horsemen with lassos dragged it back to its fate. Life had returned to normal at San Lucas.[32]

"HIS MAJESTY THE MONOPOLY" OR "MERCHANTS LIKE ANY OTHER"?

The events at Peralvillo offered sensational material for muckraking journalists seeking to boost newspaper sales, yet their accounts also provide revealing insights about Mexican society at the end of the century. Reporters naturally slanted their stories according to their political agendas, either supporting the Porfirian modernization project or opposing the dictatorship and its cronies. Much of the reporting was self-referential, as newspapers quoted and contradicted one another. Nevertheless, in order to reach a wide readership, they also drew on a combination of formal economic theory and implicit popular understandings of the market. Indeed, the importance of the meat supply, and the spectacular failure of the city to ensure it, may have allowed interest groups, from meat importers to health officials and even slaughterhouse workers, an opportunity to advance their interests in the popular press.

In a study of market discourse in Porfirian Mexico, Richard Weiner has identified three basic currents of economic thought: the científicos, the Mexican Liberal Party, and Social Catholicism. Although often considered as doctrinaire positivists, the científicos actually enunciated a pragmatic blend of liberalism, positivism, and Social Darwinism. Their beliefs that Mexico's future lay in industrial modernization and that only the vagaries of labor impeded the triumph of progress were disseminated by Rafael Reyes Spíndola's two newspapers *El Mundo* and *El Imparcial*. The latter, founded just a year before the Peralvillo episode, received financial support from the government to purchase advanced printing technology and thereby became the first mass-market daily in Mexico. Just as the científico ascendancy pushed traditional liberals from power, the redirection of press subsidies to *El Imparcial* drove many venerable liberal newspapers out of business. Weiner also examined the economic rhetoric of the Mexican Liberal Party after Ricardo Flores Magón had begun to incorporate anarchist ideas into the influential newspaper *Regeneración* (founded in 1900).

In 1897, however, surviving liberal papers such as *La Patria* and the humorous *El Hijo del Ahuizote* blended more diffuse populist language with traditional liberalism in order to gain a wide audience for their attacks against the dictatorship. Finally, the Catholic opposition press, led by *El Tiempo*, took its inspiration from Pope Leo XIII's *Rerum Novarum* (1891), which linked markets to social inequality and worker oppression.[33]

Científico publisher Rafael Reyes Spíndola provided unwavering support for the Peralvillo Slaughterhouse as a triumph of Mexican development. A front-page story in *El Imparcial*, on August 30, heralded the successful preliminary tests and contrasted the new system with the crimes against public health committed daily at San Lucas. The editors of *El Mundo* concurred in this assessment and even sent an artist to record the historic opening the following day. These drawings idealized the modernity of the new slaughter system while overlooking the chaos that resulted from its actual implementation. The market scene depicted a particularly misleading image of calm and abundance, with importers supposedly çonducting their business among large numbers of beeves hanging from overhead rails (see figure 2.5). The papers remained silent through the first week of trouble, waiting for a response to the importers' complaints by the administrator Gómez, which *El Imparcial* duly reprinted. At the end of the month, they attempted to portray the episode in a positive light by assuring readers that the city would spare no expense in correcting the problems at Peralvillo and by applauding Gómez for having carried out his duty in every way.[34]

The científico journalists blamed first the workers and then the importers as well, demonstrating both their Social Darwinism and their authoritarianism. From the very beginning, *El Imparcial* reported that the importers appeared anxious that the new system, "like all innovations, could entail some mishap in the slaughter, not by defects in the capital, but rather from the stupidity of the manual laborers (mano de obra)." At one point they described the "men of notable strength that are the majority of those destined to the slaughter," as if butchers were natural-born killers rather than skilled tradesmen. When the merchants began to question the slaughterhouse, the editors lost patience with them as well, stating that the "butchers, importers, and retailers are impervious to all innovations" and concluding with sanctimonious concern that the importers had not said a word about the two victims, although, in fact, neither had the newspaper. Moreover, when Palemón Martínez led the slaughter captains in attempting to show the superiority of San Lucas, *El Imparcial* retorted that they had "demonstrated completely the opposite, because it is evident that cattle can be cleaned better while hanging from a hook than while lying on the ground and the meat remains more substantial and tastier if not cleaned at all than if cleaned as in the past."[35]

The liberals, who had ruled Mexico at mid-century only to be pushed into opposition by the Porfirian dictatorship, shared neither the simplistic faith in industrial progress nor the callous Social Darwinism of the científicos. The *Diario del Hogar*, the foremost liberal voice remaining in Mexico at the end of the century, had been edited since 1881 by Filomeno Mata. A staunch supporter of the democratic principles of 1857 and opponent of Díaz's perpetual reelection, he had served considerable time in jail for his critiques of Porfirian politics. Despite the political divergence, the liberals' economic views remained similar to those of the científicos, and the *Diario* reprinted, word-for-word, much of the reporting from *El Imparcial*. Mata excised the worst slurs against workers and expressed genuine concern over the accidents that took place. Still, the paper remained basically optimistic about the new slaughterhouse until runaway inflation prompted fears that poorer residents would be unable to purchase any meat at all. The *Diario* thereupon abandoned classical laissez-faire doctrines and encouraged the city council to slaughter livestock on its own account to contain the rising prices.[36]

More populist liberal papers showed far less restraint and at times descended into pure sensationalism in their attacks on this new symbol of científico progress. *El Popular* described cattle carcasses dropping repeatedly from the aerial rails onto the filthy floors and reported the workers' constant fears of being flattened underneath. *La Patria*, which had lost its subsidy to *El Imparcial*, described the accidents in even more lurid detail, explaining first that Peralvillo "had been baptized in human blood" with the death of Abraham Ortiz and then announcing prematurely that Fernando Giles had "vomited blood and died." Both papers also attributed the rising prices to an importers' monopoly, which they described with populist fervor. Finally, in the aftermath, *El Globo* speculated that the disastrous affair might even claim the political career of the interior secretary.[37]

The Catholic opposition journal, *El Tiempo*, owned and edited by Victoriano Agüeros, provided the most complete reporting on the problems at Peralvillo of any Mexico City newspaper, as well as the most persistent critiques of Porfirian politics. Within a week of the slaughterhouse opening, the paper made veiled accusations of corruption within the científico-dominated municipal government. The council's subsequent disregard of complaints by the importers prompted an editorial about the lack of Mexican democracy and the illusory nature of the right to petition. After Peralvillo had closed, Agüeros attacked *El Mundo* and *El Municipio Libre* for offering commendations to Gómez, Torres Torrija, and Plowes. Speaking of these government-supported papers, *El Tiempo* observed, "when there are no elections, they say that the people have emitted their vote in the larger sense, when the people attempt to vote, it is said that they have disturbed the public order, and when a slaughterhouse is closed as unserviceable, they give a vote of thanks to the engineers and administrators who constructed it."[38]

Catholic nationalism appeared prominently as the extent of U.S. involvement in the construction of Peralvillo emerged. Even before the problems began, *El Tiempo* had complained regularly about the extent of foreign control of the Mexican economy. When meat failed to arrive in city markets, the paper pointedly questioned the "Yankee contractors" in charge of transportation. Agüeros also criticized the knee-jerk reaction to attempt to solve the problems by sending engineers or city councilmen to study slaughterhouses in the United States and Europe. The municipal government's announcement that it was considering legal action against the Pauly Jail Bldg. & Mfg. Co. prompted him to suggest that similar measures be taken against a wide range of other foreign contractors.[39]

In order to advance the political agendas of the elite, newspapers at times drew on popular beliefs about the functioning of markets. One lengthy editorial in particular, published first by *La Patria* and then reprinted in *El Popular*, blamed politically powerful merchants for the meat shortages. Using the colorful language of the streets, the article portrayed modern technology as a means to manipulate markets. Thus, the pork fat king used the telephone to dictate price increases throughout the city. Traditional forms of oppression, including militarism and clerical greed, also contributed to the negative imagery. "The people who before were cannon fodder (carne de canón) are now meat of the monopoly. Previously the revolutions tithed them, now they are tithed by hunger in complete peace." Yet the article did not consist of empty rhetoric alone;

the author correctly observed that the clique of importers owned many of the city's retail shops outright while controlling meat supplies to the rest. The wholesale merchants also held a long tradition of political influence, and the most prominent among them had reportedly spent upwards of $20,000 to gain election to the national congress, a scarcely veiled reference to Serapión Fernández. With this economic and political power, the editorial concluded: "The children of labor are nothing more than slaves to His Majesty the Monopoly."[40]

Yet this populist view of dictatorial economic power did not go unchallenged. A few days later, *La Patria* published a response by Alberto Castaños Leal, who attributed price fluctuations to natural market conditions. He dismissed "the irritating belief that the livestock importers are a monstrous whirlpool [with]...the absolute power to corner the market on meat and impose fanciful prices." Instead, he described them as "merchants like any others, functioning with their capital, work, and aptitude...subject to the incontrovertible laws of supply and demand."[41] The argument proved persuasive, at least to the editors of *La Patria*, who abandoned their populist line and embraced the importers as natural allies in the struggle against científico power. A few weeks later, after public opinion had turned against Gómez, the paper proclaimed: "We celebrate for now the justified triumph that the importers, the press, and the public are achieving over the commissioner and over certain interested individuals."[42]

The importers wanted not merely to restore the status quo at San Lucas, but rather to use the crisis at Peralvillo to shift the balance of power away from the butcher captains and thereby gain undisputed control of the workplace. Congressman Fernández advanced this agenda during the emergency meeting with Interior Secretary González Cosío. In discussing possible alternatives, the prominent merchant insisted that the slaughterhouse contain sufficient stalls for all importers to have their cattle butchered simultaneously. Moreover, he observed that at San Lucas and Peralvillo alike, the confusion of the slaughter made it impossible to keep track of the viscera, and as a result, the importers simply considered them part of the butchers' compensation. With adequate oversight in individual pens, however, the importers could reassert their property rights to this meat and thereby "abolish the school of theft and bad faith" at the slaughterhouse.[43] In this way, Fernández dismissed the butchers as criminals for taking advantage of a traditional source of pay.

The workers knew perfectly well the importers' machinations, and the experience at Peralvillo served as an important step in their political mobilization. In previous disputes such as those of 1870, the butcher captains had followed their employers' lead, and as a result, they were dismissed as an inarticulate mob. The importers' refusal to demand a safe workplace at Peralvillo, however, prompted the butchers to present their own petition to the city council, which they did with "dignity, as Mexicans, as enthusiastic as anyone for those manifestations of genuine progress."[44] Having established their respectability before an audience of suspicious científicos, they proposed a reasonable comparison of the two systems of slaughter and were eventually proven correct, although they received little credit for their troubles. The retail butchers, although lacking this political experience, likewise became aware of class conflict when the importers tried to blame them for the price rises while simultaneously saddling them with the costs of the transition to Peralvillo. Yet the ability of these workers to use their experience to press for collective gains was limited by the uncertain future of the meat supply and the need to cooperate with the importers to influence municipal decisions.[45]

SURVEYING THE RUINS

The humiliating closure of the new slaughterhouse prompted the Mexican City council to undertake multiple investigations into the causes of the failure. José de la Luz Gómez quickly penned a self-serving account of the construction and operations at Peralvillo in which he emphasized the improvements made during the course of the month and suggested that the facility could be reopened with only a small number of minor repairs. A second, more thorough study, chaired by Councilman José Ramírez and submitted the following June, sounded a far more pessimistic note about the possibilities for returning to Peralvillo. This report described the new system of slaughtering cattle as an "inopportune importation" of technology from the United States. The Mexican preference for fresh rather than refrigerated meat required different methods of preparation, and the commission recommended the complete gutting of the slaughter and dressing chambers as well as the construction of better aerial rails and of a new drainage system. A final, comprehensive study by engineer Jesús Galindo y Villa emphasized the haste with which Peralvillo had been opened, before the operators had mastered the new technology, and called for greater deliberation in undertaking such an important project.[46]

In reconciling the differing conclusions of these commentators, it becomes clear that the experience of 1897 did not provide a comprehensive test of North American refrigerated technology under Mexican conditions. The poor implementation of the project makes it impossible to conclude, as the importers argued, that the new system was inherently inappropriate. In the context of the meat industry, the first slaughterhouse at Peralvillo was most significant for the precedents it set and for the way it mobilized importers, slaughterhouse workers, regulators, and consumers for future encounters with the modernization of meat supplies.

Historical perspective also reveals broader flaws in the development strategy of Porfirian state capitalism. The speculative investments of José Teresa de Miranda and Pablo Maceda, founded more on political connections than on technical expertise, were poorly suited to assuring Mexico City an adequate meat supply. The self-destructive results of this strategy are particularly evident in the case of Maceda, for the delays in constructing the vital railroad links between Peralvillo and Mexico City effectively destroyed the market for working-class housing that he had planned to develop around the new slaughterhouse. The contracting of foreign capital, a second basic tenet of Porfirian development, proved equally misguided in this case. Not only was U.S. technology inappropriate for the local meat market, but Edgar Hahn essentially ran a fly-by-night operation for one of the most important infrastructure projects in Mexico City. After ten years and nearly a million pesos, the city council had accomplished virtually nothing.

The experience at Peralvillo also offered a prelude of future dealings between the Porfirian regime and Mexican butchers, from the wealthiest importers to the lowliest slaughterhouse workers and retail meat cutters. Leading cattle merchants clung firmly to the liberal discourse of competition in order to maintain their cozy arrangement at the slaughterhouse. They succeeded in convincing the public, or at least the independent press, that they represented the best guarantors of the meat supply, but only because of the obvious failings of city officials on this occasion. Moreover, the antiquated slaughter methods that helped diffuse rivalries between the importers were destined sooner or later to be replaced by more modern techniques that would favor industrial concentration. For slaughterhouse workers, this change portended a loss of workplace independence, as the negotiations between the importers and the secretary of the interior clearly demonstrated. Meanwhile, the attempt by the importers to pass the costs of modernization on to the tablajero vendors—and to consumers—demonstrated the unfavorable position of small-time retailers in the market. These workers clearly faced a difficult collective struggle to claim their rights as citizens under the repressive Porfirian regime.

And change was inevitable, for despite the numerous and expensive repairs needed at Peralvillo, San Lucas simply could not accommodate the long-term demand for meat. In 1899, engineer Ignacio Burgos began construction on a new road to connect the slaughterhouse with the city center, although to divert criticism, the council decreed that when Peralvillo reopened, importers would be free to slaughter in whatever manner they saw fit. The councilmen might just as well not have bothered issuing new regulations, for the land itself seemed to pass judgment on their efforts. On the morning of January 24, 1899, an earthquake shook the Valley of Anáhuac. At Peralvillo, the tremors flattened the meat market, leaving only a cement floor and a few supporting columns as reminders of the structure that had caused such problems. After floods and human sacrifices, the trembling earth provided an appropriately biblical end to the first slaughterhouse at Peralvillo.[47]

CHAPTER THREE
The Terrazas Trust

On July 8, 1902, *El Imparcial* published a lengthy letter from Felipe de J. Ortega and Theodore W. Osterheld warning of a Chihuahua-based corporation that was poised to take over the Mexico City slaughterhouse and thereby monopolize the sale of meat in the capital. The impending contract with the city council offered a twenty-five-year concession in return for investing a mere $500,000 to refurbish Peralvillo—this after the city had already sunk twice that amount in the facility. The company stood to make an annual income of $200,000 on butchering quotas alone, Ortega and Osterheld calculated, yielding a profit of $4,500,000 over the life of the contract. Such a windfall threatened to be a "decisive element to kill the competition, completely master the meat market, and arbitrarily manipulate prices." Although this language may have seemed appropriate to the muckraking journalism of the day, the authors went on to praise the Chihuahua group as "well-known capitalists and worthy of esteem for their entre-preneurial spirit." Ortega and Osterheld, industrialists themselves, simply called for open bids on the slaughterhouse contract "to encourage com-petition, to resolve [the matter] with calmness and maturity, and not with haste 'behind closed doors.'"[1]

The very next morning, Rafael Reyes Spíndola published a front-page editorial disclaiming responsibility for the letter and assuring readers of the council's good faith in working to correct the defects of the slaugh-terhouse. In particular, he disavowed the reference to the customs of Porfirian state capitalism, in which government officials and prominent businessmen arranged deals in the banquet rooms of exclusive French restaurants. The alacrity of the disclaimer reflected not only the tren-chancy of the critique but also the influence of the unnamed interests, for the Chihuahua group was headed by Luis Terrazas, the only former rival of Porfirio Díaz to survive his long presidential administration with both political and economic power intact. By 1902, management of the Terrazas family empire had largely passed to Enrique C. Creel, the nephew and son-in-law of don Luis. Known as the "Mexican J. P. Morgan," Creel resembled the New York financier physically, although without the bulbous nose, and also sought to establish a number of U.S.-style trusts in Mexico. Morgan's schemes to unite producers within an industry under a single trust company in order to rationalize competition and maximize profitability had great appeal for the development-minded científicos, of which Creel was a prominent member.[2]

Industrial concentration in the United States led to widespread debate about the threat of corporations to the public. The tremendous growth of factory production after the Civil War made it impossible to maintain the ideal of "perfect" competition between large numbers of buyers and sellers. Fearing ruinous price wars, businesses sought to protect their huge capital investments by dividing up markets through pools and corporate mergers. At the same time, they worked to improve efficiency by vertically integrating all aspects of production and distribution within a single firm. Along with railroads, steel, and sugar, the meatpacking industry became a prominent trust when the firms of Armour, Swift, and Morris combined their operations to form the National Packing Company in 1903. This attempt to monopolize the meat industry prompted government investigation under the Sherman Anti-Trust Act of 1890, but the resulting report, issued in 1905, proved a bitter disappointment to reformers. Not until the following year, when Upton Sinclair published *The Jungle*, did public outcry about sanitary conditions in the packinghouses lead to a comprehensive meat inspection act.[3]

In Porfirian Mexico, by contrast, concern focused less on the threat that such corporations posed to consumers than on the competition between rival elite clans, known as *camarillas*, for control of these lucrative enterprises. The centralizing tendencies of the Díaz government made the contract for rebuilding Peralvillo into an essential foundation stone for any potential meat trust in Mexico. To savvy observers, Reyes Spíndola's hasty disclaimer may have provided a clear indication that the Terrazas clique rather than established importers would win the Peralvillo contract. The timing of this decision was particularly important because the opening years of the twentieth century marked a crucial transition in the Porfirian regime, in which the alternation of power between competing clans began to give way to a monopolization of power by a few select insiders. This trend toward centralization extended to politics as well as business. At the same time that a private firm gained control over the municipal abattoir, a 1903 law transferred authority over municipal functions in Mexico City from the elected council to an administrative board composed of technocrats and headed by the Federal District governor. Nevertheless, the Terrazas soon discovered the limits of their control at Peralvillo, for Díaz still required them to negotiate the everyday administration, at least with the most prominent of the local importers.

Lacking political connections, small-time merchants and consumers struggled simply to gain access to work and food in the face of monopolist corporations and authoritarian inspectors. Butchers whose profit margins were slim in the best of times found themselves driven into the underworld of clandestine slaughter by the newly imposed health regime. As the common people knew all along, law enforcement worked for the benefit of the elite, and inspectors pursued minor offenders while allowing large businesses to set their own standards for wholesome meat. Working-class efforts to protect their communities likewise aroused considerable suspicion by the authorities, who feared traditional popular practices as well as the importation of disruptive trade unions. Thus, in the case of the meat supply, Porfirian modernization served to suppress the growth of a middle class on which many believed that the country's development depended.

CAPITALISTS FROM THE NORTH

Luis Terrazas began his career in 1849 as a Chihuahua City butcher and within fifty years had become the greatest cattle baron in the world. The son of a local merchant and slaughterhouse owner, he married into a wealthy *hacendado* family and ultimately accumulated more than ten million acres of land and four hundred thousand head of cattle. He was elected governor of Chihuahua in 1861, while only thirty-two years old, and was soon immersed in national politics when President Juárez took refuge in the state during the French Intervention. Despite his refusal to support the Díaz rebellion in 1876, Terrazas regained control of the state palace through a local coup in 1879. When the president finally succeeded in installing a loyal governor in Chihuahua in the mid-1880s, Terrazas shifted his focus from politics to business and proceeded to monopolize the economic resources of the state and thereby continued to undermine his local rivals. A firm grip on the country's largest cattle range and ready access to technical expertise from his North American neighbors gave don Luis the ideal levers for taking over the Mexico City meat market at the turn of the century.

Historian Mark Wasserman has catalogued the vast extent of the Terrazas family fortune during the Porfirian era. Their haciendas comprised some of the most fertile lands in the state, which they had acquired at low cost through the Lerdo Law of 1856 and the Survey Law of 1883. These laws were intended to facilitate the development of Church property and vacant public lands, but the Terrazas used their political clout to steal the common lands of many towns as well. With consummate timing, don Luis built his ranching empire at the end of decades of Apache wars and the beginning of a transformation in the United States from open range to cultivated fields, which created a heavy demand for Mexican cattle. In the 1880s alone, the Terrazas earned between half a million and a million dollars shipping livestock north on the newly built Mexican Central Railroad. These profits allowed the family to diversify into finance and other industries. By 1900, Enrique Creel had gained a virtual monopoly on banking in the state and had become a leading stockholder in the Banco Nacional de México. The family also profited from the rich mineral resources of Chihuahua, although they preferred to hire engineers from the United States to manage these operations or simply speculated in government mining concessions by selling the rights to foreign investors at large markups. Indeed, the Terrazas had a stake in virtually every enterprise in the state, from mining to manufacturing and railroads to retailing.[4]

The meatpacking industry became a vital link in the Terrazas economic empire, helping to maximize profits by connecting their ranching interests with the railroads and retailing operations. For years the family had exported young cattle to the United States, thereby losing the potential income from fattening and butchering the animals. In 1897, the Terrazas incorporated the Compañía Empacadora la Internacional (International Packing Co.) in the state of Chihuahua with a capital of two million pesos. Don Luis's son, Alberto, managed the business and the outside shareholders included John F. Brittingham, who utilized by-products from the slaughter in his soap manufacturing business near Torreón. Just as they employed foreign technicians for their mining ventures, the Terrazas contracted A. J. Morris of Kansas City to build their first packinghouse in the city of Chihuahua. Construction began in 1899, assisted by Mexican government concessions to import machinery tax-free, and the plant began operating at the end of the following year with a daily capacity of 280 head of cattle. La Internacional received a setback in 1902 when a fire destroyed the packinghouse, but Alberto Terrazas promptly set off for the United States to purchase new machinery and materials. Within a few years the company had two more slaughterhouses operating, in Torreón (1901) and Parral (1904), and planned to establish a series of branch houses for cold storage throughout Mexico.[5]

Despite this early start, La Internacional faced competition in the national market from a number of rival packing plants that were under construction as well as from municipal slaughterhouses. The Tampico Packing Company, for example, was ideally located to draw on the cattle country of the Huasteca as well as rich fisheries around the port city. The plant began exporting both beef and seafood by refrigerated ship and rail in 1905, although domestic markets for chilled meat remained doubtful. Toluca's "La Nacional" packinghouse opened in the same year to can the city's renowned chorizo sausages for sale throughout the republic and the Caribbean. The plant was built by José Castillo and reportedly contained refrigerated facilities comparable to the renowned packinghouses of Chicago and Kansas City. Also in 1905, the Swift Meat Company entered negotiations with a local merchant to open a branch house in the northern industrial center of Monterrey. The city of Zacatecas approved plans for another modern slaughterhouse in 1908. This one was completed in 1911, but many other projects never got off the drawing board. José Antonio de la Peña received a government concession to establish a packinghouse in the city of Puebla in 1903, but failed to complete work, while plans prepared in 1902 for a similar facility in Veracruz were still gathering dust as late as 1911.[6]

The failed first opening of the Peralvillo Slaughterhouse did nothing to stifle the appetite of Mexico City journalists for a modern packinghouse in their city. Carlos Díaz Dufoo, a prominent economist and associate of Rafael Reyes Spíndola, stated the case in his business periodical, *El Economista Mexicano*. Díaz Dufoo attributed the capital's meat supply problems to the "closed corporation of a medieval form" maintained by the importers. Destroying the guild would be simple, he declared, if the city only possessed an adequate slaughterhouse where all were free to slaughter cattle. Better still would be a great packinghouse like those in the

United States, Argentina, or Uruguay.[7] Nevertheless, efforts to create such an establishment in Mexico City continued to prove difficult.

SCANDALS AND SHORTAGES IN MEXICO CITY

With the law of January 20, 1897, passed before the ill-fated opening of Peralvillo, Mexico City had the regulatory framework to enforce modern sanitation standards in the sale of meat and lacked only the practical detail of an adequate slaughterhouse. The continued rapid growth of the urban population began to outpace meat supplies, causing shortages and inflation. Entrepreneurs attempted to fill the gap left by city officials, yet their private packinghouses and other technological innovations posed problems for health regulators that were as serious as the old fashioned practice of clandestine slaughter.

Mexico experienced significant rises in the price of meat about the turn of the century, which caused distress among the poor and speculation on the part of merchants and journalists. Without historical price series, reporters could only estimate the extent of the inflation; *El Imparcial* suggested with unwarranted precision that between 1868 and 1902 beef had risen by 233 percent while pork had gone up only 15 percent. Cyclical variation compounded the difficulty of such calculations, for livestock was relatively abundant in the winter months but grew scarcer by the summer. Wholesale prices of beef, which ranged from 20 to 23 centavos per kilogram in February 1902, had risen to 26 to 30 centavos by June of the same year. Even the lower winter rates translated into a retail price of 50 to 80 centavos at carnicerias where people shopped. Pork was more expensive still, wholesaling for 40 to 50 centavos at the slaughterhouse. A Porfirian journalist estimated that given the daily wage of one peso, a working-class housewife could afford to spend three pesos a month on meat, providing at best a daily allowance of 200 grams for the entire family. Even this meager allowance vanished in the summer, when prices were "in the clouds." This popular phrase for scarcity inspired a satiric cartoon in *El Hijo del Ahuizote* that depicted livestock dangling from a balloon above the outstretched hands of the common people (see figure 3.1).[8]

Explanations for these high prices varied between natural economic fluctuations and the nefarious work of monopolists. Some commentators attributed shortages to the shipment of cattle to the United States, but

3.1 "Noticia carnicera" (News from the meat market). The importers' monopoly, represented by a balloon, suspends cattle, sheep, goats, hogs, and chickens out of reach of the Mexico City poor. From *El Hijo del Ahuizote*, July 16, 1899. Courtesy of the University of Texas at El Paso Library, Special Collections Department.

since these exports came primarily from the north, beyond Mexico City's supply region, they probably contributed little to high prices in the capital. Far greater competition came from the Tampico-Havana trade, which had expanded since the Cuban War of Independence (1895–1898) had once again devastated the island's livestock industry. Shipments to the Caribbean came directly from the Huasteca region, the source of most of the cattle for Mexico City.

Whether the importers contributed to the high price of meat continued to provoke controversy. In the summer of 1898, *El Imparcial* attacked the Catholic journal *El Tiempo* for its claims that the industry was monopolized like the meat trade in Old Regime France. The científico paper insisted that the interruption of railroad communications with the Huasteca had been to blame, and concluded by insisting that meat was "subject to the invariable laws of supply and demand." Within a few years, as prices continued to rise, *El Imparcial* reversed its earlier liberal attitude and began to speak of a "plot" by members of a "trust" to menace the interests of the poor.[9]

High meat prices not only undercut living standards, they were also considered to be a genuine threat to the nation. Porfirian elites worried that industrial production depended on the nutritional health of the working classes. As one editorialist observed, with meat in such short supply, one could hardly be surprised by the feebleness of national productivity. "The truth is irrefutable: in the U.S., the number one country in meat consumption, the workers are robust and the output abundant."[10] Worse still, workers unable to afford meat filled their stomachs with pulque instead, thus contributing to drunkenness, the country's greatest problem according to many leaders. *El Imparcial* made this connection clear by calling for the Mexico City council to raise taxes on the indigenous alcoholic beverage while lowering the duties on meat, thereby encouraging the poor to drink less and eat more.[11]

Another danger of the so-called meat trust was adulterated food, a traditional concern of consumers who encountered watered-down milk and poor-quality bread, but now also a problem of modernity as food technologists produced substitutes for the pork fat that was so important to the Mexican diet. *El Imparcial* blew the whistle on the sales of "compound lard" made of cottonseed oil and coarse animal fats such as beef tallow. The article, published in January 1902, claimed that unnamed wholesalers had been passing this mixture off as pure pork fat for several months. Rafael Reyes Spíndola's other daily, *El Mundo*, soon joined in the muckraking by pointing out that this substance, although common in the United States, could be digested only with great difficulty and threatened eventually to destroy the stomach. The following month, the paper reported that stomach ailments had risen since the sale of adulterated fat began, not only in Mexico City, but also in a number of provincial capitals, especially those near the U.S. border. *El Imparcial* informed readers more cautiously that scientists from the Board of Health had determined that vegetable oil was not hazardous to the health, but that forthcoming reforms to the sanitary code would require labels so that consumers could distinguish genuine pork fat from cheap industrial substitutes.[12]

The dilemma posed by food technology was only part of a broader challenge by private enterprise against the Health Board's claims to scientific authority. An episode that demonstrated the extent of official concern over this threat took place on September 21, 1894, when an Inspector Arroyo visited the southern suburb of Coyoacán on the day of its *tianguis* (temporary market). Passing through the crowded displays, he noticed a particularly bad smell emanating from the stall of one butcher. Arroyo consulted the local market officials, Hegewich and Mondragón, who concurred that a rump of beef and its accompanying viscera were discolored and decomposing. Nevertheless, doctors Juan Revueltas and Antonio Velasco analyzed the meat, although apparently not the viscera, and pronounced it clean. The butcher, Cenobio Becerra, never did get his meat back and pressed charges with the local judge, who issued an arrest warrant, not for abuse of authority, but for issuing a false expert opinion. Arroyo was promptly freed from the local jail, but word of the scandal appeared in the pages of *Gil Blas*, one of the frequently censored but still independent popular newspapers, which delighted in deflating científico pretensions. The Health Board feared that similar incidents in the future could destroy its credibility and referred the matter to city attorneys with a note emphasizing the "transcendence of this case" for sanitary inspection.[13]

Despite occasional embarrassments, health officials scored frequent victories against butchers who violated sanitary regulations. In May 1898, for example, inspectors handed out clandestine slaughter citations to fifteen merchants, ranging from ambulant vendors to a retail outlet owned by Pedro Serrano, the city's largest hog importer. *El Imparcial* described the variety of fraudulent meats being sold, "some with falsified seals, others with the seal of the soap cauldron, and the others without any marking, which indicates their clandestine providence, some with cysticercosis (tapeworm) and not a few in an advanced state of decomposition."[14] In one revealing incident from 1900, Rafael Gómez received a $25 fine for refusing to allow the slaughterhouse guard to convey a hog with trichinosis directly to the soap cauldron. The importer explained that he simply wanted to keep it in his personal pen for another day to confirm the diagnosis. Nevertheless, regulations required its immediate dispatch for fear of its being confused with healthy animals, and the administrator at San Antonio Abad refused to dispense with the fine. Gómez then appealed on the basis of his property rights to Commissioner Jesús Galindo y Villa, who ruled unequivocally that "dangerous animals do not belong to the importers. They are under the dominion of the sanitary inspection for their destruction."[15]

Yet even as officials cracked down on small-time offenders, large-scale importers found new ways to evade sanitary controls through the construction of private packinghouses, which the city was forced to tolerate because of its inability to satisfy urban demand with the municipal abattoirs at San Lucas and San Antonio Abad. The most important private slaughterhouse in Mexico City was located at the former hospital of San Lázaro, which had been used to slaughter hogs as early as 1870 then closed temporarily about 1885 with the construction of San Antonio Abad. In 1889, Mexico's leading tocinero, Pedro Serrano, purchased the property and renovated it as a modern packinghouse with the assistance of José Castillo, later of the Toluca packing company. The Casa Empacadora Mexicana received its license to operate, subject to regular sanitary inspection and the payment of city taxes, on September 11, 1891. With the concession in hand, Serrano incorporated on September 16, bringing in a number of other prominent hog importers including Próspero Ramírez, Juan N. Zepeda, Jesús M. Bravo, Antonio García, and Francisco Pinedo. The firm of Pedro Serrano y Cia. also included as technical consultant but not stockholder one Orrin William Butt, who may have assisted with the renovations at San Lázaro, since he was the Kansas City partner of A. J. Morris, who later constructed the Terrazas slaughterhouse in Chihuahua. At the same time, Serrano negotiated a lucrative agreement with cattle merchants Hermenegildo González and Maximino Verduzco to slaughter livestock at the Casa Empacadora while works were stalled at Peralvillo.[16]

The fortunes of the San Lázaro packinghouse rose and fell inversely with the progress on the new municipal slaughterhouse. In the summer of 1892, Serrano offered to sell the Casa Empacadora to the city in lieu of rebuilding Peralvillo, but without success because of its location in a working-class neighborhood as heavily populated as San Lucas. That August, at the age of sixty-six and with failing health, he retired from the corporation, which was renamed Pedro Serrano y Cia., Sucesores. His withdrawal from the firm was completed in January 1893 with the sale of his personal interest in the Casa Empacadora for $200,000 to Ramírez and Zepeda. The two businessmen purchased San Lázaro without considering the political climate, however, for progress had resumed at Peralvillo and the city council used the change of ownership as an excuse to revoke their concession to slaughter. Nevertheless, demand for meat continued to soar and in March 1896 the city council finally relented and granted them a license, subject to annual renewal and to a monthly veterinary inspection fee of $200, which was later reduced to $150. Despite their complaints about excessive costs and unfair competition, within two years, nearly half the hogs consumed in the city were being slaughtered at the Casa Empacadora.[17]

The success of Ramírez and Zepeda tempted Pedro Serrano back into the business once he had recovered his health and retail operations. In 1897, he formed a partnership with one Paul Lourtau to take advantage of the Porfirian fad for French cuisine by producing authentic *charcuterie* for sale throughout the republic. The partnership lasted only a year, however, and the anticipated sausage factory was never built. Serrano next assembled a group of merchants to request permission to slaughter livestock in the suburb of Tlalnepantla and to take the meat to the Loreto market near the train station, where imported tocinería was sold. The importers hoped to avoid the constant fines imposed by health officials, but the council rejected their petition. Finally, by 1899, Serrano had decided to escape the restrictions at San Antonio Abad once and for all by purchasing the abandoned Nonoalco packinghouse, built a few years earlier by industrialists from the United States. Serrano renovated the structure sufficiently to pass the city's sanitary inspection, but at seventy-four, his body could no longer take the exertions. On December 22, 1900, he died of pneumonia in the tocinería on Puente de Jesús that his father had operated a century earlier. His wife had already passed away so his niece, Manuela Gómez, inherited the estate, reputedly worth $2 million. She had married Dr. Francisco Chavolla, the son of Serrano's old patron, who returned to the family business to manage Nonoalco. Having achieved a daily slaughter of more than seventy hogs, they sought to expand the factory by purchasing additional machinery from France. But on June 14, 1901, an electric motor that had arrived just two months earlier malfunctioned, causing a fire that burned the Casa Empacadora de Nonoalco to the ground and thus ended the legacy of one of Mexico's foremost butchers.[18]

With the loss of one major source of production, Mexico City consumers came to depend more heavily on pork from San Lázaro, even as municipal officials grew increasingly suspicious of Ramírez and Zepeda. An audit by the treasury department in October 1898 had revealed minor discrepancies in the weights of animals which formed the basis for tax assessments. Two years later, an inspector discovered a hundred bottles of pork fat with a combined weight of two tons that had been disembarked from a train at San Lázaro without paying import duties. Packinghouse guards even reported seeing workers remove diseased hogs from the soap cauldrons, where they had been consigned by the veterinary inspector. All the while, the two businessmen complained about the restraints imposed by the city. Despite the $200 to $250 in taxes they paid on a daily basis, they still had trouble getting animals approved for slaughter in a timely manner because of the inspector's duties at abattoirs in Mixcoac, Coyoacán, and even more distant suburbs. They considered such a situation intolerable, having installed "modern machinery beyond comparison with any other and rigorously complied with sanitary and fiscal regulations."[19]

Nevertheless, municipal authorities, concerned by the irregularities at San Lázaro, and more than a little annoyed by the complaints of Ramírez and Zepeda, referred the case to the Federal District police. Col. Porfirio Díaz, Jr., the top law enforcement officer for Mexico City, had the packinghouse placed under surveillance, then ordered a raid on the night of January 15, 1903. Domingo Martínez, chief of the reserve constabulary, an outfit of plainclothes detectives, arrived at San Lázaro about one o'clock in the morning with his deputy and a number of agents. The night watchman led them to the administrator, Guillermo Franco, and together they searched the shadowy Gothic arches of the former hospital. The first clue that something was amiss appeared in the form of a sack containing sixty-eight pairs of trotters, freshly cut. In the same room they found a metal tank with an equal number of pigskins, each representing half the animal, also freshly cut, and with the hair still attached. As the investigation continued, they uncovered quantities of meat scattered on tables, and a giant cauldron containing numerous hog's heads; the police lacked the equipment to remove them for an accurate count. The ribs, however, remained missing, making it impossible to tell if the thirty-four hogs had passed sanitary inspection. Franco denied any knowledge of their location, and referred the police to the butcher, Jesús Castelán, who also lived onsite. Leaving an officer to guard the evidence, Martínez proceeded to round up the packinghouse employees for questioning.

The three main suspects represented the tocinero's traditional division of labor: the business manager, the sausage maker, and the hog butcher. Franco, a thirty-year-old native of an important pork-production center, the city of Puebla, testified that he had gone to bed at seven o'clock the previous evening and had remained asleep until called by the night watchman. He claimed to have been unaware of the slaughter that had taken place on that or any previous night. A second suspect identified himself as Rafael Torres, twenty-five years old and originally from Calimaya, Mexico State, also the hometown of Pedro Serrano. Torres had worked at San Lázaro for eleven years, having doubtless been hired by his fellow Mexiquense, and currently managed the ham department. He admitted to having selected 122 hogs at Franco's orders, but claimed not to have witnessed the nocturnal slaughter because he had retired at five o'clock, even earlier than the somnolent administrator. Jesús Castelán turned out to be twenty-two years old, the son of the regular butcher, Ignacio, who had been unable to work for the past two weeks because of an illness. He confessed to frequent nighttime slaughters, always at the orders of Franco, and had no knowledge of whether the taxes had been paid on the hogs. He was just an employee, he explained, and did what he was told. Police Chief Martínez placed all three under arrest and conveyed them back to the stationhouse, along with large quantities of pork taken as evidence.[20]

The case against Ramírez and Zepeda grew even more serious when Health Board scientists examined the meat from the clandestine slaughter.

Seven of the thirty-four animals were found to have been condemned to the soap cauldrons, three of them with cysticercosis. The city revoked the license to operate San Lázaro and imposed a $200 fine while treasury auditors began an investigation, which revealed a longstanding pattern of tax evasion. Ramírez and Zepeda insisted on their innocence, blamed the workmen, and protested "the serious damage done to their interests, to those of the municipal government, and even to those of the city, because we have not been able to butcher hogs for popular consumption."[21] But their self-righteous claims of public service now rang hollow, and city officials consigned their business to San Antonio Abad alongside the rest of the importers. Given the gravity of their offenses, a fine and the loss of a license seems a very lenient treatment, which provides eloquent testimony to the class-biased nature of Porfirian criminal justice.

The closing of first Nonoalco and then San Lázaro placed even greater strains on the municipal slaughterhouses. The price of pork shot upward, and *El Tiempo* expressed concern that the real punishment for the packinghouse owners' crimes would fall on the inhabitants of the capital, especially the poor, who would be "sentenced to a Quaker diet, that is, preparing their dishes without pork fat." The city council appropriated funds for urgent works to expand capacity at San Antonio Abad, but then on April 17, 1903, an unusual south wind blew a forty-six meter section off the roof. A similar accident had occurred a year earlier at San Lucas, and while no one was hurt on either occasion, the need for a permanent slaughterhouse had become clear.[22]

THE RETREAT FROM LIBERALISM

Negotiations between the Terrazas interests and the Mexico City council for the reconstruction of Peralvillo began on an informal basis in 1901, unlike the public calls for bids that had been issued twice before. The meat importers failed to recognize the threat to their business until the summer of 1902, by which point the outlines of a contract had already been settled. Throughout the nineteenth century, butchers had employed the liberal language of property rights to defend their interests, but Porfirian authorities no longer accepted such arguments, having concluded that the interests of public health outweighed private property claims. In challenging the Terrazas contract, therefore, the importers invoked the constitutional protection of labor instead of capital as well as the welfare of the

municipality. This tactical retreat from liberal principles to utilitarian calculations demonstrated just how weak their position had become at a time
when the Mexico City government was increasingly under the control of
the científico bankers, with their preference for administrative efficiency
over political compromise and their open contempt for workers.

Given the deplorable conditions at San Lucas, the importers wisely
chose not to continue opposing the new slaughterhouse, a tactic that had
served them well in 1897 but clearly had little prospect for the future.
Instead, they formed their own group, headed by congressman and cattle
merchant Serapión Fernández, in order to offer an alternative project for
reconstructing Peralvillo. The importers had powerful allies within the
city council and the broader Porfirian hierarchy and therefore had high
hopes that their proposal would receive a favorable hearing. They prefaced
the bid by stating: "We ask for neither privileges nor special concessions
and still less onerous speculations for the city."[23] Their plans called for the
construction of three large chambers, for cattle, sheep, and hogs, each
divided into a number of separate lots. Importers who regularly slaughtered more than twenty-five animals per day would have private areas for
inspection and slaughter while smaller merchants would have to work
together in communal chambers. As with the Terrazas proposal, the
Mexico City merchants promised to construct an adjacent packinghouse
with refrigerated space for a thousand or more of each type of animal. At
a peso per head for cattle, the importers' slaughter fees were a third lower
than those proposed by the Terrazas, although the twenty-five centavos
charged for hogs represented a considerably higher fee, indicating the preponderance of cattle and sheep merchants over tocineros in the association. And as had been the case throughout the nineteenth century, the
importers failed to gain unanimity within their own ranks, even when
threatened by a powerful outsider. On June 20, 1902, just three days after
the importers made their collective counteroffer to the city, a prominent
firm of cattle merchants, the González brothers, filed their own plans for
reconstructing Peralvillo.[24]

Even with a united front, the local merchants would have faced a formidable challenge from the financial strength and political connections of
the Terrazas. Large, vertically integrated corporations such as La
Internacional, which controlled the Chihuahua meat industry from the
pastures to the marketplace, represented the científico ideal for business

management. That very summer of 1902, Treasury Secretary Limantour had begun negotiating the consolidation of Mexico's various railroads into a single state-owned firm. He justified this venture with a page borrowed from J. P. Morgan, arguing that the ruinous competition of price wars threatened to undermine the stability of the Mexican railroad system.[25] In a similar fashion, the financial strength of the Chihuahua group, as guaranteed by a $100,000 bond deposit, provided the official rationale when the Mexico City council awarded the slaughterhouse concession to La Internacional. The contract, signed by Mayor Emilio Pimentel and Alberto Terrazas on August 21, 1902, limited the slaughter of livestock to company personnel and set the fees for doing so at the originally proposed rate of $1.50 a head for cattle, 19 centavos for sheep, and 15 for hogs.[26]

The slaughterhouse commission of the city council promised vaguely to protect the interests of importers, who lobbied furiously to block the deal. In a series of petitions to the councilmen, the local merchants challenged the contract as a violation of their constitutional freedom to work as well as of the prohibition against monopolies. Article 4 of the 1857 charter declared all men free to practice the profession, industry, or work of their choice, while the law of April 1, 1850, specifically assured their right to butcher livestock in the municipal abattoir. By limiting the slaughter to company personnel, the contract not only infringed their basic rights, but also exceeded the legal authority of the council. This body neither had a right to contract work in the name of the importers, nor could it oblige them to pay quotas fixed by La Internacional without their consent. The merchants argued in addition that the contract violated article 28 of the Constitution, which forbade the establishment of monopolies. With a private firm both administering the abattoir and slaughtering on its own account, the other importers had little chance of equal treatment. They pointed out the opportunity to manipulate markets through the unscrupulous scheduling of livestock; although the contract required eight hours of slaughter, it did not specify which hours. The managers of La Internacional could therefore order the company's animals butchered first so that their own retailers had the only fresh meat in the markets at ten o'clock in the morning, the peak shopping hour. The importers insisted that the council could not fairly delegate the administration of the municipal slaughterhouse to a private business.[27]

The prominence of the Terrazas family hobbled the lobbying campaign of the importers, who invariably took pains to avoid personal slander against the northerners even when describing thoroughly unsavory business practices. Felipe de J. Ortega, coauthor of the July letter to the editor of *El Imparcial*, which had been disclaimed in the following issue, published a lengthy memorial to the city council, in the form of a broadsheet dated September 8, offering the most comprehensive objections to the contract. He began with the constitutional principles upholding the butcher's right to work, but quickly moved on to the fine points of municipal finances. With the slaughter fees as set in the contract, La Internacional could expect to repay its investment in just five or six years, leaving fifteen years of pure profit, accruing not to the common good of the municipal treasury but to a private firm. The rates set for butchering cattle were anyway far too high, as Ortega demonstrated through the testimony of prominent importers, who asserted that the cost of slaughter could not possibly exceed fifty centavos under the Terrazas plan and would have been even less under the rival proposal. Ortega then proceeded to lay out the case against monopoly, arguing that once the competition of the current importers had been eliminated, La Internacional would be free to set prices arbitrarily. He concluded with a series of financial projections showing that—at a time when the average corporate stock yielded 5 percent—the company could earn a tremendous return of 30 percent annually.[28]

By formulating their arguments in the científicos' language of banking, the importers succeeded in wresting some important concessions. The Terrazas had long experience manipulating both state and national courts to defend suspicious land claims in Chihuahua, so the threat of a constitutional challenge to the contract probably held little concern. Nevertheless, they agreed to a modification in the proposal setting aside a separate area for the importers to slaughter livestock using the traditional methods. The municipal government also reduced the life of the concession from twenty-five to twenty years. Finally, the Terrazas allowed a clause to be inserted in the contract reducing the slaughter fees if annual profits rose above 9 percent of the capital invested. Given the realities of Porfirian investment, as opposed to the somewhat fevered calculations made by Ortega, this may not have appeared as such a significant concession after all.[29]

The Terrazas also took steps to reassure Mexico City consumers that their arrival would not endanger local meat markets. Some of the changes were purely superficial, such as the establishment of separate corporations for importing livestock, La Abastecedora (The Supplier), and for the slaughterhouse administration, the Rastro de la Ciudad de México, S.A. (Mexico City Slaughterhouse, Inc.). Nevertheless, a valid argument could be made in favor of rationalizing industries under the control of large corporations so long as they operated in the public service by limiting the wild gyrations of supply and price, which had long afflicted the Mexico City meat markets. The Terrazas were soon presented with an opportunity to demonstrate their dedication to market stability when the health officials closed down the Casa Empacadora de San Lázaro. As the price of pork fat began to rise alarmingly, *El Tiempo* informed readers on January 23, 1903, that adequate supplies existed in the city. The apparent shortage resulted from "speculators without conscience who are taking advantage of an opportunity not to search for legitimate gains, but rather to steal." Nevertheless, the Catholic newspaper went on to list a score of "conscientious and honorable merchants" who had not joined with the "trust" and were dedicated to selling at the regular prices. Perhaps fearing an association with this supposed plot, the management of La Internacional promptly notified the editors that it had more than forty tons of pork fat available for sale at the usual price and it was prepared at any moment to rush additional supplies to the capital as needed.[30]

While the northern capitalists sought to bolster their public relations in Mexico City, important political changes were afoot that threatened the future of self-government at the city council. Historian Ariel Rodríguez Kuri has documented the "colonization" of the city council by científico bankers over the course of the 1890s. This group had controlled the municipal presidency without interruption since 1894, and a federal law of March 26, 1903, formalized the transfer of power from the local council to the executive branch. The law created a new government council, the Consejo Superior de Gobierno del Distrito Federal, comprising the district governor, Guillermo Landa y Escandón, the director of public works, engineer Roberto Gayol, and the president of the Board of Health, Dr. Eduardo Licéaga. The preponderance of technocrats in the governing council illustrated the Porfirian priority of efficient administration over political compromise. Indeed, all city property, from the municipal palace to the San Lucas slaughterhouse, passed to the new executive board, leaving the elected council as a purely advisory body.[31]

The transfer of power in Mexico City facilitated the Terrazas efforts in renovating the Peralvillo Slaughterhouse. In Chihuahua, Díaz completed the rehabilitation of don Luis in 1903 by allowing the aging general one last triumphal entry to the governor's palace before he yielded power the following year to his son-in-law, Enrique Creel. Construction began at Peralvillo in May 1903 under the direction of Harry H. Hinkle, a thirty-two-year-old associate of the Terrazas's packinghouse experts from Kansas City, Orrin William Butt and A. J. Morris. Hinkle soon demonstrated his worth by helping to convince the Mexico City Board of Health of the need for company personnel to slaughter all livestock at Peralvillo using modern techniques. The Government Council therefore offered a revised contract on November 14, 1903, which removed the company's obligation to provide a special compartment for the importers to slaughter livestock and also ceded additional land for the construction of stockyards, a packinghouse, and a meat market.[32]

The importers, upon learning of the modifications, naturally connected the loss of municipal self-government with their fears of a monopoly over the local meat markets. The Government Council responded to the protests by reminding them that the elected council had signed the original contract with La Internacional and that the changes promised to benefit the city by separating the packinghouse from the municipal slaughterhouse. The council offered to provide a comparative study of the two contracts, demonstrating the advantages of the revised version, but the promise was never fulfilled.[33] With the científicos entrenching their control over the municipal government, the importers were forced to retreat from the liberal ideology that had proved so successful over the previous century. Whether they would be able to adapt to survive in the Social Darwinist business climate of Porfirian Mexico remained to be seen.

THE RETURN TO PERALVILLO

Engineer Luis Espinosa, the director of public works for the Federal District, delivered the inaugural speech at Peralvillo on February 25, 1905. "Yesterday the doors of this important edifice opened, to cure the illnesses of the body and to alleviate the pain; today, the final touches are applied to the city's General Slaughterhouse, [which is] reclaimed for the public hygiene and for the civilization of our now populous Metropolis."[34] While touring the imposing structure and enduring the learned discourse, the importers found little to quiet their fears that La Internacional would soon monopolize the Mexico City meat supply. Nevertheless, with two years advanced warning, they had done their best to organize in their own defense. The wealthiest importers established corporations to attempt to compete with the Terrazas on their own terms, and smaller merchants, including the numerous independent tablajeros, followed the example of trade unions, which had grown increasingly active by the turn of the century. The científico elite looked benignly on the imitative efforts of the well-to-do, but closed off the more radical alternatives available to the lower sectors, thereby driving them into the illicit Porfirian underworld.

Unlike the frenzied atmosphere leading up to the September 1897 opening, Alberto Terrazas had already announced the completion of work in January 1905 and calmly awaited the return of President Díaz from his tour of the Tehuantepec Railroad to schedule the formal inauguration. The company conducted its first public test of the new system on February 8 by slaughtering fifty head of cattle, sheep, and hogs before an audience of government officials. In keeping with the Porfirian penchant for symbols of progress, the inaugural ceremonies began on the morning of February 25 with a special train from the National Palace to Peralvillo. The electric tram carried Díaz, his cabinet, and a number of prominent guests over the newly paved macadam road, while at the same time demonstrating the ease of conveying meat back to the capital. The decision to open the new slaughterhouse during the winter dry season avoided the threat of floods, which had caused such havoc seven and a half years earlier.[35]

The tour of Peralvillo astonished many visitors who were familiar with the ill-fated first slaughterhouse. Of the buildings constructed earlier, the new architect Louis P. Brauss had retained only the administrative offices and the warehouse on the northwest edge of the perimeter. For those who could remember them, the meat market and slaughter facilities must have seemed like flimsy shacks compared with the solid, two-story brick construction that now took up virtually the entire western half of the property. The eastern extension had been left uncovered as corrals for sanitary inspection of livestock and for the horses and mules used to pull the meat delivery cars. The fence around the perimeter, with stone guardhouses at each corner, remained as the only other artifact from the original works. A single smokestack towered above the large building to vent the six industrial ovens that replaced the defective Albright crematorium of the original Peralvillo Slaughterhouse.

Having examined the outside of the facility, the distinguished visitors reviewed the slaughterhouse workers, who lined up for inspection in waterproof yellow uniforms, some wearing aprons and others overalls, depending on their assigned tasks. As the butchers marched off to their stations, the dignitaries climbed a staircase that opened onto a balcony with a panoramic view of the great hall. The observation platform had been specially decorated with ribbons and banners for the inaugural ceremony, but it was intended as a permanent feature to encourage residents of Mexico City to view the modern technology used to process the meat that they consumed daily. Peralvillo soon became a regular stop on excursions through the capital, just as the La Villette abattoir attracted tourists in Paris.[36]

A second distinguished group that gathered for the inaugural ceremonies consisted of prized steers from the Hacienda of San Nicolás Peralta, owned by Ignacio de la Torre y Mier, Mexico's foremost gourmet and the son-in-law of President Díaz. While the official party looked on from their balcony, the cattle ascended a long enclosed ramp that narrowed progressively until they were pinned at the top in a single file. A door slammed shut behind them, isolating a dozen at a time, and then sledgehammers began raining down on their skulls from workers on overhead platforms. Once they had all been bludgeoned, a trap door opened beneath them, dropping them to the next level. Workers quickly secured the stunned animals by their hind legs, lifted them up by pulleys, and slit their throats with knives. After the bleeding had finished, the carcasses were lowered briefly for skinning, then raised again for dressing. The hides and viscera dropped through another level of trap doors into processing rooms, while porters wheeled the sides of beef off to market on elevated rails, all in under five minutes before the next dozen steers descended from above. Workmen dispatched hogs and sheep using similar industrial processes, although without the sledgehammers needed to stun the larger animals. Members of the Mexican Society for Prevention of Cruelty to Animals had reportedly lobbied unsuccessfully to prevent the butchers from using hammers.[37]

After the meat had been carried off to market or to the ample refrigeration chambers, workmen proceeded to scrub the remaining bits of blood and waste from the hardwood floors with powerful jets of water. The cleaning was aided by improvements in the processing of by-products, for the blood of cattle and sheep had already been drained off in wooden gutters to be dried and powdered for industrial uses. Contrary to practices in the meatpacking center of Chicago, however, the importers continued to process the hogs separately for such traditional culinary preparations as chicharrones, pork fat, and blood sausage. In addition to cleaning the floors, the water tanks at Peralvillo also flushed the sewage pipes that carried waste to the Grand Canal and supplied a fire extinguishing system that had been installed with memories of the Chihuahua packinghouse fire. Satisfied with the technical arrangements, the official party descended from their balcony for a champagne luncheon, where they encountered some of the same animals that had just been slaughtered in the form of a shepherd's broth, spaghetti au jus, *machitos* (fried organ meats), and kid cooked in blood.[38]

However impressive the inaugural day demonstration had been, the real test of the slaughterhouse lay in its ability to meet the regular demand for meat by Mexico City consumers. The contract had stipulated that the Terrazas management provide a capacity of 500 cattle, 600 sheep, and 800 hogs in eight hours with three-fifths of the meat available in markets before ten o'clock in the morning. While the hogs and sheep were dispatched without difficulty, the workers had trouble once again in adapting to the new system for slaughtering cattle. City officials attributed the slowness to their inability to learn the technical arrangements, but a far larger problem lay in the reduced workforce. At San Lucas, the butcher captains together with their numerous helpers had totaled nearly three hundred workers, while in Peralvillo there were fewer than fifty in the entire cattle chamber. La Internacional doubtless hoped to justify the smaller numbers with greater industrial efficiency. Nevertheless, the work of cleaning and dressing the carcasses remained as labor intensive as ever, since the mechanical apparatus merely assisted in the actual slaughter and in conveying the sides of beef to market along elevated rails.[39]

Consumers soon felt the effects of the troubles at Peralvillo, for within two weeks of the opening, the price of meat had doubled in some retail outlets. *El Tiempo* proclaimed with alarm: "Meat shortage. Is this a plot of the importers?" Some vendors blamed the wholesale merchants for trying to pass on the rising costs of slaughter quotas, inspection fees, transport tariffs, "and who knows what other requisitions." Others attributed the problem to the irregularities of supply resulting from the new system of slaughter.[40] *El Imparcial* laid the blame flatly on the small retailers, who "take advantage of whatever circumstance to sell more expensively and obtain at times immoderate profits." The editors ran through the litany of tablajero complaints: that two companies dominated the market; that small competitors could not slaughter on their own account; that meat from Peralvillo arrived late and cost more; and that the new washing techniques caused it to lose weight. "The truth is that our reporters have made investigations that permit us to assure that the price of meat in the slaughterhouse has not remained almost without alteration from which we can deduce that the retail sellers could very well have conserved the old prices."[41]

The ambiguity of this statement, which was buried in an otherwise sharp indictment, may well indicate that Reyes Spíndola, the científicos' chief mouthpiece, knew more than he was prepared to tell the public. Two companies did in fact dominate the wholesale cattle business: the Terrazas' La Abastecedora and Nacional Ganadera, S.A. (National Cattle Company, Inc.), established with $500,000 in capital by Luis G. Padilla and Adolfo Fernández, heir to the aging don Serapión. Less than a week later, on March 20, the Mexico City importers sent a petition to the secretary of the interior complaining about unfair treatment at Peralvillo. They alleged that the managers invariably scheduled the slaughter so that livestock from La Abastecedora arrived first in the markets. Workers did not attend to cattle from La Nacional until after taking a leisurely brunch, so that their meat did not reach the market until nearly closing time. "Thus, La Abastecedora takes advantage of the best hours for sale without competition, raising the prices during those two or three hours, and when the cattle from La Nacional arrive on the market they lower the prices in order to harm us with an unequal competition."[42]

The importers' worst fears of monopolization at Peralvillo had indeed come to pass, but the Porfirian government acted decisively to limit the harm to consumers, at least temporarily. A week after receiving the petition from Padilla and Fernández, the interior secretary ordered the director of public works to ensure that La Internacional accorded equal treatment to both importing companies. To achieve this end, the schedule was changed so that the two companies went first on alternate days, and the resulting competitive struggle soon caused prices to fall. In reporting the fortuitous effects of this price war, however, *El Tiempo* warned that the two companies would surely reach an *acuerdo*, or secret agreement, to divide the market between themselves, thereby sending prices back into the clouds. Indeed, before the summer had ended, the opposition newspaper announced that the two companies had joined together to raise wholesale prices once again.[43]

Independent confirmation of these muckraking claims is difficult to obtain. Unfortunately, systematic price data on meat markets are available only for part of 1902 and not again until 1907. Díaz Dufoo's *El Economista Mexicano* did publish weekly pork fat prices, which remained relatively steady throughout 1905, but this preserved article serves as a poor proxy for more volatile fresh meat prices. Without corroboration from other newspapers or sources, the accusations of monopolistic behavior made by *El Tiempo* must be viewed with caution.

Nevertheless, the treatment received by small-time butchers contrasted sharply with the científicos' conciliatory attitude toward more prominent importers. Shortly before the opening of Peralvillo, city officials announced a vigorous campaign against clandestine slaughter and other violations of the 1897 sanitary ordinances. They started in January 1905 by disseminating the provisions of the code, including the new requirement that all meat imported from outside the district had to be taken directly to Peralvillo for inspection before it could be sold. To emphasize their point, officials then fed the press a series of reports about fines handed out for sanitary violations; these stories invariably concluded by stating that the butchers involved had protested the penalties in vain. On February 4, 1905, for example, the newspapers informed readers that the police had discovered an entire clandestine slaughterhouse operating within the city. The suspected owner, Francisco Alfaro, had fled, but his alleged accomplice, police inspector Mariano Aguila, had been arrested and consigned to Belén prison. The news reports ended abruptly on the very day that Peralvillo opened, although one can only speculate on the timing. Officials may have manipulated the press in an attempt to create the impression that although the old sanitary regime was open to abuse, the new slaughterhouse would solve these problems. After all, the

Porfirian establishment worked hard to preserve the illusion of order. Alternately, the government may have discontinued the press releases to cover up genuine troubles at Peralvillo.[44]

Tocineros likewise complained about unfair treatment from both health inspectors and the management at Peralvillo, but their negotiating position with the Porfirian government was far weaker than that of prominent cattle importers. The dispute concerned the disposition of animals with minor infections. Formerly, the meat from hogs with small lesions could be cleaned, or if that was not safe, the butchers at least had the option of removing the fatback to be rendered down into lard. Under the new regulations, authorities destroyed all hogs that appeared unhealthy, resulting in a total loss to the importers. The merchants complained that they were losing $400 to $500 daily, and would soon be driven out of business. In keeping with the fashion for incorporation, they formed the Cia. "Unión del Ramo de Tocinería" ("Union of the Industry of Hog Butchers" Co.), a curious blend of medieval and modern corporate language. Timoteo Zepeda served as president and other members included Próspero Ramírez, Rafael Gómez, and Jacinto Pineda. When the government denied their petition, the number of hogs butchered at Peralvillo dropped precipitously, raising fears of clandestine slaughter. Finally, on June 22, sanitary authorities restored the more lenient standards used at San Antonio Abad. Nevertheless, officials remained concerned that once started, the clandestine slaughter would continue unchecked. Police caught Jacinto Pineda with 150 hogs ready to be sacrificed, and other butchers were arrested with smaller numbers.[45]

The tablajeros likewise attempted to form a union to put an end to their own ruinous competition, but without much success. On August 23, 1905, the tablajeros met at the Xicontécatl social club to discuss the competition between them. They complained that while the law granted anyone the right to slaughter livestock at Peralvillo, nobody was willing to do so because the combination of La Abastecedora and Nacional Ganadera had threatened to cut off their supplies. Another form of competition developed from the new restaurants that opened in the Porfirian era. Because they purchased in bulk, the restaurateurs demanded discounts, which the tablajeros could scarcely provide and still cover their own costs. Nevertheless, the hundred and eighty odd retail vendors could achieve nothing on their own because of internal rivalries and to reach any agreement at all they had to turn to Adolfo Fernández. The manager of Nacional Ganadera succeeded in establishing a board of directors for the organization but declined to serve as president. Fernández had an interest in preserving the trade because so many of the retailers operated on credit with his company. Moreover, by helping to direct the association, he could ensure that they did not carry out any serious collective action that might threaten the control of the importers. Not surprisingly, although the tablajeros failed to arrive at any substantial market-sharing agreement, prices reportedly continued high through the fall.[46]

The political reorganization of 1903 had caused upheavals in the meat supply throughout the Federal District. Health Board inspectors found slaughterhouses in outlying towns to be completely inadequate, often simple corrals in the center of town, without adequate water supplies and drainage, and at times polluted with large amounts of accumulated, putrefied waste. The town of Tacuba, just west of the capital, constituted one of the worst offenders, and in 1905, officials ordered the facility closed until renovations could be completed. This threatened a political crisis if local merchants had to travel to slaughter livestock in nearby Azcapotzalco, which had formerly been subject to the authority of Tacuba. To prevent such a reversal for this traditional head town, the council members sued to preserve their autonomy in the same way they had appealed to colonial courts to protect their common lands from Spanish incursions. District officials finally succeeded in closing the slaughterhouse in 1907, and the town of Tacuba did not regain the right to butcher animals until the following year.[47]

As sanitary inspectors attempted to extend their jurisdiction into the surrounding countryside, they came up against deeply engrained popular practices, thereby revisiting Francisco Carbajal's struggle to restrict chito during the 1848 celebration of the Virgin of Guadalupe. What officials condemned as an illegal and unsanitary tax evasion, campesinos considered to be a vital part of traditional holiday festivals. Witness the February 1907 arrest of Antonia Rojas and four men who butchered two hogs for Carnival in the village of Magdalena Mixihuico. The inspector who caught them in the act provided no details, but culinary ethnographer Diana Kennedy has described how Mexicans butchered livestock in the countryside. One of the men cut the animal's throat, then Antonia probably filled a bucket with blood and stirred in salt crystals to prevent coagulation.

Tucking up her skirts, she waded into a nearby canal to wash the organs her male companions had extracted. Finally she dried them on rocks while the men prepared the meat. Nothing was wasted in cooking such mouthwatering festival foods as *tamales, flautas,* and *pozole.*[48]

The politics of home butchering became considerably more complicated in the cities. From the very beginning, Terrazas had sought guarantees of adequate sanitary inspection to ensure that the Peralvillo Slaughterhouse retained its monopoly. By the end of 1906, the plant manager Hinkle complained that clandestine slaughter had reduced the volume of hogs at Peralvillo by a third. This practice threatened serious losses to municipal revenues, endangered public health, and, because of the need to transport animals through the streets, even caused public disturbances. On one occasion, residents of the working-class Colonia Santa Julia saw their butcher chasing after a mortally wounded steer that was trying to escape down Matamoros Street. Nor was this practice limited to small vendors; Hinkle accused the city's largest hog merchant, Próspero Ramírez, of continuing to engage in the illicit commerce for which he had lost the license to operate the San Lázaro packinghouse in 1903.[49]

With the competition of Nacional Ganadera for the premium markets and clandestine slaughter on the low end, profits at Peralvillo fell far short of expectations. Rumors had already surfaced by the end of 1905 that La Internacional would sell out to an unnamed company from San Francisco. The company did succeed in squeezing efficiency gains on the work floor, reducing the number of cattle butchers from nearly fifty at the opening to just thirty-three in 1907. Yet such modest improvements hardly offset the effects of a world depression. With banks everywhere calling in loans, the company was forced to seek court protection in July of that year. The management then began to ponder a restructuring plan to emerge from bankruptcy by eliminating the slaughterhouses in Torreón and Parral and by concentrating on core markets in the cities of Chihuahua and Mexico. Dreams of a national meat trust based on North American refrigerated technology had certainly vanished.[50]

ORDER AND PROGRESS AT PERALVILLO

The opening years of the twentieth century found traditional liberalism in full retreat in the Mexico City meat supply. After a decade of progressively increasing their control over the capital's electoral machinery, the cientifico elite consolidated their hold on the city by centralizing authority in a governing commission made up of federal technocrats while reducing the local council to a powerless debating society. The científico goal of establishing a modern corporate business structure likewise took shape with the replacement of individual livestock traders, as the liberal generation of Serapión Fernández and Pedro Serrano handed power to Nacional Ganadera and assorted Sucesores. From there it was a relatively small step to the creation of industrial trusts under the authority of científico leaders such as the Terrazas-Creel clan. Emilio Pimentel illustrated the interlocking directorship between these groups; he first signed the contract granting control of Peralvillo to La Internacional in 1902, then after stepping down as municipal president, he went on the company payroll as a consultant.[51] Labor, while not part of the Porfirian blueprint of progress, responded in Mexico as it had in Europe and the United States by asserting its collective voice. Nevertheless, petty retail meat merchants found it more difficult to organize independent unions than did mine and textile workers.

Even as the goal of economic progress seemed near fruition, the Porfirian elite also worked to instill order, but the government's authoritarian system of justice worked to the advantage of the powerful rather than of ordinary people. In the case of prominent businessmen, only the most egregious of legal violations such as the clandestine slaughter of diseased animals and systematic tax fraud incurred the notice of police inspectors. Small-time offenders, however, were routinely harassed as a matter of policy, in order to bolster the public image of a modern, orderly Mexico. The double-standard of the judicial system also appeared in the case of punishments, as Próspero Ramírez and Juan Zepeda were allowed to continue to work out of the San Antonio Abad slaughterhouse despite the evidence of their clandestine slaughter, while retail butchers lacking political connections were incarcerated for lesser infractions. Nevertheless, once obscured in the murky underworld of clandestine slaughter, butchers could continue to practice their trade as long as the public accepted such gray-market commerce as necessary for their regular supply of meat.

Events at both the height of Porfirian political economy and in the depths of the criminal underworld thus served to emphasize the essential role of the state in guaranteeing order and progress in Mexico. The moderating power of the presidency was particularly important to the meat importers, who had initially feared that the tremendous political and economic influence of the Terrazas family would quickly drive them out of business. Instead, the government functioned as a relatively impartial arbitrator, at least between the most powerful firms. Yet this careful arrangement was soon destabilized with the arrival of meatpacking interests from the United States.

CHAPTER FOUR

The Popo Challenge

When John Wesley DeKay arrived in Mexico City in August 1901 representing the North American Beef Company of Chicago, he gained a personal audience with Porfirio Díaz to discuss his investment plans. The president often received such foreign visitors at Chapultepec Castle in an effort to dispel the stereotype of Mexico as a backward and bandit-ridden country. His personal charisma overcame his halting English and he won the friendship, and the investment capital, of such prominent businessmen as mining engineer John Hays Hammond and construction magnate Sir Weetman Pearson. Díaz certainly charmed the twenty-seven-year-old DeKay, who proceeded to lay out his vision for transforming the Mexican meat industry through a network of packing-houses modeled on those in the United States. By using refrigerated railroad cars to bring the meat to retail markets, DeKay hoped to eliminate those inefficient and untrustworthy middlemen, the local importers and butchers. At the same time, he sought to convince Díaz of his own trustworthiness in providing the people of Mexico with wholesome and fairly priced meat. DeKay left Chapultepec armed with letters of introduction and fired with enthusiasm for Porfirian progress and for his own role in bringing it to fruition.[1]

While DeKay's future in Mexico seemed bright, his past remained shrouded in mystery. He later claimed to have been born in the small town of New Hampton, Iowa, a hog-raising area in the northeastern corner of the state, but he did so with an urgent need to demonstrate U.S. citizenship. There was no way to check because the Chickasaw County courthouse had conveniently burned down in 1880, six years after his birth. At least two writers have attributed British citizenship to DeKay, and he may well have come to the meatpacking capital of Chicago in the hopes of emulating the illustrious career of Sir Thomas Lipton. The son of a Glasgow grocer, Lipton traveled to the United States as a young man in the 1860s before building one of the first modern retailing chains, with nearly 250 outlets throughout the United Kingdom. His success derived in part from the sale of cheap, new industrial processed foods, such as tinned pork from his own private packinghouses in Chicago. Yet Lipton depended even more on the innovative use of advertising, and in this DeKay proved to be a talented understudy. Regardless of his place of birth, the ambitious young meatpacker belonged to, or perhaps better aspired to, the turn-of-the-century, transatlantic financial elite, equally at home in New York and London, and dedicated more to global capital markets than to either nation state.[2]

Few industries offered better prospects for wealth than supplying the British meat market about the turn of the century. The Argentine example demonstrated how quickly such an industrial complex could be established. For centuries a center of dried meat exports, the province of Buenos Aires possessed great herds of cattle, but they were still scrawny, underdeveloped animals when British capitalists began establishing refrigerated plants in the 1880s. With the lure of European markets, the quality of livestock had improved drastically by 1900, and the outbreak of the Boer War offered huge profits to packers able to supply the British army. Investors thereupon began feverish construction on a new series of refrigerated packinghouses, just in time to benefit from the loss of U.S. exports around 1906, when Upton Sinclair's exposé made European consumers hesitant to trust Chicago meat. In addition to capturing domestic markets in Mexico, DeKay hoped for a share in this Latin American beef bonanza, which ultimately supplied as much as 80 percent of British consumption by the 1920s. Yet he had to overcome huge logistical problems in order to bring Mexican beef to London's Smithfield market.[3]

The technical difficulties of constructing a modern packinghouse in the remote cattle country of western Mexico were matched by the political challenges of establishing an industrial enterprise subject to Porfirian political economy. Although foreign investors had received extremely favorable concessions during the early years of the Díaz regime, the government had become far more restrictive by the dawn of the twentieth century. In a broad study of the North American colony in Mexico City, William Schell Jr. has depicted the majority of these outsiders not as proconsuls of capitalism but as often-unsuccessful supplicants to the favor of President Díaz.[4] Edward Beatty has followed an even more revisionist tack, arguing that Porfirian industrialization was not simply a haphazard process of favoritism, whereby politically connected individuals received privileged monopolies. He argued instead that the científicos established the basis for economic development through an explicitly designed and fairly administered industrial policy comprising tariffs, patent laws, and tax concessions for new industries. Through a statistical analysis of new industry awards, Beatty concluded that the Porfirian development bureaucracy did not give undue preference to politically connected elites.[5] But his cliometric study failed to adjust for the competition between rival elite factions, whereby Díaz played off his subordinates through the denial as well as the awarding of favors. Because most concessions were never developed anyway, it is far more revealing to look at the implementation of these grants than at their assignment. As DeKay quickly discovered, the rule of law in Mexico led directly to Porfirio Díaz.

THE URUAPAN PACKINGHOUSE

"Uruapan should qualify as the paradise of Michoacán," wrote the geographer of that enchanting state, José María Pérez Hernández, in 1872. "The purity of its crystal waters, the aromatic chirimoyo trees, whose scented perfume blends with that of a thousand flowers... [provide] the observer one of those eloquent and sublime pictures that move the souls of exquisite sensibility and make one comprehend the capacity of the omnipotent hand of the Supreme Creator."[6] For promoter John W. DeKay, by contrast, the crystal waters of the Rio Cupatitzio offered 7,500 horsepower to drive the machinery, while the aroma of the countryside derived from 1,700,000 cattle and 300,000 hogs that were "tributary to the company's first packing house."[7] To transform these resources into profits, however, strained the capacity of many human hands, which proved to be far from omnipotent.

Theodore W. Osterheld, sometime partner of cattle merchant Felipe de J. Ortega, who also owned an hacienda in Michoacán, obtained the original concession for a packinghouse in Uruapan. Renowned since the colonial period for the ceramics produced by Purépecha Indians, the town became an important coffee-growing center in the nineteenth century and even won a gold medal for its coffee at the Parisian Exposition of 1900. A branch of the Mexican National Railroad arrived in 1899, but the harvest had already been greatly reduced by crop diseases, which ruined many growers. The declining fortunes of coffee left the livestock raisers preeminent, and on May 2, 1899, Lic. Salvador Cortes Rubio, acting as attorney for Osterheld, signed a contract for the packinghouse with Governor Aristeo Mercado. The agreement provided a number of favorable concessions, including a ten-year tax holiday, allowances of waterpower from the Rio Cupatitzio, and an exemption on import duties for livestock entering the state on the condition that the meat was later exported.[8]

As was often the case in the Porfirian era, obtaining the concession proved far easier than organizing the capital to exploit it successfully. In 1900, Osterheld prepared a prospectus for a Michoacán Packing Company, but apparently he could not find financial backing, despite a possible association with A. H. McKay of the Mercantile Bank Company. It was not until the following April that Osterheld informed the state government, as required by the contract, that the North American Beef Company would begin construction shortly. Nevertheless, the company's representative, John W. DeKay, did not arrive in Mexico until August 1901 and he brought with him more grandiose claims than actual capital. In March 1902, one Cornelius S. Palmer visited Morelia, presenting himself as the president of a Chicago packing company. He declared his intention of purchasing the concession, and thereby prompted a flurry of speculation in the press. *La Patria* announced that a Mexican engineer, Gustavo Roth, had received a commission to build the packinghouse, while *El Economista Mexicano* reported that it would be undertaken by Charles C. Mallory of the Clark Construction Company at a cost of $500,000. Neither prediction proved accurate, but the North American Beef Company did retain the services of a prominent local attorney, Luis Méndez, to protect its concession. When the Mexico City council published the draft of its contract with La Internacional in the summer of 1902, Méndez successfully argued for changes to ensure that refrigerated meat from the Uruapan packinghouse could be imported into the city.[9]

DeKay continued to build his connections within the Porfirian elite, even as construction work languished in Uruapan. By 1903, Osterheld had left the company for unknown reasons, perhaps rivalries with DeKay's new mentor in Mexico, Alfred Bishop Mason, the president of the Veracruz and Pacific Railroad and a promoter of tropical agriculture. A native of Chicago who may have known DeKay previously, he instructed the newcomer on the fine points of cultivating the native elite; together they hosted a banquet at the Hotel Asquera in Morelia for Governor Mercado to ensure favorable treatment of a licensing request. Mason's interest became apparent on April 6, 1903, when Lic. Méndez obtained a contract with the secretary of development adding federal incentives to the state concession for the Uruapan packinghouse and also providing for the construction of a second facility alongside the Veracruz and Pacific Railroad. DeKay had already purchased pastureland in Michoacán and hired a cattle buyer, F. L. Bael, to supply the packinghouse. The construction engineer, Ernest Abe-Hagen, had informed the *Monterey News* that the plant would be finished by October of 1903, but reports emerged in the summer that rains had delayed work.[10]

Bad weather was only the beginning of the problems at Uruapan. Writing several years later, a British engineer considered it "no slight feat to have begun in a wilderness some hundreds of miles away from any workshops, the erection of a large factory of this kind." The company imported from the United States virtually all of its construction materials down to the bricks for the buildings as well as the machinery for the meatpacking operations. The construction workers' lack of familiarity with these materials apparently compounded the problem, although the engineer did not specify whether the hired hands were Mexicans, African Americans, or Chinese, all of whom helped to build so many of the railroads in Mexico as in the United States. Nor were the laborers the only ones having trouble; by 1905, John's younger brother Henry E. DeKay had taken over as superintendent of construction. Historian José Napoleón Guzmán Avila found that the DeKays also experienced difficulty in buying land from a local rancher, Manuel Campos, to gain access to the banks of the Rio Cupatitzio and the waterpower needed to run the machinery.[11]

The actual ownership of the North American Beef Company remains a mystery, one that John DeKay did little to clarify. He informed the *Monterey News* that the company had "$1,000,000 of American capital" but denied any connection with the so-called beef trust when news broke in 1905 of a U.S. government anti-trust investigation of the Chicago meatpackers. There seems little reason to doubt him on the latter point, for at least one of the "Big Five," Swift and Company, had failed in a previous attempt to set up operations in Mexico. On October 18, 1905, Lic. Méndez filed a request with the Mexican government to change the company's name from the North American Beef Company to the United States Packing Company. Once again the paper trail is muddled because the state of Michoacán had already accepted the transfer in 1903 and the names were used interchangeably in the press for the next two years.[12]

The most likely explanation for the mystery is that the million dollar capital fund existed only in DeKay's imagination, which would account for the construction delays far better than the vagaries of weather or workers. By 1903, DeKay's original backers for the North American Beef Company, possibly including Cornelius Palmer, had apparently lost interest in the Uruapan packinghouse. At about the same time, with the Veracruz and Pacific Railroad on the edge of bankruptcy, Alfred Bishop Mason had sold out to Treasury Secretary Limantour's consolidated Mexican National line. The pair then proceeded to New York in an attempt to recapitalize the packing company, but it was not until 1905 that DeKay succeeded in subscribing a US $600,000 bond issue for the company, and that probably accomplished little more than refinancing the existing debt.[13]

DeKay's fortunes changed abruptly in 1906 with the publication of Upton Sinclair's novel *The Jungle*. As British consumers read lurid accounts of the conditions in Chicago packinghouses, the prospect of Mexican beef exports gained instant credibility.[14] DeKay incorporated under the laws of New Jersey, and by December of that year had secured the backing of a consortium of London bankers. The company issued US $2,000,000 worth of twenty-year gold bonds at 5 percent interest, with US $700,000 going to the previous bondholders while the remaining US $1,300,000 were sold in London, primarily to the British and Mexican Trust Company. Lafayette Hoyt DeFriese, a New York lawyer with extensive connections in London, served as a director for the trust and probably took the lead in arranging the British capital. The trust company board also included Sir William F. Haynes Smith, chairman of the Egyptian Land and General Trust, Campbell P. Ogilvie, an expert on Argentine cattle and director of the Buenos Aires and Rosario Railway Co., and Vincent W. Yorke, a director of the Mexican Railway Co. At the request of his London bankers, DeKay changed the company's name in March 1907 to the Mexican National Packing Co. to avoid any possible association with the discredited U.S. exporters.[15]

In the years that DeKay struggled to finance the company, Mexican counsel Luis Méndez remained busy securing regular extensions of the contract deadlines from the secretary of economic development. The original agreement of April 6, 1903, required the company to complete work at Uruapan within three years. On November 15, 1905, then again on March 17, 1906, the Mexican government granted extensions of the deadlines for beginning the Veracruz project and for completing the packinghouse in Uruapan. In a contract dated November 24, 1906, another extension was granted, and since British capital was already forthcoming, the company asked for and received an additional concession to build a plant in the northeast, either in Nuevo León or Tamaulipas. The projected network of packinghouses expanded yet again, under a contract dated June 21, 1907, to include a plant in central Mexico, in Hidalgo, Querétaro, or Mexico State.[16]

Once DeKay had secured British financial backing, construction sped rapidly to a conclusion at the end of 1907. The Uruapan plant consisted of two main buildings, for slaughter and by-products, each with a fronting on the railroad tracks. An elevated ramp led up from the stockyards in the back to the two-story slaughterhouse, which also contained extensive refrigerated storage. The by-products building included separate departments for making lard, sausage, and margarine, as well as a detached fertilizer house. Although a planned canning department had not yet been completed, the facility had an appraised value of $1,350,000. A Mexico City branch house, located in the Rancho del Chopo industrial park along the railroad line on the northwestern side of the city and valued at $150,000, had ample refrigerated space to supply local retailers. In addition, the company had purchased fifty refrigerated railroad cars to deliver the meat for a total of $240,000. Other properties included a refrigeration plant at San Luis Potosí, machinery for fifteen more cold storage houses, and the haciendas of Santa Catarina and Santa Bárbara near Uruapan (see figure 4.1).[17]

After more than five years of stop-and-go construction, an entirely favorable balance sheet could hardly have been expected. A second London bond issue in December 1907 brought the company's debt to just under $10 million. Of that, real estate, plant, and equipment amounted to a mere $2.3 million, while other Mexican assets, including livestock, cash, and receivables, added another $1 million. With the equivalent of $3 million still uncollected from London investors, the company had spent two pesos for every one of value received. DeFriese presented the calculations in a more favorable light, observing that "the actual cash investments of

4.1 "Compañia Empacadora Nacional Mexicana: Del rancho a la mesa" (Mexican National Packing Company: From the ranch to the table). El Popo's packinghouse in Uruapan, Michoacán. From *El Imparcial* January 19, 1908. Courtesy of the Latin American Library, Tulane University.

the Company have amounted, as nearly as possible, to 70 percent upon the par value of the bonds issued." Given the tremendous difficulties of constructing the packinghouse in the Mexican countryside, he concluded, "I think you will agree with me that the net moneys invested from the proceeds of the Company's bonds are more than creditable."[18] As with most investments, DeFriese based his valuation not on immediate returns but on future prospects. Yet as DeKay had already learned, Porfirian investment, more than most, depended on a favorable political climate.

CULTIVATING THE PORFIRIAN ESTABLISHMENT

Because Díaz was already seventy years old and had held office for sixteen uninterrupted years when DeKay met him, the presidential succession was the foremost political question in Mexico. Although the científicos, led by Treasury Secretary Limantour, dominated the Porfirian cabinet, traditional liberals had a powerful candidate in General Bernardo Reyes, former secretary of war and governor of the northern industrial state of

Nuevo León. Neither científicos nor liberals formed a genuine political party but rather loose associations of camarillas, cliques centered on a powerful individual like Limantour or an extended family such as the Terrazas-Creel clan. Moreover, Díaz actively encouraged rivalries between these various groupings in order to ensure his own paramount status. In this political vipers' nest, an outsider like DeKay had to move very carefully indeed.

In a typical move designed to complicate the political picture, Díaz had chosen a dark horse for vice president, Ramón Corral. With only a primary school diploma, Corral held dubious claim to the title "científico." He had risen to prominence in his home state of Sonora in the mid-1880s with campaigns to pacify the fiercely independent Yaqui Indians. After serving two terms as governor of the northern state, Díaz appointed him to run the Federal District in 1900. When the district government was reorganized in 1903, Corral was promoted to secretary of the interior, a powerful cabinet position responsible for relations with Congress and the states as well as internal security. His meteoric career was capped the following year, when the aging Díaz named him vice president and heir apparent.[19]

His enormous power notwithstanding, a black cloud hung over Corral. Although only fifty when elected vice president, with his grey hair and lined face he appeared as old as Díaz. Sophisticated residents of Mexico City furthermore considered Corral a barbarian from the northern frontier. They spoke quietly of his brutal suppression of the Yaquis, sold off to slavery on the henequen plantations of Yucatán, where the life expectancy was a year or two at best. While governor of Sonora, he had grown rich on commissions from businessmen, and his reputation for graft followed him to the Federal District, where he had reportedly used his position as governor to collect protection money from gambling and prostitution rings. He had served as Díaz's political hit man, fabricating the evidence used to discredit a potential rival, General Reyes. Rumors also circulated that Díaz had appointed the vice president as a stooge to assure his own position as the indispensable man of Mexico. Corral nevertheless retained enormous influence as secretary of the interior, which he used to promote Porfirian progress. Just how far he would go to support Mexican industrialization became apparent only later.[20]

As an outsider himself, DeKay naturally gravitated to the powerful figure of Corral. Because the vice president's portfolio at the secretariat of interior included regulating the Mexico City meat supply, it seemed imprudent to offer him a position on the Mexican National board of directors. Instead, DeKay appointed a staunch Corral partisan, Tlaxcala Senator Jesús F. Uriarte, to look after his interests. Sebastián Camacho received the post of vice president of the board, having acquired some knowledge of the meat industry while serving as president of the city council during the disastrous first opening of Peralvillo in 1897. More recently, this prominent científico had been named president of both the Mexican senate and the Banco Nacional de México. Other Porfirian notables on the board of directors were lawyers Luis Méndez and Francisco Alfaro as well as General Fernando González, the governor of Mexico State and son of a former president. Two non-Mexican board members, appointed for their expertise rather than for political connections, were George I. Ham, president of the United States Banking Co. of Mexico City and Horace Potter Chesley, former general manager of the St. Louis stockyards.[21]

Not content simply to pay directors' salaries, DeKay also employed his literary proclivities to curry favor with the Porfirian elite. In 1906, he financed the publication of a small, leather-bound volume entitled *The Men of Mexico and the Land They Love.* He described his subjects with language drawn from the serialized adventure stories popular at the time. Of Corral, he wrote: "his hair is gray; his eyes are keen, frank, piercing; his face strong, rugged, resolute."[22] In an attempt to ingratiate himself with existing cattle merchants, DeKay also included photographs of the cartel's aging patron, Serapión Fernández (see chapter 1) and his mansion in the palatial suburbs west of Mexico City. With its emphasis on the stability of the Porfirian regime, the book served as an advertisement for investment in Mexico. The message was clear that capitalists from the United States could trust their money in a country governed by resolute men like Díaz and Corral. *The Men of Mexico* thus fit within a genre, analyzed by historian William Schell Jr., of U.S. businessmen attempting to boost the value of their interests in Mexico by encouraging other investors to join them in a tropical pyramid scheme.[23]

Another example of mixing literature and business illustrates DeKay's modus operandi in Mexico. On June 2, 1907, the aspiring packer sent President Díaz a clipping from the *New York Commercial* with the headline "Mexico and Peace." In the editorial, DeKay refuted contemporary U.S.

newspaper stories accusing Díaz of provoking a conflict with Guatemala. The next day, he forwarded to the president a detailed study analyzing the inefficiency of Mexico's antiquated tanning shops, which processed an annual output of thirteen thousand tons of raw hide down to a mere six thousand tons of finished leather, far less than the yields achieved by factories in the United States and Europe. Having established his loyalty to the Porfirian regime, while at the same time pointing out a glaring deficiency in Mexican manufactures, DeKay proceeded to advance a mutually beneficial proposal. If the government would grant him tax exempt status under the New Industry Act, he would establish modern tanning factories, thereby improving national productivity and enhancing the balance of payments. In a stern paternal tone, Díaz responded that the proposal contained just one flaw, as the report itself made clear: tanning was not a new industry in Mexico. DeKay failed to appreciate the scrupulous constitutionalism of the Porfirian dictatorship; Díaz regularly flaunted the spirit of 1857, but took care to avoid violating the letter of the law.[24]

An incident from the following year further demonstrated the counterproductive nature of uninformed sycophancy. In 1908, Díaz informed journalist James Creelman that he was ready to step down from the presidency and encouraged the formation of an opposition party in the 1910 election. The interview, published in *Pearson's Magazine* and intended to establish his democratic credentials for a U.S. audience, provoked an uproar when it was translated by the Mexican press. Middle-class groups, excluded from office, took the president at his word and launched a flurry of political activity that threatened to upset the delicate Porfirian balance of power. Unaware of the domestic political repercussions, DeKay had a thousand copies of the inflammatory interview printed up and circulated them to Mexican state governors and other prominent politicians—the last people Díaz wanted to remind of his hasty offer to retire from politics. In attempting to gain favor, DeKay succeeded instead in alienating the most powerful man in Mexico.[25]

Whatever his personal misgivings about DeKay, the president turned on the charm when the Mexican National Packing Co.'s financial backers arrived on the Montezuma Express from New York City on December 31, 1907. The party included British and Mexican Trust directors Lafayette DeFriese and Campbell Ogilvie, as well as Eustace Finnes, M.P., London solicitor William Capel Slaughter, and Hiram R. Steele of the New York

Life Insurance Co. As a demonstration of the importance of their project for Mexico's development, Díaz found time in his schedule to receive them at Chapultepec Castle on New Year's Day. He assured his guests that the packing company enjoyed the protection of his government and that British capitalists could invest in it with safety. Moreover, he promised to lend his personal prestige to the enterprise by escorting Madame Díaz to the company's retail meat shops when they opened in the capital. Such favorable publicity would be a vital step in convincing Mexican customers of the value of the new methods of preparing meat. Finally, to ensure that local butchers learned the lesson, he would instruct the Board of Health to issue regulations requiring the trade to be organized according to the company model.[26]

For the inaugural ceremony in Uruapan, scheduled for January 18, 1908, DeKay chartered a special train from Mexico City with Vice President Ramón Corral as the guest of honor. Also attending the opening were District Governor Guillermo Landa y Escandon, Health Board medics Domingo Cervañanos and Jesús Monjarás, public works engineer Miguel A. Quevedo, and the long-time slaughterhouse inspector José de la Luz Gómez. The train stopped briefly in Morelia to pick up Governor Mercado and his entourage, then continued on to Uruapan, where it was met by a crowd of three thousand. After passing through the coffee groves south of town, the party arrived at the three-acre site on the banks of the Rio Cupatitzio. A giant electric welcome sign illuminated the side of the ice plant, while evergreen garlands decorated all the buildings. The dignitaries inspected the slaughterhouse and the cooling rooms, filled with sides of beef from a trial run earlier in the week. The inevitable champagne lunch featured roasts carved by skilled butchers from the United States.[27]

DeKay hurried back to Mexico City to conclude a few final arrangements with the government before the grand opening of his retail operations. On February 7, 1908, he finalized a contract with Vice President Corral so that all meat produced at the Uruapan slaughterhouse would undergo federal inspection and thereby avoid delays when it arrived at retail markets in Mexico City. Ten days later, he met at the Treasury building with Limantour to consider an ambitious contract to provision the Mexican Army and other public institutions for twenty years at prices 10 percent below retail value. They also discussed a schedule under which the company would receive a five-year tax holiday, after which taxes would gradually increase to a maximum of one centavo per kilo of meat. DeKay expressed the hope of having all four projected plants running at 50 percent capacity within five years, but the question remained of how Mexican consumers would react to the novelty of refrigerated meat.

BETRAYAL

As former chief clerk of freight for the Mexican National Railroad, J. F. McGinnis had long experience dealing with the vagaries of local customs officials. The newly hired traffic manager of the Mexican National Packing Co. therefore quickly perceived the danger when treasury agents seized an entire trainload of refrigerated meat arriving from Uruapan at the end of February 1908, scarcely a week after the first shipments had begun. Melting ice dripped on the railroad siding like a ticking time bomb as company employees struggled frantically through the labyrinth of Mexican bureaucracy to release the meat before it went bad. DeKay informed Méndez, who insisted that under the terms of the concession, they owed no additional taxes to the government. Treasury Secretary Limantour responded with a dramatic gesture by ordering the destruction of the entire shipment. Seven years of meticulous planning, hard work, and abject flattery may have passed through DeKay's mind as the train made its way across town to the Peralvillo Slaughterhouse, where the carefully aged sides of beef were duly incinerated.[28]

DeKay had known from the very beginning that the packing company's success depended on winning the favor of Mexico City consumers, and to that end he formulated a savvy and elaborate marketing plan. The refrigerated branch house served as the hub for receiving meat from railroad cars and passing it along to local butchers. For this wholesale depot DeKay purchased a prime industrial location at Rancho del Chopo near the Mexican National Railroad terminal on the northwest side of the capital. The company began its retail chain small with just two outlets, but they were carefully chosen for maximum exposure. To educate the masses about U.S. standards of hygiene, DeKay established a model market on the busy thoroughfare San Juan de Letrán, which ran just east of the Alameda Park, a popular gathering place for all levels of Mexican society. A second, more upscale shop opened on Viena Street in the exclusive Zona Rosa (Pink Zone). DeKay intended the shop to cater at first to the large colony of U.S.

expatriates living in the district, but counted on the Mexican penchant for foreign fashions to add a native clientele as well. The El Popo brand name, recalling the majestic volcano rising above the Valley of Mexico, became a regular feature in the prominent English-language daily, the *Mexican Herald*. This advertising campaign emphasized the company's dedication to supplying the public with "clean, wholesome, and properly prepared meats."[29]

The Popo marketing strategy mirrored the larger Porfirian development project aimed at inculcating the Mexican masses into modern European lifestyles. The foreign colony and the elite were supposed to demonstrate such benefits of modern technology as refrigerated meats to the local middle classes, who in turn served as an example for the working classes, indoctrinating them in the manners of the gente decente. Diffusing the ideals of polite society was essential not only to avoid class conflict but also to ensure the success of mass production in Mexico. DeKay's business model depended on selling large quantities of meat at low prices, and an elite clientele alone could not provide sufficient demand to utilize fully the Uruapan packinghouse. To reach this mass market, he later diversified his advertisements beyond the English-language press to include *El Obrero Mexicano*, a newspaper directed at working-class readers and supported by Federal District Governor Guillermo Landa y Escandón. DeKay thus hoped to establish Popo-brand refrigerated meat as an essential element of the modernity advocated by the paternalistic Porfirian government.[30]

The Mexican National's business plan also depended on winning the support of livestock producers. In a *Mexican Herald* advertisement, DeKay explained the benefits of El Popo "to the cattlemen of the Republic. The establishment of this Company's system of packing houses will insure to the growers of cattle, hogs, and sheep of the Republic a steady and reliable cash market."[31] The unspoken point of this advertisement was the cartel of importers, who dominated the marketing of livestock through secretive personal ties rather than through an open wholesale market. DeKay hoped to circumvent these middlemen and approach the ranchers directly, with the ultimate goal of raising the quality of Mexican livestock in order to compete in the European export market. The vast majority of local cattle, particularly in the Huasteca and in Michoacán, were Creole breeds descended from the original herds introduced by Spanish conquistadors in the sixteenth century. Although the annual Coyoacán livestock exposition featured Herefords and Aberdeen Angus, importers refused to pay a premium for such animals, and therefore ranchers had no incentive to improve their livestock and produce export-quality beef.[32]

Given the Porfirian infatuation with symbols of progress, the opening of the Mexican National Packing Co.'s refrigerated branch house on February 20, 1908, went strangely unnoticed in the press. Díaz himself may have attended the inaugural ceremony at Rancho del Chopo, but the event received no mention, even in the *Mexican Herald*, which had already collected advertising revenue from El Popo. Only the *Mexican Daily Record*, a small newspaper financed by company director George Ham, reported on the event. According to their story, which may well have been written by DeKay, Mexican butchers already stood waiting in line at dawn for the wholesale market to open, and those who arrived after ten o'clock were turned away. Not surprisingly, the article read like advertising copy: "customers are delighted with the flavor and quality of the Popo products while the fact that the meat is prepared under the most modern and sanitary conditions...is proving a great attraction to that section of the public who are anxious to obtain the most healthful food products."[33]

Even without independent reports on the public reception of Popo meat, one can easily imagine the concern of the slaughterhouse management about the potential competition. The Terrazas had no sooner opened the abattoir in the spring of 1905 than a costly price war broke out against the Mexico City importers. The northern capitalists ultimately reached an accommodation to share the market with the most powerful of the local cattle dealers, Fernández and Padilla, but less prominent merchants, particularly in the hog business, resorted to clandestine slaughter, causing a constant drain on revenues. Far from reaping monopoly profits as the importers had initially feared, La Internacional found itself in bankruptcy court by 1907. The global depression strained the Mexican family's capital reserves, leaving them even less prepared to sustain an extended competitive battle with the British-financed Mexican National. Such a struggle seemed all the more one-sided because the foreigners held the technological advantage of refrigerated railroad cars, which allowed them to halve their freight costs by shipping only the meat, without worrying about losses from transporting livestock.

DeKay interpreted the unexpected tax levy and the seizure of meat from Uruapan as a crude government attempt to gain a competitive advantage for the local company, but Limantour envisioned a more subtle and ambitious plan, a forced merger between the ironically named firms, the Terrazas's La Internacional and DeKay's Mexican National Packing Co. Such a deal seemed obvious to the Porfirian banker, ever alert for mutually profitable joint ventures between domestic and foreign capital. The attempted merger by packers in the United States to form the National Packing Co. seemed to prove yet again the benefits of consolidation over unrestrained competition. By successfully constructing the Uruapan packinghouse, DeKay had demonstrated both the technical qualifications and the financial resources to modernize the Mexican meat industry. The Terrazas would naturally remain junior partners in the concern, although their local expertise deserved suitable compensation, perhaps through the sale of the Mexico City slaughterhouse contract. With the outlines of a deal worked out, the treasury secretary had only to convince the British investors that it was in their interest to cooperate with the Terrazas. Nevertheless, these negotiations needed to be conducted with great care to avoid damaging Mexico's reputation as safe for foreign capital.[34]

The key to this industrial confidence game lay in Díaz's role as arbiter of the Mexican political economy. Just how he accomplished the trick remains unknown, for DeKay implausibly claimed that the president consulted Lic. Méndez on the tax question, accepted his legal opinion that the company owed nothing, and then ordered Limantour and the Terrazas to reach an agreement with the Mexican National Packing Company. In fact, the company eventually paid more than $100,000 in back taxes, but the packer still maintained his faith in don Porfirio, or perhaps, with several million pesos already sunk in Mexico, he simply had no choice. Regardless, on Friday, March 14, DeKay sent Limantour a draft proposal for the purchase of the Mexico City slaughterhouse, and they met the following Monday at the Treasury offices to work out the details. Vincent Yorke, a British and Mexican Trust Company director, approved the plan when he arrived a few days later, having booked passage from London immediately after the crisis broke. On March 25, 1908, DeKay departed for London, armed with official statistics of Mexico City meat consumption as well as renewed assurances from Díaz and Corral, in order to convince the rest of the board to support the acquisition of La Internacional.[35]

The contract proposal revealed that industrial efficiency based on vertical integration formed the cornerstone of DeKay's strategy for winning the Mexico City market, just as it had for the Chicago meatpackers a few decades earlier. Although the purchase price for the slaughterhouse concession remained open to negotiation, the company promised to sell beef wholesale at just twice the going rate for live cattle, and in any event, the retail price would not rise above 30 centavos per kilo over the twenty-year life of the contract. Given that dressed meat constituted slightly more than half the weight of the live animal and that Mexico City retail prices averaged a peso or more, this proposal offered a tremendous savings to consumers. In return, DeKay asked for a monopoly on the slaughter of meat in the city, exemption from federal taxes, and a tariff on imported meat either from elsewhere in the republic or from the United States. One final but significant provision of DeKay's memorandum requested a government regulation requiring all meat sold in Mexico City to be refrigerated.[36]

The importance of this last clause became clear the following month as an advertising war broke out between Popo meats and the Mexico City slaughterhouse. The Mexican National had been promoting its brand heavily in the press since January with repeated references to government inspection and to scientific and hygienic methods, thereby catering to the Porfirian ideals of order and progress. Illustrations of the Uruapan packinghouse and of the refrigerated railroad cars used to carry the meat to Mexico City further emphasized this image of modernity. But in April two of the most influential daily papers, *El Imparcial* and the *Mexican Herald*, carried advertisements questioning the new product. "Refrigerated meat is useful on long sea voyages or to send to distant markets, but understand it well, it is only as a matter of absolute necessity." The advertisements not only implied that the Popo brand tasted inferior to freshly slaughtered beef, they also cast doubt on the company's claims of sanitary benefits from refrigerated meat. "It loses its juice, it becomes discolored, it is insipid and acquires a rare tenderness, due, perhaps, to the beginning of decomposition. How can a government inspector answer for the good sanitary condition of meat ten or fifteen days after inspection?"[37]

The public attacks by La Internacional against the Mexican National appear quite at odds with the secret negotiations underway for a merger that promised to benefit the Terrazas far more than the foreigners.

Furthermore, abattoir superintendent Hinkle was still trying to work through government channels to block the sale of Popo meat in Mexico City. Alberto Terrazas may well have left his manager in the dark about the negotiations in order to keep pressure on DeKay, for the respective market shares would help determine the final sale price of the slaughterhouse. Moreover, the advertising copy carefully avoided making reference to either company, thereby allowing the slaughterhouse owners to attribute the campaign to local importers. Indeed, the traditional meat distributors may have provided far more innovative and effective promotional work than expensive newspaper placements, which anyway appeared only briefly. In May, for example, the Mexican National offered a $100 reward for information leading to the arrest and conviction of "certain persons, falsely representing themselves to be Agents or inspectors of the Superior Board of Health of Mexico, [who] have visited several butcher's shops saying that refrigerated meat is unhealthy and liable to decomposition."[38]

As the Mexican butchers carried on their struggle against Popo in the summer of 1908, the Mexican National proceeded to buy the slaughterhouse out from under them. DeKay persuaded his London bankers to approve the deal, assuming he could negotiate a reasonable price, and set sail from London on June 19, accompanied by DeFriese. Arriving in Mexico City, they called on Porfirio Díaz to repeat their assurances that the company would act in the public interest. Their meetings with Limantour were perhaps less cordial, as he refused to concede any of their three basic demands, either a monopoly on wholesale meat, an exemption from federal taxes, or a refrigeration requirement for all meat sold in Mexico City. Meanwhile, the London bankers insisted on doubling the retail price ceilings, from thirty to sixty centavos, with a contingency for further increases to account for possible scarcity of livestock. The company did gain some concessions, a legal title to the slaughterhouse property and tax-free importation of machinery, including unlimited supplies of tin plate to be pressed into cans for meat. Yet these must have seemed minor consolation when Alberto Terrazas demanded $2.5 million for the slaughterhouse concession—five times the cost of construction.[39]

Paying such an outrageous price went against DeKay's entire strategy for providing low cost meat from small, efficient packinghouses in the livestock raising areas of the country. Nevertheless, General Fernando González, the governor of Mexico State and a director of the Mexican

National Packing Co., explained to him the need to adapt his U.S. business model to local conditions. Of course the Terrazas demanded far more than the actual value of the slaughterhouse—they always charged staggering commissions—but the company had no hope of dominating the national cattle markets without their acquiescence. By the same token, González explained, the prestige of owning the Mexico City slaughterhouse concession was worth several times the monetary price. Armour and Swift might control the U.S. market from packinghouses in Chicago, St. Louis, and Kansas City, but no French company could do the same without the La Villette slaughterhouse in Paris. Bolstered by these arguments and convinced of the future potential, Lafayette DeFriese signed a contract with Alberto Terrazas on July 25, 1908, obliging the British and Mexican Trust Company to pay the full $2.5 million for the Compañía del Rastro de la Ciudad de México.[40]

Although ill from the effects of Mexico City's altitude, DeFriese remained to oversee the transition while DeKay carried the contracts back to London. In a Compañía del Rastro board meeting on September 17, the new owners left the management essentially unchanged under Frank E. Humphrey and Harry H. Hinkle. Alberto Terrazas likewise retained his directorship in the company. By about the same time, DeFriese and his New York partner, Judge D. A. Holmes, had concluded negotiations with the secretaries of the treasury, interior, and economic development to extend the slaughterhouse concession until December 31, 1926. The company agreed to pay the Mexican government $228,500 for the land at Peralvillo plus $105,941 in "accrued slaughter taxes," that being the formula they settled on to resolve the dispute that had begun the entire episode. Sir William Haynes Smith, chairman of the British and Mexican Trust Company, accompanied DeKay to Mexico City for the final signing ceremony on October 23, 1908.[41]

The peripatetic meatpacker did not remain long in the Mexican capital; scarcely a week had passed before news arrived from Chicago that DeKay was touring the Union Stockyards with Sir William and don Alberto, who had been invited onto the board of the Mexican National. To complete the merger, a tentative agreement had been reached with La Internacional to purchase the packinghouses in Torreón and Parral. General Manager Frank Humphrey had also accompanied the party to the United States to purchase machinery for upgrading the Mexico City slaughterhouse. On top of all the publicity surrounding the slaughter-house concession, DeKay unveiled a marketing coup in the form of an exclusive, five-year contract with some of the leading importers in Mexico City. The González brothers, Felipe Zepeda, Inocencio de la Vega, Ramón Mireles, and several other meat merchants announced that they would sell only Popo products.[42]

On January 7, 1909, DeKay ended an exhausting year of travel at Winchester House, on Old Broad Street, in the heart of the City of London, chairing a bondholders meeting of the Mexican National Packing Co. He began with an "inspiring narration of the progress, achievements, and projects" of the company, from the construction of the Uruapan packinghouse, to the rapid takeover of its principal competitor, the long-term contracts to supply government institutions, and the beginnings of a retail chain that would eventually extend throughout the country. "Broadly speaking," he concluded, "there is consumed in the Mexican Republic more meat than can be supplied in five such packing houses as we now have in operation in Uruapan, so that the question of a local market for all that we may produce for many years to come is one which does not admit of doubt, and which does not require to be developed."[43] To supply that market, he requested a second bond issue of US $5 million, which his creditors readily approved. The plaudits of the London financial community must have done much to erase the painful memories of the previous year.

Although DeKay never doubted the superiority of Popo meats over those of rival butchers, local demand for company products was not at all a foregone conclusion. The poor generally obtained what meat they could outside of regular markets, while better off consumers had long preferred the taste of freshly slaughtered meat.[44] In the summer of 1908, the foreign packer pointed to the declining numbers of livestock slaughter at the municipal abattoir to prove that demand was strong for Popo meat. A newspaper advertisement proclaimed already in June that the Mexican National had captured half the meat sales in the capital. In testimony given years later, DeKay had inflated Popo's share to a fantastic 85 percent of the market, but even the smaller figure would represent a remarkable achievement after just a few months. The official bulletin of the Council of Government indeed indicated that while more than 11,000 head of cattle were butchered in each of the first three months of 1908, the numbers

CATTLE SLAUGHTERED AT MEXICO CITY RASTRO

MONTH	AVG CATTLE 1898-1902	CATTLE 1908	AVG PRICE 1908
January	9830	11760	0.25
February	8071	11674	0.20
March	8347	11059	0.22
April	7561	8458	0.23
May	7893	6944	0.26
June	7376	6884	0.28
July	7549	5391	0.23
August	7723	5028	0.27

4.2 Livestock slaughter and wholesale prices at Peralvillo, 1906–1908. Sources: AHCM, vol. 3764, exp. 39, vol. 3775, exp. 589, 599, vol. 3776, exp. 618; *Boletín Oficial del Consejo Superior de Gobierno del Distrito Federal*, 1908.

began to drop rapidly in April. Slaughterhouse workers processed fewer than 7,000 in June and scarcely more than 5,000 in August, although hog supplies remained steady throughout the year. Yet DeKay's claims sound much less impressive after factoring in seasonal variations, which regularly reduced the summer slaughter to about 75 percent of the winter high (see figure 4.2). Moreover, if competition from Popo was undercutting the local importers, one would expect prices at the Peralvillo to drop significantly. In fact, they rose throughout the spring before leveling off in the summer, a strong indication that the decline in slaughter at Peralvillo resulted from overall market scarcity rather than cutthroat competition from Popo.[45]

Even an additional 25 percent fall in cattle at the slaughterhouse represented at best a qualified success for the company. Much of the demand for Popo came from government contracts to supply schools, prisons, and the army—scarcely an indication of consumer preference. Another significant market for the company's meat lay in the so-called American colony, which numbered upwards of ten thousand people by this time. Expatriates from Canada, Britain, and the United States commented frequently on the poor quality of work by Mexican butchers and were delighted to purchase familiar cuts of aged beef. Admittedly, the exclusive contracts with several local merchants augured well for the future, although they had probably been secured with promises of heavy discounts. Nevertheless, DeKay contradicted his own claim of the superiority of refrigerated beef from Uruapan over the freshly slaughtered products at the Mexico City slaughterhouse. Despite the price advantage of shipping refrigerated meat over livestock, when he purchased the slaughterhouse from Terrazas, he immediately converted the Michoacán packinghouse to the preparation of canned meat, an indication that he already understood the struggle he faced in converting local consumers to U.S. tastes. The greatest betrayal may therefore have been not the Porfirian government forcing him to purchase Peralvillo at an inflated price but rather the Mexican public, which remained skeptical of the promises of refrigerated meat.[46]

PORFIRIAN BUSINESS LESSONS

John Wesley DeKay seemingly exemplified the Porfirian goal of economic progress through foreign investment. Having mastered the technology of meatpacking in its most advanced center, Chicago, he came to Mexico, where the butchers' art remained antiquated by comparison. Financial backing was just as important as technological prowess, and DeKay demonstrated his skill at securing investment capital in both New York and London. This flair for salesmanship also served him well when marketing the Popo brand in Mexico City. Learning to operate in the Mexican political environment was also crucial to his success, and he assiduously cultivated the local elite despite cross-cultural misunderstandings such as his failure to appreciate the political significance of the Creelman interview. One measure of his overall success can be found in the prominent científicos, including Sebastián Camacho, Julio Limantour, and Joaquín Casasus, who ultimately came to serve on the board of directors of the Mexican National Packing Co.

DeKay's most significant miscalculation lay in his failure to understand Mexican business practices, in particular, the Porfirian elite's aversion to cutthroat Yankee competition. His dogged belief that Limantour must have been an investor in La Internacional, and therefore forced him to acquire the Peralvillo slaughterhouse at a greatly inflated price, revealed a simplistic view of the interlocking directorship that governed Mexican industry. The days in which Díaz gave the economic keys to the kingdom away to foreign investors had passed by 1908, if they had ever really existed. Limantour's insistence that the Mexican National pay $100,000 in back taxes made that point perfectly clear to all concessionaires. And from the Mexican point of view, a merger between the two companies made perfect sense. Mexico City would achieve its long time goal of a modern slaughterhouse, and the foreign businessmen would gain extensive privileges in return for technical expertise, while assuming their fair share of the risk if the venture failed.

Success ultimately depended on whether DeKay could capture enough of the Mexican market to achieve the economies of scale needed to drive independent importers out of business. In the United States and Britain, the packing corporations had achieved that critical mass, transforming the supply chains from fresh to refrigerated meats and thereby pushing the local butchers and livestock raisers to the edge of the market.[47] In Mexico, by contrast, the importers had long experience operating on the edges of the legal trade through semi-clandestine slaughter. Moreover, the Porfirian government did not provide the dictatorship that DeKay had counted on. In particular, he regretted the government's refusal to require that all meat sold in Mexico City had to be refrigerated. But the Health Board had a far more realistic view of the limits of sanitation than did DeKay, and in any event, the Mexican elite did not share his taste for U.S.-style cuts. El Popo's future therefore depended on converting the consuming public before exhausting its financial reserves—an uphill battle, even without the opposition of the local meat trades.

CHAPTER FIVE

The Sausage Rebellion

In 1911, Rafael Torres still lived and worked in the otherwise abandoned ruins of the San Lázaro packinghouse, where he had been arrested for clandestine slaughter eight years earlier. After the city government revoked Próspero Ramírez's license, Torres made sausage and hams for other importers until he had saved enough to begin trading hogs on his own account. The master tocinero from Calimaya specialized in morongas and morcillas, rustic blood sausages favored by the lower classes. Obtaining raw materials became difficult after the Mexican National took over at Peralvillo and cleaned out the slaughter chambers where importers had formerly collected their by-products. Unable to practice his trade legitimately, he no doubt woke the neighbors of San Lázaro on many occasions with the shrieks of dying hogs. Yet this source of supply grew risky as private detectives employed by the packing company prowled the city in search of clandestine slaughter. So when the Porfirian dictatorship fell to revolutionary insurgents, Torres and his comrades felt emboldened to challenge the company's authority over the slaughterhouse. The sausage makers' rebellion embodied a cross-class alliance of livestock importers, slaughterhouse workers, and retail meat cutters, all determined to regain control of the Mexico City meat supply from El Popo's foreign owners.

The butchers' insurgency against the Mexican National Packing Co. was just one episode in the epic Revolution of 1910. This broad social movement began when Francisco Madero, the offspring of one of Mexico's wealthiest landowners, challenged the aging president in the election of 1910. During his campaign, Madero gained widespread support across the social spectrum, including middle-class groups excluded from power by the perpetual reelection of Díaz and his cronies, urban workers demanding an end to the repression of their unions, and peasants whose lands were threatened by Porfirian modernization. When Díaz stole the election, Madero called for an armed rebellion in November to overthrow the dictatorship. The guerrilla movement spread quickly through the countryside, and forced Díaz into exile, leading to a new election that Madero won easily. Although he viewed the revolution narrowly as a triumph for Mexican democracy, newly elected members of the Mexico City council took a more activist stance and joined with the meat cutters to bring about genuine change at Peralvillo.[1]

As a struggle between local butchers and foreign meatpackers, the sausage rebellion engages an academic debate regarding the significance of popular nationalism in the Revolution of 1910. In his exhaustively documented study *Empire and Revolution*, John Hart has demonstrated widespread popular attacks against U.S.-held property. Alan Knight, while agreeing that the popular classes took the forefront in revolutionary activity, has argued that anti-American sentiment was strongest among the Mexican elite and that xenophobia only spread to the masses in the wake of U.S. military interventions.[2]

In the case of the sausage rebellion, the foreign ownership of the Popo packing company played an important role in uniting butchers and importers. The Terrazas family, although carpetbaggers from the north, shared enough of a common culture to co-opt the leading cattle importers and gain a dominant position in the capital's meat markets. The Mexican National, by contrast, alienated slaughterhouse workers and importers with their efficiency campaigns while making implacable enemies of the tablajero vendors through their efforts to modernize retailing. The company's monopolistic practices not only united the formerly divisive trades, they also drove the importers to a definitive break from their liberal heritage. As foreigners usurped the Health Board's regulatory authority by imposing U.S. meatpacking methods, the importers demanded that first the Porfirian state and then its revolutionary successor abrogate the company's property rights and assert control over Peralvillo. Nevertheless, the documents provide little conclusive evidence of popular mobilization at the slaughterhouse independent of the paternalistic influence of elite importers.

For DeKay and the butchers alike, the revolution entered a new stage in 1913 when the government of Francisco Madero fell to a military coup led by the Porfirian General Victoriano Huerta. Having clung desperately to the company through years of revolutionary upheaval, DeKay immediately offered to sell his stock to the newly installed military government. At the time, the dictatorship had little interest in operating the slaughterhouse, and concentrated instead on suppressing the renewed uprising. Nevertheless, as the insurrection gained strength, the meatpacker conceived an audacious scheme to procure war materials in Europe for the beleaguered Huerta government in return for buying out his stake in the company. As a result, DeKay found himself caught up in one of the most controversial episodes of the revolution, the Ypiranga affair, when the United States Navy occupied the Mexican port of Veracruz to prevent the delivery of arms to the Huerta government.

The revolutionaries vanquished Huerta, and in the decades that followed they worked to build a more inclusive state in order to gain popular support for development policies similar to those of the Porfirian regime. The government established a corporatist system of trade unions and agrarian leagues, which held out the promise of labor and land reforms while at the same time attempting to impose discipline on peasants and workers mobilized by a decade of revolutionary fighting. Indeed, class conflict returned to the meat trades soon after the Mexican National Packing Co. lost control at Peralvillo. Without a common foreign enemy, the temporary alliance of tablajeros, importers, and slaughterhouse workers collapsed amidst economic troubles and the revival of old rivalries. In keeping with the corporatist model, the government encouraged workers to organize unions while the merchants formed chambers of commerce. Yet rather than serve as an impartial mediator between the two groups, the revolutionary regime tended to privilege developmental goals by supporting capital in industrial disputes.

For consumers, the sausage rebellion preserved traditional supplies of meat, but within the political context of the corporatist system. To sustain its revolutionary legitimacy, the ruling party established an elaborate welfare bureaucracy intended to cushion the effects of rampant inflation and stagnant wages by providing subsidized food to urban workers. Although these programs began as a New Deal–style attempt to limit price fluctuations in basic foodstuffs, they eventually grew into a massive food processing conglomerate. The Mexico City slaughterhouse formed a crucial link in this system by facilitating traditional methods of supplying meat through importers and tablajeros. Consumers thus became another link in the ruling party's corporatist base of support. But recalling the ideals of moral economy from the colonial abasto (monopoly) also entailed considerable political risk, not least because of the pervasive corruption within the system.[3]

FORGING A BUTCHERS' ALLIANCE

"Today in Merrie England," the *Mexican Herald* reported on October 7, 1909, gracing "the ends of traditional English boards is roasted beef from the plains of Mexico."[4] Within a year after taking over the Peralvillo Slaughterhouse, the Mexican National Packing Co. delivered the first shipload of meat on a multi-million-peso contract with Britain's foremost distributor, Lipton, Ltd. Meanwhile, Popo had launched an ambitious campaign to expand its own retail operations in Mexico City and the surrounding suburbs. To supply both domestic and export markets, the company had undertaken extensive renovations to the Peralvillo Slaughterhouse to bring it into conformity with U.S. industrial standards. Once again, the importers viewed the changes at Peralvillo as a threat to their existence, but unlike previous renovations, the Mexican National simultaneously challenged the retail butchers with ruinous price competition. The traditional rivalry between tablajeros and importers for a share of the consumer's peso suddenly gave way to a common interest in driving out the foreign company. Confronted by this vengeful alliance of butchers, DeKay turned for succor to the Porfirian state he had cultivated so assiduously, but internal divisions within the governing elite limited the assistance they could provide.

After his successful meeting with bondholders in January 1909, DeKay remained in London to conclude negotiations with Sir Thomas Lipton. On February 5, they signed an agreement appointing the British company as general sales agent for Popo meats outside of Mexico. Lipton not only offered to buy $2.5 million worth of meat in 1910 and $5 million the following year, he also made a substantial investment in packing company bonds. Nevertheless, the contract depended on improving the quality of Mexican livestock, which fell far short of the standards expected by British consumers. Cattlemen in northern Mexico such as the Terrazas had already begun to improve their breeds to supply calves to U.S. feedlots, as had the Argentines who were shipping refrigerated meat to Britain. DeKay counted on Mexican stockmen likewise to invest in Hereford and Aberdeen Angus given regular demand from the Mexican National Packing Co.[5]

A more immediate problem awaited DeKay at Peralvillo, which still functioned as both municipal slaughterhouse and private packinghouse, making it difficult for the new management to assert control. Already in

MEXICO GETS INTO ENGLISH MARKET IN EARNEST

5.1 "Mexico Gets into English Market in Earnest." Popo advertisement depicting John W. DeKay delivering a shipload of meat to English retailer Sir Thomas Lipton. From *Mexican Herald*, October 7, 1909. Courtesy of the Latin American Library, Tulane University.

December 1908, the common requirement of Popo and the importers to pass their meat through sanitary inspection revealed the conflict of interest between the two. As the Mexican National began killing greater numbers of livestock to supply its packing operations, it ran up against the ten o'clock deadline for completing the slaughter, despite its intention to refrigerate the meat rather than sell it immediately. The Board of Health agreed to hire two additional inspectors, as long as the company paid their salaries, to allow work to continue until six in the afternoon. It took several months to train the new veterinarians, but a far more important long-term concern arose over the pre-dawn starting times. DeKay argued that slaughtering livestock in the early morning hours did not allow sufficient light for sanitary inspection, and therefore the workday should run from six in the morning until six in the afternoon. Health officials privately agreed, having ordered a similar reform in 1890 only to reinstate the early morning slaughter when consumers complained about the lack of fresh meat in the markets. This information naturally galvanized DeKay's demand for daylight shifts, because it would assist his larger goal of converting Mexicans to refrigerated meat.[6]

A second renovation that pitted the company's profitability against the importers' interests involved the processing of by-products from slaughtered animals. Chemists had developed a remarkable range of industrial products including fertilizer, margarine, glue, soap, pepsin (a digestive aid), and even more esoteric items. Transforming the blood, bones, and other wastes in this manner also diminished, although by no means eliminated, the pollution from butchering animals. About 1898, Pedro Miranda obtained a contract from the city government to collect for industrial uses the slaughterhouse waste, which had formerly been carted off to the city dump. The importers promptly asserted their property rights to the profits from these sales, but the council responded that the revenues scarcely covered the cost of cleaning up the mess. Indeed, Miranda failed to make any profits from the deal and stopped collecting the waste a year before the contract expired in August 1901.[7]

Industrial establishments had more success in this regard, although the question of property rights still hampered their development. Because the San Lázaro packinghouse operated privately, Próspero Ramírez did not have to worry about sharing the profits when he invested in advanced equipment for extracting hog fat to make soap. Harry Hinkle installed machinery at Peralvillo to dry cattle blood for fertilizer, and in 1907, he offered to collect condemned livestock from outlying slaughterhouses in the Federal District and dispose of them at no cost in return for the right to use their by-products. The tocineros' long experience using hog by-products impeded comparable innovations because the Health Board consistently ruled that these materials belonged to the importers. Nevertheless, few merchants bothered to collect the blood, and when DeKay took over the municipal slaughterhouse, he had to dispose of as much as forty tons of accumulated waste. Therefore, while reorganizing the hog butchering department to improve efficiency, he ordered private tocineros out of the workplace entirely and had the most commonly used by-products, such as the intestines for stuffing sausages, delivered afterwards with the meat.[8]

DeKay's renovations expanded the slaughterhouse workforce to allow increased production of refrigerated beef. The company employed about 250 people at Peralvillo, including managers but not health inspectors. Nearly a third of the total worked in the cattle slaughtering department:

a foreman, thirty-four skilled butchers, eight peons assigned specifically to cleaning the carcasses, twenty more for general work, and eight porters. In contrast to the anticipated demand for beef, the hog department foreman oversaw only a single butcher, eight shavers, and seven skinners, and because the importers continued to slaughter their own sheep, a single person ran that department. Information about by-products remains sketchy, but there were fourteen employees listed for the hide salting department. The maintenance department was quite large, with fourteen mechanics, and an assortment of carpenters, bricklayers, and electricians. Thirty people worked full-time cleaning, and an equal number provided security. Only about ten employees came from the United States and Canada, but they dominated all the leading management positions, starting with the president's younger brother, Louis F. DeKay, who had taken over as plant superintendent by the summer of 1909.[9]

The company's attempts to reform the Mexican meat industry even extended to the popular spectacle of the *corrida de toros* (bullfights). Like many foreigners, DeKay protested the cruelty of the Spanish custom, and although unable to stop the practice entirely, he campaigned at least to prevent the consumption of animals killed each Sunday in the city plaza. Not only did fighting bulls have tough, stringy meat, but also the procedures for dressing the carcasses constituted an offense against public health. The dead animals piled up over the course of the afternoon so that they finally arrived at the slaughterhouse in an early state of decomposition. Hinkle presented the case to the Board of Health in March 1909, reminding the officials that the company's contract stipulated that all livestock in the city had to be slaughtered at Peralvillo. As good *científicos*, they undertook "experimental studies of the effects alluded to by the manager [Hinkle] that the meat of toros could produce when ingested by distinct animals [presumably dogs and cats] and until now have not had the expected result." In other words, the test subjects were just fine. Although clearly inferior to properly dressed beef, meat from the corrida helped feed many poor residents of the capital, and so without definitive proof of a health hazard, the board recommended that its sale be limited to special, clearly labeled market stalls.[10]

The ruling did not satisfy DeKay, who directed the guards at Peralvillo to refuse to admit the bulls from the following Sunday's corrida. Without the support of the Health Board, however, this unilateral sanitary reform merely earned the management a fine by city officials. Moreover, the company's humanitarian image, proclaimed in newspaper advertisements and supposedly the reason for attempting to suppress bullfighting, concealed cynical motives. In petitions to Díaz and Corral, DeKay emphasized the danger that the consumption of meat from the corrida de toros posed to the company's European exports. They stood to forfeit a market that was potentially worth millions of pesos if competing packers from Argentina or the United States spread the word that Mexican beef was tenderized by picadors. The vice president passed along the petition to the Health Board, but once again the scientists declined to ban the meat, arguing instead that the carcasses should be dressed immediately after being removed from the arena. Finally in September, even as shipments to Europe had begun, Corral satisfied DeKay by arranging a regulation against exporting the meat of fighting bulls.[11]

The Mexican National meanwhile underwent further reorganization to finance the slaughterhouse renovations and marketing campaigns. In May the company issued a £500,000 mortgage debenture on top of the US $10 million consolidated bonds that had been sold in two equal installments in 1908 and 1909. At current exchange rates of roughly £1 to US $5 to $10, the company's debt therefore amounted to $25 million Mexican pesos. The denomination of the mortgage bonds in sterling reflected the company's transition from New York to London capital. The association with the Terrazas family had never panned out, and rather than purchase La Internacional's facilities in Torreón and Parral, DeKay obtained a government concession to build a packinghouse in nearby Monterrey. About this time, the former Terrazas manager, Hinkle, left the Mexican National for an ill-fated venture to build a Guadalajara slaughterhouse, Empacadora del Pacífico, S.A.[12]

Flush with cash from the mortgage bonds, DeKay launched his Mexican retail campaign in September 1909. The company opened its first suburban shop in Azcapotzalco and soon followed with outlets in Tacuba and Tacubaya, towns just west of the capital. The *Mexican Herald* reported enthusiastically that these "Popo meat shops [were] crowded daily with purchasers"—although these repetitive articles may well have been paid advertisements disguised as news, a common practice. The stories certainly echoed DeKay's voice, emphasizing the purity of Popo meats and denouncing traditional butchers for selling "offal and impure meat products such as would not be disposed of for human food in any other part of the world."[13] Sanitation still remained the central theme of the company's promotional literature, which, like most advertising, stretched the truth considerably. These newspaper spots claimed, for example, that the only safe meats for sale in the city were Popo meats, as if the livestock slaughtered on the importers' accounts at Peralvillo were not government inspected as well. Another ad juxtaposed photos of the Mexican National's modern automobile and tram delivery cars with one of the competitors' horse-drawn carts (inaccurately) labeled: "doing the meat business *contrary to law*."[14]

Nevertheless, the greatest attraction for the Mexican masses was price rather than quality, for Popo sold meat "at such low prices as to make competition impossible."[15] In contrast to independent tablajeros, who charged upwards of a peso per kilogram of beef, Popo retail shops practically gave it away for as little as twenty centavos. DeKay indeed seemed determined to buy the goodwill of Mexican consumers; when a flood devastated Monterrey, he contributed $5,000 worth of Popo hams to a relief fund. As another promotional device, he established a lottery with inexpensive, hand-cranked sewing machines for prizes. Tickets were available with each purchase of Popo brand meat from company stores and other authorized retailers. The Mexican National took over Luna Park on the fashionable Paseo de la Reforma for the first drawing, on October 17, and handed out free samples of Popo meats and bread to thousands of visitors. Encouraged by the large turnout, the company scheduled future lotteries on a monthly basis.[16]

Paradoxically, El Popo's retail campaign had little significant effect on wholesale meat prices in the city. The cyclical pattern of winter abundance and summer scarcity seems to have had the greatest influence on prices (see figure 5.2). In the winter of 1908–1909, prices fell from their previous summer's highs, recorded during the supposed competitive struggle against La Internacional, even though the foreign managers were preoccupied by renovations at Peralvillo. Prices rose again the following summer even as industrial capacity came online. Despite his claims for the benefits of refrigeration, DeKay therefore remained dependent on the vagaries of Mexican livestock supplies.

Moreover, the importers and tablajeros, long accustomed to defending their interests, with violence if needed, were not about to surrender to the

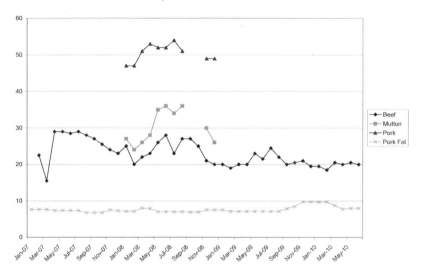

5.2 Mexico City wholesale meat prices, 1907–1910. Sources: AHCM, vol. 1278, exp 6–9; *Boletín Oficial del Consejo Superior de Gobierno del Distrito Federal*, 1907–1910; *El Economista Mexicano*, 1907–1910.

foreign company without a fight. Hog butchers, in particular, saw this as merely the continuation of their struggle against La Internacional, which they carried on largely through clandestine slaughter. Cattle merchants, who had formerly reached an understanding with the Terrazas, also joined the struggle against the Mexican National. Theft constituted one serious problem, as DeKay explained to city officials: "hundreds of people come in to the grounds of the rastro [abattoir] and wander all about the plant stealing whatever they can under the guise that they are coming to a public rastro and that they have a right to."[17] The packer attributed these losses to a conspiracy of importers, although much of the theft may have been carried out by poor residents of the city, who had long been motivated by differing ideas of moral economy. Regardless, on August 18, 1909, the management issued a series of new regulations intended to contain the problem. Importers had to advise the company in advance of the number of animals they planned to butcher and show receipts to prove their ownership. At the time of slaughter, the meat received seals identifying the importer, which had to be reviewed by the management before it could leave the premises. Despite the cumbersome nature of these checks, the new regulations limited the time that meat could remain in the wholesale market at Peralvillo to no more than two hours.[18]

This attempt to regularize the administration, an obvious stock control system for any large business, alienated virtually every group working at the slaughterhouse. Importers unaccustomed to maintaining elaborate documentation for their livestock were refused admittance to the slaughterhouse, putting them out of business at least temporarily. Health inspectors were likewise unable to complete their work, but unlike the importers, they had actual power. On Saturday, August 21, they ordered the market to remain closed until they finished their work, and as a result, the company failed to make the ten o'clock opening required by regulations. The following Monday, emboldened by the conflict between packers and city officials, a number of slaughterhouse workers went on strike, closing the market once again and costing the company a $100 fine from the city for the successive violations. DeKay protested the penalty, citing the inspectors' own refusal to open the market on time the first day and blaming the strike on "intimidation and inducement by the importers."[19] Yet one hesitates to credit the implicit assumption that slaughterhouse workers felt much loyalty to the new management given the model of labor relations in U.S. packinghouses. After all, any efficiency gains DeKay achieved at Peralvillo probably came through tighter factory discipline rather than technological improvements. It seems likely, therefore, that at most the importers fanned existing discontent to precipitate the strike.

The Porfirian establishment responded to the strike with genuine restraint, reflecting both the balancing of rival camarillas and concern for avoiding instability in the food supply prior to the upcoming presidential election. Although Corral still supported the Mexican National, the importers had a powerful ally in Federal District Governor Guillermo Landa y Escandón. As a director of the National Railways, he had long experience doing business with livestock shippers. The científico governor rejected outright DeKay's attempts to alter the slaughter schedule and insisted that the government respect the interests of the meat merchants. Perhaps at his behest, public works director Guillermo Puga received the importers at home on the evening of the strike, although they were unable to reach an immediate solution to the impasse. Nevertheless, the decision to fine the company rather than blame the workers automatically indicated a more flexible stance than usual in the Porfirian government's dealings with labor unrest.[20]

The hog importers, led by the prominent firms of Gómez and Váldez, Colin and Cueva, and Ramón Pineda, presented the most vociferous complaints about the company's conduct. They accused the Popo management of attempting to transform the municipal slaughterhouse into a private packinghouse in order to monopolize the meat market. The company also refused to return the blood and other viscera traditionally used in sausage making, and even the meat came out of the slaughterhouse in poor condition. Worse still was the so-called Mexican National's usurpation of the government's regulatory authority. They referred to the foreign manager as a "cacique," a pre-Hispanic word that could be applied to a respected leader but used sarcastically meant a tyrant. This "greasy foreigner, lacking civility (falto de educación) and ignorant of the language of the country" had no right to dictate slaughterhouse regulations, much less to tell the importers how to run their businesses.[21]

The retail meat cutters likewise joined the struggle with the onset of cutthroat price competition, intended to create a monopoly for Popo. They organized the Gran Liga de Tablajeros de la Ciudad de México (Great League of Meat Cutters of Mexico City), and as their first act, demanded the closing of Mexican National outlets. But this was simply a cover for more direct action. Sanitary regulations intended to guarantee adequate ventilation facilitated their attacks by requiring the front door to remain open although protected by iron gratings. Vandals simply tossed iodine through the bars at night, making it impossible to open the shop until the floors had been disinfected and deodorized. On another occasion, they used syringes to spray acid over the meat. Nor did the tablajeros limit their attacks to property; DeKay complained that "at night when I am going home to Tacubaya my car is stoned, sticks are thrown at me and in my yard night after night men prowl about and I repeatedly go into the streets of Tacubaya and get the police to come and see what can be done to insure the safety of our lives."[22]

The DeKays had trouble simply maintaining control at the Peralvillo slaughterhouse. José Zakany, a public works delegate who sympathized with the management, observed: "The night watchmen almost never appear at their posts, and those of the day frequently stand guard in taverns near the abattoir."[23] An unidentified knife wielder even attempted to murder Louis

DeKay on the slaughterhouse floor. After such serious threats, the final straw came on October 11, 1909, when petty officials stopped a company tram delivering meat to Tacubaya despite the company's tax exemption. Remembering the experience with Limantour that had embroiled him at Peralvillo to begin with, DeKay sent a letter to Vice President Corral listing his many grievances. To emphasize the importance of the packinghouse for the larger Porfirian project, he explained that Thomas Lipton himself was planning a visit to Mexico, but if the situation did not change, DeKay would have to recommend that the British merchant cancel his trip.[24]

Reprimanding a petty tax official was easy enough for the interior secretary, but guaranteeing the company's security was another matter entirely. Despite the Porfirian government's attempt to maintain the image of order and progress, the Mexican people had long experience evading the controls of the governing class. Lipton never did come, and DeKay would ultimately have to reach an accommodation with the Mexican meat trades if he hoped to continue in business.

The *Mexican Herald* published two notices in December 1909 that neatly summarized the mixed prospects of the Mexican National as it closed its books on a second year of operations. The first appeared on December 6 under the headline: "Splendid endorsement of Popo Company by Geo. I. Ham," which consisted of a letter from the U.S. Banking Co. president to a potential investor assuring him of the packing company's financial stability. The banker stated that he held on his own account nearly 20 percent of the $5 million mortgage bonds issued in May, and he praised DeKay as "an aggressive but very conservative and able business man." Despite this glowing testimonial, an advertisement appeared on December 28 with the familiar logo of the Mexican National and its Uruapan packinghouse over a prominent sign reading: "For Sale." After the initial shock of seeing this supposedly sound corporation up for auction, the newspaper reader found a rather circular endorsement for Popo meats in the small print. But doubts may have remained for many readers about whether the ambiguous advertisement foretold the future more accurately than the banker's optimistic prediction, and the answer was soon forthcoming.

POPO UNDER SIEGE

Lines of people running out the door and into the street mean big business for merchants and big trouble for bankers. George Ham fell decidedly into the second category on the morning of Saturday, January 22, 1910, as nervous depositors clamored for their savings. The United States Banking Co. had stunned the Mexican financial community with its radical policy of treating all customers equally, and Porfirian widows and clerks, unaccustomed to such democratic treatment, opened small accounts that added up to millions of pesos. These ordinary depositors made a sudden run on the bank when rumors broke that a major industrial firm could not cover its short-term debt. With cash on hand of $2 million, Ham made it through the first day, then brooded over the Sabbath. Unable to face the hostile crowds on Monday morning, he checked into the Lavista Sanatorium in suburban Tlalpan. The Mexican banking system shuddered, as did the Mexican National Packing Co., whose insolvency had triggered the run in the first place.[25] DeKay struggled to shore up the company's finances, but this sign of weakness encouraged the butchers to renew their attacks on Popo even before the Maderista insurgency toppled the Porfirian regime in the spring of 1911, thereby depriving the meatpacker of his powerful patron, Ramón Corral.

The Mexican National was clearly pushing the limits of its credit in January 1910. Whatever remained of the $25 million in bonds after the purchase and renovation of Peralvillo had gone to finance the price war against the importers and tablajeros in the fall. By year's end the company was operating on $2 million in short-term, unsecured loans from the U.S. Banking Co. Although rather unusual, these debts appeared minor compared with the $22.5 million in paid-up stock listed in a financial statement that was cited in December 1909 by U.S. Consul General Arnold Shanklin. The source of this additional capital remains a mystery, however, for while the British bondholders informed Limantour in 1908 that the stock was held in a New York trust, more recent press reports credited both stocks and bonds to London financiers. What should really have alarmed auditors was the offsetting claim in the balance sheet for assets worth more than $40 million—ten times the cost of Uruapan and Peralvillo, even at the inflated price paid to Terrazas. It was a dry winter in Anáhuac, but the Mexican National stock was watered to the breaking point.[26]

The troubles at Popo could not have come at a worse time for the U.S. Banking Co. At a shareholders meeting on Saturday, January 15, Ham had just declared a $1 million profit and a 7 percent dividend, but only by falsifying the balance sheets. The panic withdrawals started a week later and continued on Monday, January 24, after he failed to appear at the bank. When James Forsyth of the Bank of Montreal, Ham's largest creditor, finally took over on Tuesday, many depositors went home erroneously believing that their savings were guaranteed. In fact, that same afternoon the U.S. Banking Co. was unable to cover its $400,000 clearinghouse obligations, having paid out an estimated $3 million, one third of its deposits, in the three-day run. Depositors returned the next morning to find signs in the window announcing the bank had closed. Limantour hastened to reassure investors that the Mexican economy remained sound and that the failure of a single, unchartered institution would not affect the entire banking system.[27]

The treasury secretary offered little solace to the bank's remaining depositors, but the board of directors for the Mexican National promptly set to work controlling the damage. Claiming a temporary lack of liquidity because of the bank failure, the corporation filed for bankruptcy on February 2 in the state of New Jersey, where a sympathetic judge appointed Henry E. DeKay as receiver. When Mexican attorneys in charge of liquidating the U.S. Banking Co. protested the selection of such a biased trustee, Judge Carlos García chose Ham's personal lawyer, Francisco Alfaro, as supervisor (interventor) for the case. Yet this decision did little to protect the interests of the failed bank's depositors because Alfaro also served as counsel for the packing company. Corral expressed his own concerns about the length of time needed to resolve the bankruptcy and suggested separating the slaughterhouse contracting company from the rest of the Mexican National to prevent any interruption in the Mexico City meat supply. The upcoming presidential elections made stability in the markets for basic consumer goods particularly important. Nevertheless, the directors must have convinced him of the company's viability, for the vice president did not insist on carrying out the plan.[28]

Even the appointment of public works director Guillermo Puga as receiver, as Corral had briefly considered, would not have appeased the importers, who took the news of the bankruptcy as an excuse to demand the absolute revocation of the slaughterhouse concession. In a petition of February 19, 1910, prepared by Lic. Ricardo Guzmán, they repeated their complaints of the previous fall about the monopolization of the slaughterhouse. Now with its declaration of bankruptcy, no doubt could remain about the deficiencies of the management. Perhaps the government should never have given up this important administrative duty, they suggested, before concluding that the opportunity now existed to reclaim the abattoir for the city. Having invoked the tenets of classical liberalism throughout the nineteenth century, the livestock importers now found themselves requesting government intervention in the economy. The irony of this turnabout was not lost on Ramón Corral, one of the most powerful officials of a Porfirian state that rarely missed an opportunity to consolidate its own authority. In a brief letter dated March 10, the vice president explained that the slaughterhouse was private property and therefore the government was powerless to act.

This curt reply provoked the importers far more than had the previous six months of silence, and they fired back a lengthy and impassioned petition. Where before they had merely questioned the deficiencies of the Popo management, they now denounced the "disastrous administration, which reveals the most supine ineptitude or the grossest speculation." As proof of this malfeasance, they pointed to the company's stated capital of $37 million. With their intimate knowledge of the livestock business, the importers immediately perceived what the frock-coated accountants from London had apparently overlooked, that given an annual consumption of 140,000 cattle, with a value of $40 each and an average profit of $3, the company could not be earning more than 1 percent return. "And if this [$37 million] has existed in reality, what could have been its destiny?" The importers had plenty of suggestions for improvements at Peralvillo such as a stockyard for fattening cattle, but their representatives had not even been received by the company managers, who anyway spoke only English. The foreigners had done nothing for the nation or the city, and contrary to advertising claims, their meats "were not subject to any scientific procedure that improves them." After Mexican butchers performed the slaughter, the meat went out to shops in the same manner that it had "since time immemorial." The importers concluded not with a timid suggestion that the government might find it convenient to reclaim the slaughterhouse services, but with an unequivocal demand for state intervention. Supplying the city with meat "is a difficult task that imposes grave responsibility on its management, and it is more difficult still to know how to guard, without pecuniary motives (mercantilismo), the interests of the public and above all of the impoverished people...when [the administrators] are the directors of a private corporation.... These services should always be in the hands of the government."[29]

Corral dismissed the petition as improper at the same time that DeKay was traveling aboard a Cunard steamship from Liverpool after having arranged yet another financial package with his bankers. Attorney Robert B. Miller of the British and Mexican Trust arrived from London to carry out the reorganization in July when all Mexican eyes were fixed on the presidential elections. Díaz won an easy reelection—his seventh—having jailed his popular opponent Madero. The plan was to transform the Mexican National into a completely British enterprise managed by the firms of Van der Bergh, Ltd., Poel & Webster, and W. & J. Biggerstaff. The equity of the new company would remain roughly the same as the old, at £2,450,000, including both common and preferred stock, yet it was to be allocated in a revealing fashion. The prospectus called for the conversion into preferred shares of 40 percent of the London mortgage bonds and all of the New York consolidated bonds with a total face value of £2.2 million. Meanwhile, the remaining £300,000 of mortgage bonds were to be transmogrified into a "second mortgage income debenture stock" paying 6 percent interest. The bankers would thereby dispose of the mysterious Popo stock, but they offered only slight hope for additional capital by allowing the creation of a new First Mortgage bond issue of £600,000, assuming it could be subscribed in the face of current financial difficulties. Perhaps as a result, the plan was never carried through. With this option denied, Miller could offer only a cash payment of $1.4 million in return for Henry DeKay signing over the company's property in Uruapan and Rancho del Chopo to the British and Mexican Trust. To stretch this relatively meager sum, John DeKay announced his intention to use the bankruptcy protection to pay just 30 percent of the $5.5 million owed to the U.S. Banking Co.[30]

With such precarious finances, the DeKays knew they had to regain complete control over the slaughterhouse and defeat the importers quickly. Together with José Zakany, their ally in the public works department, they adopted a bold offensive strategy of dealing with the troublemakers in their own shops rather than at Peralvillo. The plan was to get the Mexican authorities to arrest the leading hog importers for violating the sanitary codes, thereby solving their problems as well. Dissatisfied with police efforts to stop clandestine slaughter, Zakany took a page from U.S.

industrialists and employed "un *detective*," Antonio Montiél, to penetrate suspected establishments and capture the culprits "*in fraganti*" (sic). The Frenchman certainly looked the part of the private eye; the photo on his license resembled a bulldog with a Porfirio Díaz mustache. For two weeks in September, while the city center was festooned with crepe paper and confetti to celebrate the centennial of independence and the eightieth birthday of the president, he patrolled the back alleys in search of clandestine butchers.

Zakany and the DeKays must have read the reports with great satisfaction as Montiél accumulated evidence against their rivals. "September 10, 1910. I continue the surveillance of the shops of 'Gómez and Váldez' and 'G. Meenen,' whose establishments are close to one another and I should report that yesterday and last night they did not smuggle in live hogs.... At the last hour I have learned of another clandestine slaughter by C. and Cuevas, whose shop is near the Penitentiary; it is known that they kill there daily and that they brought in and sacrificed ten hogs. More detailed information will follow shortly." And so the butchering continued: "September 11, 1910. Yesterday afternoon Colin and Cuevas had more than a hundred hogs in their shop, and today at 3 A.M. they were killing." The butchers were well aware of Montiél's presence and sought to evade his watch: "September 23, 1910. Inocencio Anaya, of the Barrio de San Simón, changed his location to the Colonia de Vallejo, and there it follows he has his clandestine slaughter." There even appeared to be some coordination between the various illicit butchers: "September 25 and 26, 1910. On Saturday, that is the day before yesterday, 'Gómez and Váldez' killed; yesterday the only one that did so was Anaya, and today at dawn 'Meenen.'"[31]

This narrative of illegal activity held little interest for the Porfirian bureaucracy, to the chagrin of the Mexican National managers. Part of the problem lay with Zakany's decision to take these reports not to his own superiors at the Government Council but to the revenue officials, who might be more inclined to prosecute the delinquent importers. This "highly unusual" visit surprised the treasury supervisor, unaccustomed to dealing with petty functionaries from other departments, but he forwarded the documents to the district officials in charge of slaughterhouse collections. They took the report as an allegation of their own negligence and ridiculed the claims as either exaggeration or error, concluding that if some agent had witnessed criminal acts he should have arrested the perpetrators. The embarrassed treasury supervisor passed the story back to Zakany's superiors at the Government Council and instructed them to use the proper channels for any future allegations of clandestine slaughter.[32]

Despite this rebuke, Montiél had earned a permanent position as security director at the Mexican National, where he worked closely with José Zakany to advance the company's interests. In March the private detective was deputized to the Mexico City police to keep watch for illicit butchers, although he often had confrontations with regular officers. His first step was to enforce discipline among the slaughterhouse guard, a continuing problem given the night watch's habit of sleeping on duty. On one occasion, Montiél and Zakany stationed patrolmen at the slaughterhouse gate, only to have a rival policeman, José María Hernández, order them away. When the pair confronted Hernández, he replied: "Go to hell, that's not my responsibility."[33] Zakany also clashed with teamsters who accused him of giving preferential treatment to company cars and even of arranging the schedule to cause confusion among competitors' stock cars. The resulting collisions often caused injuries to work horses, prompting a strike in January 1911. But to his credit, Montiél made at least one successful arrest, catching Pedro Urquiano and Fortino Acuautla in the act of smuggling condemned pork out of Peralvillo. Urquiano confessed to police that he was using the meat to make chorizo.[34]

Meanwhile, the company's financial situation remained bleak despite a reorganization attempt based on a new corporation, the Mexican National Packing Co., Ltd., domiciled in the state of Maine. DeKay's plan to transfer the slaughterhouse concession was blocked by the protest of William E. Stavert, an executive for the Bank of Montreal, who acted as receiver for the U.S. Banking Co. Hoping to reclaim some of the $5.5 million owed to the failed bank, Stavert reached an agreement with one of the Mexican National's principal London creditors, Linklater & Co. Unlike Miller's proposal the previous summer, their reorganization plan discounted the existing capital heavily, converting both the company bonds and the U.S. Banking Co. claims into £970,000 of common stock. To cover expenses and develop the business, the reorganization plan allowed for a new mortgage bond issue of £400,000 to be sold at 85 percent. Finally, the creditors agreed to fire the entire board of directors, starting with John W. DeKay. This plan was completely unacceptable to the founder and president of the Mexican National, and in May 1911, he traveled to Montreal to present an alternate proposal to the parent bank. DeKay's plan preserved the £2,450,000 capital and allocated primarily non-voting preferred stock to the failed bank's liquidators. In addition, he asked for a new mortgage issue of £500,000, again at 85, including payments of £90,000 in cash to himself and his brother Henry. The Canadian banker rejected this "extravagant over-capitalization," doubted their ability to subscribe the new bonds, and questioned the large cash payments to the DeKays. The matter remained pending as Stavert's attorney S. C. Norsworthy filed suit in Mexican court.[35]

While the Mexican National lingered in legal limbo, the Díaz government suffered a rapid decline. With democratic options closed by the fraudulent election of 1910, Francisco Madero escaped to the United States and issued a call for revolution to overthrow the dictatorship. Guerrilla fighting began in November, and by the spring of 1911, the Porfirian army had been stretched thin suppressing the insurgency. When rebel forces captured the border port of Ciudad Juárez in May, Díaz and Corral resigned their positions and went into exile in France. Even as an interim government prepared for new elections in the fall, which Madero handily won, workers began making revolutionary demands for social justice.

The Porfirian bureaucracy continued to function as usual even after the president's departure, and during a routine meeting on June 14, the Health Board considered a question that appeared minor but had far reaching consequences for the Mexico City meat supply. Amid reviews of monthly inspections, Dr. Jesús Monjarás brought up the petition of one José Torres, Actually, the claimant was Rafael, and the mistaken name provides an indication of the apparent insignificance of the request. Torres sought permission to use the blood of hogs killed in the city abattoir to make the sausages popularly known as morcillas and morongas. The Health Board secretary had examined the question, and from a public health standpoint, there was nothing inconvenient in the request. The legal situation was equally clear; clause fifteen of the contract of November 14, 1903, with La Internacional required the Peralvillo concession holder to allow importers to collect by-products from the slaughter. One of the learned doctors raised the question of just whose hogs Torres intended to collect blood from, and the board specified that importers had the right to by-products from their own animals only. The scientists may also have paused for a moment to consider the gastronomic merits of morongas and morcillas, but Monjarás did not record the conclusions of any such discussion in the board's report to the District Government Council.[36]

Council delegate José Zakany passed the decision along to the DeKays, who responded that Torres's request was impossible to fulfill. In an official statement delivered August 4, the Popo management explained that with the modern machinery at its command, it sacrificed 120 hogs an hour or one every half minute. To collect the blood would require the hog to remain stationary for more than thirty seconds, thereby interrupting the industrial process and preventing the company from fulfilling its requirement of having the meat ready in the market by ten o'clock. Moreover, the industrial process of slaughter made it impossible to separate out Torres's hogs from those of the other importers.[37]

Torres countered this claim and offered to demonstrate to Health Board officials just how he would collect the blood. He also explained that he had contracted with a number of other importers to use the blood from their animals, presumably not all of it in making morongas—even the greatest aficionado could only consume so much blood sausage. In any event, he proceeded to meet with Dr. José E. Mota of the Peralvillo sanitary inspection service, and then confronted Zakany, but the latter official denied him entrance. Despite a renewed decree by Dr. Licéaga, Louis DeKay continued to insist that allowing Torres access to the slaughterhouse would violate sanitary precautions and risk spreading infection through the city.[38]

However much of an inconvenience Torres had become, Popo confronted a far greater threat as the Mexican courts slowly unwound the affairs of the failed U.S. Banking Co. The case had remained deadlocked since the spring. With a majority of the voting shares still held in his trust, DeKay continued to use the bankruptcy protection to veto Stavert's plan to reorganize the company. The bank liquidator, in turn, had frustrated the meatpacker's rival plan by blocking the transfer of the slaughterhouse concession to the newly incorporated Mexican National Packing Co., Ltd. When the administration of President Francisco Madero took office in November, Stavert's attorney, Norsworthy, informed Secretary of Development Rafael Hernández that "the plan recommended by Mr. DeKay will result in a capitalization *thirty times greater* than the value of the assets and can only result in a second insolvency." The new president reviewed the case and concluded that by transferring the rights without prior authorization, the company had violated its contract and forfeited the concession. In an official notice of December 29, 1911, the company received fifteen days to appeal the decision. The new revolutionary administration thus seemed poised to grant the demand made by the importers for the past two years.[39]

MUCKRAKING IN REVOLUTIONARY MEXICO

Dr. Felipe Gutiérrez de Lara took the oath of office as a Mexico City council member on January 1, 1912, determined to fulfill the democratic promise of the recent revolution. The Maderista party had swept the municipal ballot held in December, although the council's notorious lack of authority had discouraged voter turnout, unlike the national elections held the previous October. Moreover, the ten new delegates composed only half the council, and they promptly lost their first battle when the incumbent Porfirian mayor, Pedro Lascurain, defeated the incoming Carlos Herrera in the vote for the municipal presidency. Nevertheless, Madero had promised the return of local autonomy, and the progressive Gutiérrez intended to transform the municipal government from the rubber stamp it had been under the old dictatorship into a genuine voice for the people. He forged close ties with working-class organizations and headed the committee to establish a civic militia, thereby hoping to revive a longstanding tradition of liberal citizenship.[40] Yet Gutiérrez also looked forward to new meanings of citizenship tied to consumer issues, and with his medical credentials, he formed a health commission to investigate fraud in the Mexico City food supply. He denounced El Popo, in particular, for a longstanding practice of selling adulterated pork fat and contributed to important legislation by the Mexican Congress to ensure pure food for consumers.

Gutiérrez had scarcely settled into office when the deadline passed for DeKay to justify the transfer of the slaughterhouse concession. Unfortunately for the aggrieved importers, the incoming Madero administration had absolutely no desire to intervene at Peralvillo and thereby set a precedent for labor activists in other industries, particularly the capital's strategic electricity and streetcar networks, where strikes threatened. As a result, the existing management remained, by default, in control of the slaughterhouse. The Mexican Supreme Court later described the Limited Company's anomalous position as a "mere holder or de facto caretaker of the interests of the Mexican National Packing Co."[41]

The importers may never have known just how precarious the company's legal situation had become, for they surely would have used such information in their ongoing battle. Instead, they drew ammunition from an ironic source, industrialists in the United States. In January 1912, the *Mexican Herald* followed the trial of Chicago's meatpacking pool under prosecution for violating the Sherman Anti-Trust Act. The English-language newspaper revealed during the course of the proceedings that no more than 3 percent of the packers' profits came from the sale of meat. The rest derived from industrial by-products such as blood and hoofs—over 40 percent from the fat alone.[42] While the importers had long felt they were being cheated, they had not suspected the full extent of the duplicity. Not only did they receive no compensation for any by-products except the hides, but in the case of diseased animals, they even paid to have the carcasses burned, after which the company sold the sterilized fat.

Rafael Torres promptly made use of this knowledge in his struggle against the company. In a petition dated January 20, 1912, he denounced the Popo management's claims about the impracticality of collecting blood as nothing but a subterfuge. Their true motive for preventing him from claiming his contractual rights to the blood was their own lucrative business selling it as fertilizer. Torres had obtained as evidence a receipt indicating the company received $130 per ton for the dried blood. The tocinero insisted that the Government Council issue the decrees allowing him access to his rightful property and warned that his entire guild took an interest in the matter.[43]

Indeed, before the month had ended, Ignacio Mendoza filed a complaint on behalf of the hog importers with Secretary of the Interior Jesús Flores Magón. The petition revealed not only their anger at the company's profits, but also their hopes for the recent Maderista revolution. He explained that El Popo took animals destined for the oven in violation of the sausage makers' property rights. Sanitation authorities could prevent diseased animals from being used as human food, he conceded, but that did not give the company the right to profit from the property of others. He concluded by asking for the return of the carcasses to their legitimate owners, which alone would serve justice and vindicate the new government's good name. Officials nevertheless displayed little enthusiasm for the sausage makers' plans to enter the soap business. Slaughterhouse delegate Arturo Ibáñez conceded that they deserved compensation for their animals' by-products, but he was not prepared to release the infected carcasses, fearing attempts to sell the meat for human consumption.[44]

Even the more limited campaign to allow Torres to collect the blood from his hogs made little progress. Health Board secretary Rafael Norma spoke personally with Louis DeKay on February 14, but when the importer appeared at the slaughterhouse a few days later with bucket in hand and two witnesses by his side, the foreign manager flatly denied him entrance. The company meanwhile commissioned a twelve-page legal brief from Lic. Manuel Escalante justifying its refusal to hand over the blood. When that failed to persuade the government, DeKay tried another legal maneuver, arguing that the claim against the Mexican National Packing Co. did not apply to the new company of the same name, Ltd. This was a bold strategy, given that the government had not even recognized the transfer, but it made little difference. Not even the direct orders of Interior Secretary Flores Magón could force DeKay to budge, and when, on May 31, the government imposed a $400 fine—the legal maximum—Popo appealed for judicial protection (amparo). Undersecretary Jesús L. González concluded with disgust in August that it was impossible to make the company respect authority, although in fact, an excessive concern for legal process had hamstrung the administration's efforts, as was true of Maderista reforms in general.[45]

The feebleness of the government in enforcing its will encouraged the people to adopt an assertive new attitude, as Alan Knight and John Lear have demonstrated. The importers had always been combative in this regard, and when a veterinary inspector named Irigoyen proved too zealous in condemning hogs, they suspended slaughter until the city council replaced him. Ordinary employees and teamsters also began to voice their dissatisfaction with city council delegate Arturo Ibáñez, whom they considered a tyrant and a stooge for the Mexican National. An investigation ensued and by August they had succeeded in having him fired. Merchants in suburban Azcapotzalco similarly denounced the abuses of the "notoriously irascible and despotic" meat inspector Agustín Zimbrón.[46]

Popular activism combined with federal inactivity also opened a potential space for the Mexico City council to reclaim a measure of authority, particularly over local issues such as food adulteration. The first target of Dr. Gutiérrez de Lara's Health Commission was the Universal Corn Manufacturing Co., which had requested the government's permission to sell tortillas made with pulverized corncobs, a common feed for cattle, added to the dough. An analysis by the Health Board found the supplement to be completely devoid of nutritional value, and on March 27 the council adopted a resolution written by Gutiérrez urging the Superior Council to "pursue and exterminate this scandalous and criminal fraud."[47] Nevertheless, on May 17, President Madero issued a decree allowing the addition of foreign substances to bread and tortillas up to 25 percent of the volume. This ruling cited a positive recommendation of the Board of Health, apparently a reversal of their earlier position.[48] Gutiérrez immediately condemned the decision, accused the council of duplicity, and asked for a second opinion from the National Medical School. This body ultimately concurred with Gutiérrez, but by that time the administration had already reversed itself, and on June 13, Interior Secretary Flores Magón resumed the ban on food adulteration.[49]

A fortuitous mistake allowed Gutiérrez to expand the scope of his investigation into the abuses of the Porfirian food-processing industry. In August 1912, the Mexico City council received a request from a Nuevo Laredo businessman named R. González asking for an exemption from import duties on cooking fat sent to the capital. He wished to compete in the lucrative market, he explained, but believed that the $250 fee charged on each carload of cottonseed placed him at an unfair disadvantage compared to producers within the city. The municipal secretary replied that such fees fell under the jurisdiction of the secretary of the treasury and not the city government. Nevertheless, this simple mistake by a provincial businessman, unfamiliar with the Mexico City bureaucracy, alerted Gutiérrez to a potentially explosive issue: the widespread adulteration of the pork fat used by virtually all cooks in the city.[50]

The Board of Health, jealous of its authority and perhaps fearing for its credibility, immediately launched an investigation of its own. On August 22, the Federal District Government Council, including Governor Federico González Garza, public works director Luis Salazar, and several members of the Health Board, performed an early morning inspection of the Peralvillo Slaughterhouse. Manager Louis DeKay, accompanied by two lawyers, demonstrated the various machines used to make the compound lard. The company employed separate pressure cookers to sterilize the wastes of hogs and of cattle and sheep. The highest quality pork fat was mixed with cottonseed oil at a 40 to 60 ratio, then blended in a centrifuge and filtered to remove impurities. Although packaged by Popo under the label "cooking fat," most retail stores sold it from a generic lard bin.

DeKay also took the opportunity to demonstrate to the assembled notables the impracticality of Torres' request to collect blood from hogs. To ensure sanitation during the slaughter, powerful hoses poured a continuous stream of water on hogs, so any blood he collected would inevitably be diluted and impure. Moreover, DeKay noted, many hogs vomited and defecated when butchered, which would also contaminate the blood. Finally, he pointed out, pre-slaughter inspection revealed only the most obvious lesions and symptoms, while many other diseases showed up only in the post-slaughter examination, by which point it would be impossible to separate out the unhealthy blood. Because the company cleaned, dried, and packed the blood for industrial uses, particularly fertilizer, it made the most economical sense to continue with the present system.

Despite DeKay's efforts to show the company in a positive light, the subsequent Health Board report castigated the Mexican National in the finest muckraking tradition. Secretary Norma stated that "on the day of the inspection the slaughterhouse contained not a single gram of lard, understood to be the pure fat of the pig." Nor could the company pass the blame to small-time retailers by arguing the technical accuracy of their label, "cooking fat." Under Mexican custom, the only fat used for cooking was that from the pig, and so the Popo product should properly be labeled "tallow and cottonseed oil."[51] Nevertheless, the report neglected to mention that the Board had approved these same procedures for several years.

Based on this revelation, Gutiérrez gained approval from the city council to pursue an investigation of both the Mexican National Packing Co. and the Board of Health. An official inquiry, on September 21, featured testimony from Dr. Nicolás Ramírez de Arrellano and two Health Board colleagues. They stated that years earlier both Gerard Meenen and John DeKay had separately requested permission to sell a cottonseed oil mixture labeled as lard. The board had rejected both petitions on November 4, 1909. This decision had ended Meenen's industrial ambitions, but DeKay, in his hour of need, had turned to an old friend, Ramón Corral. The secretary of the interior obliged by verbally ordering the

Health Board to halt the inspection of cooking fats. For three years, beginning in November 1909, businessmen had flooded Mexico City with adulterated lard without fear of official retribution.[52]

This revelation of Porfirian corruption, no doubt intended to halt the investigation, produced the opposite effect. Gutiérrez could now smell blood, and using his municipal credentials, he demanded access to Health Board documents. These files revealed a rot deeper than even he had suspected. He reported back to the council on October 1 that sales of adulterated lard had gone on not just since 1909, but for at least eight years. Under Article 120 of the Mexico City Sanitation Code, the board had permitted manufacturers to sell for human consumption fat that been extracted from diseased animals. Gutiérrez also observed that when health inspectors had attempted to crack down, they invariably targeted small-time vendors instead of the industrial producers responsible in the first place. The council member lambasted the board's conduct and demanded a municipal decree resuming the inspection of lard throughout the city.[53]

With this declaration, Gutiérrez had gone too far. The Health Board, recognizing the threat to its public credibility, sent a parade of officials before the council. Slaughterhouse inspector Dr. José Gómez testified that "El Popo" used only uncontaminated meats to produce its cooking oils. José Mota explained that he personally saturated the corpses of trichinosis-infected swine with petroleum to prevent their sale for human consumption. He offered further assurances that the company maintained complete records of all diseased animals to prove that they were used exclusively for industrial purposes. Not content with having refuted Gutiérrez, the board consulted lawyers, who concluded that he had overstepped his authority by demanding access to Health Board files. After all, despite the stunning revelations, the city council remained an advisory body without any formal powers. Gutiérrez offered a formal apology but kept the investigation open nevertheless.[54]

The activist council member finally saw his efforts vindicated on November 16, 1912, when Interior Secretary Flores Magón published a new code for the sale of food and beverages in the Federal District. This law, comparable to the United States Pure Food and Drugs Act of 1906, imposed harsh penalties on the sale of adulterated products. Although the regulations did not outlaw the sale of cottonseed as cooking oil, misrepresentation was no longer tolerated. Manufacturers had to label their products and clearly list the contents. To assure clarity and further assist those unable to read, the law stated that any given store could sell either pure lard or seed oil products but not both. Rafael Norma summarized the new standards in the Health Board's official publication and warned that violators would face certain punishment.[55]

As a result of the council's revelations, the advertising claims that Popo sold only pure pork fat and that the company was "determined to impede the sale of impure or adulterated pork products" lay exposed as the lies of a duplicitous foreigner.[56] Nevertheless, the scandals did not receive coverage from Mexico City newspapers, perhaps because consumers purchased pork fat from retail-shop tubs rather than from neatly marked Popo packages. Even in elite households, the company's advertising campaigns may have had little effect on the working-class servants who did the shopping. The price cutting of previous years had no doubt benefited many poor Mexicans, but DeKay refused to adopt local practices such as offering credit on retail sales. As a result, most customers still probably maintained their relationships with their local butchers, even if they did purchase cut-rate Popo meat on the side.

Meanwhile, DeKay perceived a glimmer of hope when Stavert finally compromised on the reorganization plan. The banker from Montreal, hoping to salvage something from the deal, agreed to fold all outstanding debt into US $12,750,000 in stock, plus a new bond issue of US $2,900,000 to provide working capital. With this question resolved, the Madero government finally assented to transferring the concession to the Mexican National, Ltd., on November 11, 1912. Leaving his brother Louis still holding off the importers, John DeKay returned to London hoping to subscribe the new bonds.[57]

"WITH THE CANAILLE"

The democratically elected government of Francisco Madero, having drifted from one crisis to the next, was finally extinguished by a military coup in February 1913. The presidency then fell to General Victoriano Huerta, a bald and crusty relic of the Porfirian army who sought to restore the old dictatorship. Revolutionaries throughout the country repudiated the new regime, yet from the chaos, John DeKay glimpsed the possibility of an escape from his ill-fated Mexican investment. While in London, trying vainly to raise capital, he made contact with Huerta's financial agent in an attempt to sell El Popo to the government. Although initially rebuffed, he bided his time until autumn. Then, as the rebellion gained strength, toppling federal strongholds in the north, he approached Huerta personally. If the dictator would take the company off his hands, he offered to travel to Europe to purchase munitions that were desperately needed for repressing the insurgency. The proposition seemed particularly enticing because financial assistance and arms purchases had been cut off by the United States government. Nevertheless, after the meatpacker had departed, Huerta lamented to the German minister, "Respectable people don't come to me, and hence I must rule with the canaille (rabble)."[58]

The military coup by Huerta, and the subsequent murder of Madero and his vice president, led to rebellion in the provinces. As the general moved to repress possible opponents, a number of reformers resigned from the Mexico City council; Gutiérrez de Lara remained, but without his former activism. Although most of the Maderista governors accepted the new president, Venustiano Carranza mobilized the state militia of Coahuila and declared himself the leader of a Constitutionalist revolution. The bulk of the resistance to Huerta, however, came from partisans such as Francisco "Pancho" Villa and Emiliano Zapata, who owed only nominal allegiance to Carranza. The rebel movement gained an early boost from the incoming president of the United States, Woodrow Wilson, a constitutional scholar who refused to acknowledge Huerta's seizure of power. Indeed, Carranza could not have chosen a revolutionary slogan better calculated to gain Wilson's support. With U.S. financial markets closed off, Huerta turned for assistance to Europe, where governments took a less principled view of his position. In June, a consortium of banks, including the European office of J. P. Morgan, arranged a syndicated loan of $200 million under the condition that the government not issue additional bonds until 1915. The bankers accepted $60 million immediately, but most of this initial tranche went to retire existing debt, leaving less than $10 million available to the Huerta government. Worse still, European investors subscribed a mere 16 percent of the bonds, forcing the bankers to swallow the rest, and ensuring that the remaining $140 million would never be paid out.[59]

The financial plight of Mexico held particular interest for John DeKay as he continued his search for a European loan. Meanwhile, his embattled brother Louis held off government claims on behalf of the local importers. On May 29, 1913, the Mexican Supreme Court ruled in favor of Rafael Torres, denying judicial protection to the Mexican National. At this point the management agreed to pay the fine, a trivial $400, but still refused to change the company's operating procedures. When an official appeared at Peralvillo to insist on compliance with the court order, Louis DeKay replied that "he did not believe himself obligated to recognize the authority of the secretary of the interior" in this case. The foreign manager added that if Torres wanted to reclaim the blood, he could do so in the waste tank.[60] At the end of July, Health Board officials Rafael Ortega and Edmundo Aragón ordered the company to construct a special room for the return of blood and other by-products. DeKay had grudgingly complied by October, but promptly insisted on a return to the former system for sanitary reasons. After an inspection, Aragón reported to the contrary that of the forty-three hogs he observed, only one had begun to urinate when slaughtered, and in that case the worker had made a simple adjustment to prevent contamination of the blood tank.[61]

The importers might well have taken advantage of the government's impatience with the packing company by working together to establish an alternative to Peralvillo, at least for processing by-products, but they squandered this opportunity through rivalries within their own ranks. On several occasions, beginning in January 1912, Ignacio Mendoza had spoken for the hog importers to protest El Popo's illegal expropriation of their property. Edmundo Aragón had accepted in principle the argument, but the importers could not agree on the financing of such a project. A few ambitious ones tried instead to establish meat monopolies of their own in the suburbs. The González brothers proposed constructing a modern slaughterhouse in the town of San Angel to replace all of the antiquated municipal abattoirs in the southern and western areas of the Federal District. Rafael Torres meanwhile petitioned for the right to build a similar facility in the north at La Villa de Guadalupe. Neither plan came to fruition, but one justification for them lay in the increasing disorder at Peralvillo, as the cash-strapped DeKays neglected even basic maintenance. At the end of June, the city delegate had already described "conditions of genuine abandonment and slovenliness."[62]

With virtually no prospects for reviving El Popo, DeKay tried once again to sell out to the government in the fall of 1913 by promising to use his European connections to purchase arms for the embattled federal army.

Constitutionalist victories in northern Mexico prompted Huerta to give the meatpacker a more favorable reception, despite his personal misgivings. DeKay made his best sales pitch for the company's future profitability, but a Commerce Department accountant, Antonio Phillipe Serrano, remained skeptical. The doubts began when Serrano arrived at Peralvillo to examine the books, only to be told by the manager that "no balance was ever taken." The only available documents consisted of some loose sheets listing the slaughter of cattle to date in 1913, with itemized statements of the previous few months, and a number indicating the net profit for the previous two and a half years: $136,000. DeKay attributed this poor return on equity to the recent political disorder and the temporary revocation of their concession by the Madero government. He assured Serrano that the military government could swiftly end the dispute with the importers, rebuild the export market, and thereupon achieve the projected profits that had convinced British investors to subscribe the bond issue five years earlier. The accountant summarized this rosy scenario for his superiors, projecting a possible annual profit of $1.5 million, then discounting the cost of servicing the existing bonds, an unknown liability given the lack of a proper balance statement. He also cautioned that the anticipated profits depended not only on a successful conclusion to the current insurgency but also on the installation of a "wise administration" at the slaughterhouse to make it capable of competing against U.S. and Argentine packers. Serrano ultimately recommended purchasing the Mexican National based on the political need for arms rather than any economic benefits.[63]

Thus, the Mexican government took control of the financially dubious packing company with a legally questionable bond issue of $25 million. On January 10, 1914, DeKay concluded the deal by signing two contracts with Undersecretary of the Treasury Pascual Luna y Parra and with Secretary of War General Aurelio Blanquet. The first $10 million of the bonds went to DeKay in return for his 51 percent holding of El Popo stock. The government assumed responsibility for the company's bonded debt, while leaving DeKay personally liable for any other debts that might surface, a clause that may have been suggested by Serrano in view of the meatpacker's cavalier accounting practices. DeKay received the remaining $15 million of the bond issue with the condition that he use the funds to purchase munitions for the government. In the second contract, Blanquet provided a shopping list of arms needed to suppress the Constitutionalist revolt: a quarter of a million Mauser 7 mm. rifles with a thousand rounds of ammunition for each, a hundred Mondragón mountain guns with half a million shells, and five hundred Hotchkiss machine guns, for which ammunition was already available from a Mexico City factory. With these two contracts, DeKay tied his fortunes irrevocably to the Huerta regime.[64]

The nationalization of Peralvillo did little to reverse the continued decline of the Mexico City meat supply. The situation remained relatively stable through the winter of 1913–1914, primarily because large-scale revolutionary fighting had not yet reached the capital's traditional sources of cattle. The Huasteca region had its share of insurgents, most notably the Cedillo brothers of San Luis Potosí, but the importers nevertheless succeeded in evading their requisitions. Huerta made a brief attempt to run the slaughterhouse, in the same way he ran everything else, with military discipline. To halt the drain on revenues caused by clandestine slaughter, in January 1914 police began to round up all concealed livestock in Mexico City, ultimately impounding more than 150 animals, mostly hogs being raised on kitchen scraps. After that rather derisory campaign, he left the business to concessionaires, who fought over lucrative military and prison meat contracts. Even Próspero Ramírez took the opportunity to reopen the San Lázaro packinghouse in March 1914, arousing once again the complaints of the neighbors.[65]

John DeKay had meanwhile proceeded to Europe with his commission for the Huerta regime. In February, he met with M. Camberfort, managing director of La Compagnie des Forges et Acieries de la Marine et d'Homecourt (St. Chamond). The French arms maker welcomed the continuing business, but reminded DeKay that the Mexican government already owed the company nearly US$2 million for previous contracts. Moreover, the new bond issue effectively repudiated the promise made the previous summer that Mexico would contract no additional debt until 1915. Nevertheless, Camberfort continued, by a fortuitous chance he was also vice president of one of the participating banks, Comptoir National d'Excompte de Paris. After brief consultations, he agreed to take the bonds at 70 percent of face value as part of the 1913 bond issue and to hold them until 1915 as security for Mexico's outstanding balance and new orders. The meatpacker arranged a similar deal through the Banque

Cantonale de Berne, Switzerland, with Georges Leroy of Cartoucherie Française, which unlike St. Chamond, promised immediate delivery.[66]

DeKay had to work fast to wrap up the complicated arrangement and cash out his Mexican investment, for the Constitutionalist revolution continued to gain strength in the spring of 1914. In early April, the Cartoucherie Française weapons, together with a supply of arms originally purchased by Huerta agents in the United States and transshipped through Odessa, Russia, were loaded aboard the Hamburg-America Line steamers *Ypiranga*, *Kronprinzessin Cecile*, and *Bavaria*. As the arms began their seventeen-day journey across the Atlantic, DeKay returned to London to launch a public relations campaign in favor of the Huerta government and its bonds. He began by publishing a book entitled *Dictators of Mexico*, an updated version of *Men of Mexico*, his laudatory account of the Porfirian elite from 1906. The new volume sought to convince the British that, news accounts notwithstanding, Huerta held an iron grip on the country and a Federal victory over the Constitutionalists was inevitable.[67]

This optimism notwithstanding, Huerta's cause promptly took a turn for the worse when President Wilson used a diplomatic incident as a pretext for military intervention. During revolutionary fighting at the port of Tampico, sailors from a U.S. warship had been mistaken for Constitutionalists and briefly detained by the federal garrison. Although they were quickly released, Wilson used the episode to demand once again Huerta's resignation. Then, when the U.S. president learned of the imminent arrival of the steamship *Ypiranga* with its load of arms, he ordered the navy to occupy the city of Veracruz on April 21. The following morning, DeKay, who was staying at Regents Park, heard the news of the seemingly imminent war between the United States and Mexico. He immediately consulted with his associate, the barrister Sir William Haynes-Smith, who advised him that having contracted for the arms, he could legally request their return to Europe. At noon on April 22, he wired the Hamburg-American Steamship Company to that effect. In fact, the *Ypiranga* offloaded its arms at Puerto México on May 27, but too late to save the federal army.[68]

Huerta fled to a European exile in July 1914, and a few weeks later, the Constitutionalist financial agent in London, Miguel Covarrubias, repudiated the former dictator's debts. The steamships *Kronprinzessin Cecile* and

Bavaria returned their load of arms to Europe, where they were deposited in Bilbao, with both transportation and insurance costs billed to DeKay. The Spanish government later handed these weapons over to the Constitutionalist agent Juan Sánchez Azcona, who sold them to the Allies in World War I for a tidy profit. Diplomatic officials warned that foreigners with ties to Huerta should leave the country, and Louis DeKay quickly complied, along with several other Popo managers. This exodus left Charles Mallory, head of the livestock department and a former commission agent from Chicago, in charge at Peralvillo on August 15, when the Constitutionalist army entered Mexico City.[69]

THE LEVIATHAN AT THE STOCKYARDS

The Constitutionalist revolutionaries went on to form a one-party state that remained in power until the end of the century, yet this Mexican leviathan proved curiously reluctant to enter the stockyards at Peralvillo. The economic nationalism that inspired the expropriation of industries such as petroleum was muted by the peculiar circumstances under which the slaughterhouse passed into government hands. In conflicts between labor and capital, the state frequently assumed the role of social mediator, but here too, the government intervened only in moments of crisis. This laissez-faire policy had reversed by mid-century as the state began providing cheap food to guarantee political support, making the consumer movement yet another component of the ruling party's corporate structure. Even as food subsidies helped importers and tablajeros to provide Mexico City with fresh meat, industrial practices from the United States, including feedlots, packinghouses, and supermarkets, gradually infiltrated the country. Therefore, when economic crisis provided an excuse for neoliberal technocrats to amputate the welfare bureaucracy, traditional methods of meat provisioning quickly fell apart. The resulting system—a modernization by default—brought prime cuts of marbled beef to wealthy Mexicans, while allowing the masses only refrigerated portions from lean Huastecan cattle.

Far from a rampaging leviathan, the Mexican state virtually ceased to exist soon after taking control of the Peralvillo Slaughterhouse. After the fall of Huerta, the revolutionary coalition promptly disintegrated into a bloody civil war that centered on Mexico City. Merchants responded to the turmoil by closing shop, and women spent their days in search of food. In an attempt to provide relief, Peralvillo's administrators began handing out blood from slaughtered animals. As many as fifteen hundred women waited in line outside the gates each morning to collect a liter of blood, which they boiled down into a black pudding to help feed their families. Rumors of hoarding arose, particularly against foreigners such as Colin and Meenen, who remained active in the meat trade.[70] Yet importers did not monopolize the blame for high prices; tablajeros were accused of buying meat at Peralvillo for $2 a kilo then reselling it for as much as $6 to $8.[71]

The Constitutionalist government gradually asserted its authority at Peralvillo, although instability remained throughout the country. In January 1915, the Health Board had even encouraged the formerly emasculated municipal government to take charge during the interregnum of federal authority. Sanitary officials particularly feared the sale of unwholesome meat to desperate consumers. By the fall, once the Constitutionalists had largely defeated their rivals, interim Governor General Cesar López de Lara attempted to increase the supply of meat by limiting slaughter in outlying towns and ordering all available livestock shipped to Peralvillo. When the Carranza government finally appointed Hipólito Aguirre to take over the slaughterhouse, in April 1916, he discovered the facility was being run by Antonio Montiél, the Porfirian private detective, and Henry O'Rourke, a twenty-two-year-old Canadian mechanic.[72]

Years of neglect had left Peralvillo in a dreadful state according to José M. Rodríguez, head of the newly created federal Department of Health. His 1917 report sounded reminiscent of the complaints issued twenty years earlier about the old slaughterhouse of San Lucas. The wooden slaughter floors were in a deplorable condition, filled with potholes in which the blood pooled and coagulated. Slaughterhouse personnel had not been provided new apparel in years, and their work clothes were encrusted with blood and other substances. The machinery was equally run down, and even with spare parts salvaged from the abandoned packinghouse at Uruapan, a general overhaul was needed to restore the plant to working condition. Rather than invest in such a costly undertaking, Carranza settled instead on the nineteenth-century expedient of contracting the slaughterhouse out to private enterprise, thereby ignoring the problems. The government did not undertake significant repairs at Peralvillo until 1924.[73]

Labor conflicts between slaughterhouse workers and livestock importers flared throughout the 1920s. Butchers formed the Sindicato de Trabajadores del Rastro (Slaughterhouse Workers Syndicate), and because the government still contracted out the management at Peralvillo, they negotiated directly with the chamber of commerce for importers and commission agents, the Asociación de Introductores y Comisionistas del Rastro. The two sides reached a contract in August 1922 which still maintained a piecework schedule of sixty centavos per steer, divided among the workers, and also included payment in kind—the old custom of giving butchers the viscera, including the "gallo" (literally, "rooster," the point of the loin) and the marrow. Both of these retrograde labor practices angered the union, but they were minor nuisances compared to the 1925 attempt by importers to cut back on benefits by informing the slaughterhouse administrator that workers were stealing these cuts of meat.[74]

In July 1927, the various meat unions joined together to shut down the entire Mexico City meat supply. The protest included more than three thousand workers in five separate unions, including slaughterhouse workers and technicians, the teamsters who delivered meat, and retail meat cutters and their employees. In response to this challenge, President Plutarco Elías Calles nationalized the slaughterhouse so that the meat cutters, as federal employees, would be forbidden to strike. Thus, the federal government finally claimed jurisdiction at Peralvillo on September 21, 1927, a decade after the revolutionary Constitution of 1917 had authorized the transfer of authority, and even then, it came not as a nationalist response to foreign control of the meat supply, but rather as an excuse to repress labor activism.[75]

The government undertook renovations again following a major earthquake in 1931, but the fundamental inequalities between labor and capital remained. For butchers on the killing floor, perhaps the greatest improvement came from the simple installation of emergency lamps, thereby ensuring that the regular power outages would not allow cattle to escape control in the dark. For importers, the new slaughterhouse consolidated their control on the market for another generation. With population growth, the annual consumption of cattle in the Federal District had risen to more than 200,000 by 1932, but given the deplorable conditions at the municipal abattoir, suburban butchers had taken up the slack. The slaughter at Peralvillo had actually fallen from its 1910 level to just over

100,000 head of cattle, while the Tacuba Slaughterhouse, which had been closed in the Porfirian era for lack of sanitary facilities, processed 42,000 cattle and workers at Tacubaya added another 27,000. The government therefore negotiated a market sharing agreement between suburban importers and the Mexico City clique.[76]

Nevertheless, the administration sought to bolster its revolutionary credentials among the working classes, even as guild traditions survived. Although the serial method of slaughter, dividing each task among specialized workers, had become firmly installed at the remodeled Peralvillo, the chief cattle butcher, Eusebio Martínez, may well have been a relative of Palemón Martínez, the butcher captain who led the protests against the original slaughterhouse in 1897. A state-sponsored magazine, *Resumen*, published a photograph of him standing next to his boss, General Fortino Uribe. The slim, wiry Martínez, much smaller than the rotund revolutionary, had reportedly worked at Peralvillo for twenty-three years, having started at the age of sixteen. The journal embraced his working-class heritage as well as his upstanding citizenship, noting that he was a husband, father, and homeowner. Other social benefits included a profit-sharing plan for workers and a meeting hall for the Unión Sindical Cooperativa de Obreros y Empleados del Rastro (Syndical Cooperative Union of Slaughterhouse Workers and Employers), which also became a site for worker's education, cultural events, and classes on health and personal hygiene. The construction of a sports field on the empty adjacent lot encouraged the formation of sports teams such as the butcher baseball squad, the Federal District champions of 1931 (see figure 5.3).[77]

The ruling party next sought to draw consumers as well as workers under its corporatist wing through the creation of a welfare bureaucracy intended to subsidize urban food supplies and prevent social unrest. Revolutionary General Lázaro Cárdenas laid the foundations for this bureaucracy during his presidential administration (1934–1940), but even with subsidies, inflation took a heavy toll on Mexico City residents. The cost of living rose more than 50 percent during the Cárdenas years, and shortages grew even worse when Mexico entered World War II, as the government diverted agricultural production from staple grains to oilseeds and other crops needed for the Allied war effort. Already by 1943, corn shortages had caused riots in Mexico City while the Peralvillo Slaughterhouse rationed tablajeros to half a side of beef every other day.[78]

5.3 Rastro union workers exchange their knives and saws for bat and gloves to win the Federal District championship of 1931. Fondo Plutarco Elías Calles, álbum 44, vol. 2/4, foto 52. Courtesy of Fideicomiso Archivos Plutarco Elías Calles y Fernando Torreblanca, Mexico City.

Taking responsibility for the urban meat supply entailed political risks, not only from popular complaints about shortages but also from prominent officials who enriched themselves on the black market. Wartime accusations of corruption extended all the way up to President Manuel Avila Camacho. In July 1943, as rumors of profiteering spread through the city, a popular magazine charged Secretary of Economy Francisco J. Gaxiola with manipulating grain and meat prices. The scandal became a cause célèbre, and Gaxiola was ultimately forced to resign. Historian Stephen Niblo has uncovered evidence that the president's brother, General Maximino Avila Camacho, may well have pointed the finger at Gaxiola to divert suspicion from his own illicit dealings, and the perspective from Peralvillo supports this conclusion. The Avila Camachos came from the town of Teziutlán, in northern Puebla, and they had acquired enormous ranching interests in the Huasteca region. Maximino was known as a brutal and corrupt businessman, enriching himself through his cabinet portfolio as secretary of communications and transport. Another brother, Rafael Avila Camacho, served as official mayor of the secretary of economy, and in October 1943, the opposition newspaper *La Nación* accused him of using the position to administer the meat monopoly. Other journalists referred more discreetly to anonymous "Teziutlán stockmen" as the beneficiaries behind the black market. Thus the revolution revived both the ideal of moral economy and the reality of corruption embodied in the colonial abasto.[79]

The leviathan of the Mexican ruling party, known as the Partido Revolucionario Institucional (PRI), reached its pinnacle of influence during the boom years following World War II. Rapid economic growth allowed the state to funnel even greater sums into urban food subsidies, which were necessary because the government refused to support workers' demands for wage increases to keep up with inflation. Industrialization fueled urbanization, and as the population of Mexico City tripled from 1.5 million to 5 million between 1940 and 1960, the need for a new slaughterhouse became clear. In 1955, the government inaugurated the new Rastro Ferrería, located in the northern suburb of Azcapotzalco, and Peralvillo was demolished to expand the Campo Deportivo Plutarco Elías Calles, originally built as a sports facility for the butcher workmen. The dualistic nature of Mexican meat supplies, already evident in the colonial and Porfirian eras, kept apace with the rapid urbanization. Although tablajeros maintained their shops in working-class barrios, U.S.-style supermarkets began to open in affluent neighborhoods. Modern refrigerated packinghouses likewise began to open up, primarily in the north, to meet export demands to the United States for "manufacture beef" used in fast food hamburgers and other industrial processed foods. To ensure that imported meat complied with U.S. standards, the Mexican federal inspection law of 1953 was simply a translation of USDA regulations. Although Mexican herds of cattle had increased to 17 million head by 1960 and almost 30 million by 1980, annual per capita consumption increased only modestly from 9.1 to 14.6 kilograms over the same two decades.[81]

By the 1980s, the economic boom had given way to bust, and neoliberal administrations, inspired by the policies of Margaret Thatcher and Ronald Reagan, sought to eliminate the welfare bureaucracy, including the Mexico City slaughterhouse. After three decades of service, Ferrería had accumulated a deficit of US $16 million, and replacing it would cost at least another US $5 million. Rather than gaining a new facility, the capital would henceforth have to rely on refrigerated meat from packinghouses in the provinces.[81] Residents of Azcapotzalco rejoiced at the imminent closing of the abattoir that had long blighted the neighborhood, contaminating ground water and spreading horrific odors into nearby suburbs. The government scheduled the closing for March 15, 1992, during the Lenten season, when meat consumption reached its lowest point, to minimize disruptions in the supply system. But economic crisis, rather than religious observance, did the most to restrict demand during the transition. Scientific progress had updated the Porfirian slogan of "meat in the clouds" to a new image of "stratospheric prices" without changing the basic fact that a kilogram of meat cost twice the minimum daily wage paid to most workers.[82]

As the date approached, Carlos López Reyes and other leading importers campaigned to preserve their bailiwick, taking out a full-page advertisement in *Excelsior* warning that the closing of Ferrería would result in meat shortages, inferior products, and clandestine slaughter. A number of tablajeros expressed similar fears that their customers would refuse to buy frozen meat or that unscrupulous competitors would begin a large-scale commerce in contraband. Journalists at *Excelsior* meanwhile denounced López Reyes as the "eternal middleman," and expressed the hope that the change might finish off the Mexico City black market once and for all.[83] Socialist Congressman Ramón Jiménez López simply objected that the decision had been taken without considering the views of the majority of the people who, denied their preference for fresh meat, "will be acquiring meat that has been refrigerated for days."[84]

Ultimately, the government of Carlos Salinas de Gortari closed Ferrería according to plan. The chaos and shortages predicted by the importers did not come to pass, but neither did the end of the black market or clandestine slaughter. Although established livestock merchants such as López Reyes began to decline in importance, they were soon replaced by a new generation of importers more skilled at handling refrigerated meat. Meanwhile, the continuing economic crisis hastened the final closing of the welfare bureaucracy, and in 1999, the government abolished the final subsidy on the staple corn tortillas. One year later, the PRI lost its seven-decade monopoly on the presidency.[85]

THE REBELLION IN RETROSPECT

The sausage rebellion followed a circuitous path from political protest to violent rebellion and ultimately a return to traditional practices, thereby reflecting the broader course of the Mexican Revolution of 1910. The movement began with protests and political maneuvers within the Porfirian establishment in an attempt to prevent El Popo from monopolizing the meat supply. With the success of the Maderista movement, the meat trades quickly adopted revolutionary language in their attacks on the foreign company, condemning the Health Board as a creature of the Porfirian establishment and insisting on their rights as citizens to carry out their traditional meat trades. Mexican consumers likewise joined in the movement, albeit less overtly, through their choices in favor of fresh rather than refrigerated meat. They gained the support of local Maderista politicians, who ultimately enacted reform legislation that set a precedent for consumer protection as a civic right. The opportunity was lost, however, with the coup that brought Huerta to power and the subsequent campaigns to overthrow him. The revolutionary movement brought the downfall of El Popo and eventually the rise of a corporatist state that treated consumer issues as a source of political patronage, but one that had to be balanced against the interests of labor and capital. By mid-century, the single-minded pursuit of development had brought business to the forefront and food subsidies became simply a method to help hold down wage increases. Worse still, the trickle-down industrialization scheme failed to create a competitive business structure, and in the ensuing economic crisis, the welfare bureaucracy was dismantled too quickly for importers and tablajeros to adapt their supply chains and preserve the consumer preference for freshly slaughtered meat.

The Mexican National Packing Co. offered a clear blueprint of the neoliberal future of the meat supply, both its promise and its drawbacks, but it came half a century too soon. John W. DeKay had arrived in Mexico with a proven business model, but he miscalculated the difficulty of transforming consumer tastes from fresh to refrigerated meat. Meatpackers in the United States had effected this transition in urban consumption habits as early as the 1880s, and London underwent a similar change in the decade following World War I. Industrial production and refrigerated transport attained such overwhelming cost advantages that the entire distribution network was altered to facilitate the new sources of supply. Once that adjustment had been made, individual stockmen found it difficult to get their animals to market at all, let alone to dislodge their giant competitors.[86]

Given the complex nature of the transition from fresh to refrigerated meat, it is impossible to isolate a single cause for Popo's failure, whether poor management, market competition, consumer resistance, or political pressure. The failure of the Terrazas to create a national packing network, and the closing of their unprofitable packinghouses in northern Mexico, demonstrated the difficulty that the refrigerated model faced in overcoming consumer preferences. Chicago packers, notwithstanding their heavy advertising campaigns, ultimately succeeded by driving independent butchers and freshly slaughtered meat from the market. Even with better management, DeKay lacked the deep financial reserves to carry out such a campaign that Swift and Armour developed through the sale of cured pork and through geographical diversification which underwrote losses in regional beef markets.[87] Unfortunately for DeKay, Mexican butchers proved even more resilient than their North American counterparts. Ultimately, the aspiring packer counted on the regulatory power of the Porfirian health establishment to enforce U.S. standards, but the dictatorship proved unable or unwilling to make the people eat refrigerated meat. Despite the vaunted ideals of order and progress, the government could not even adequately police the Peralvillo Slaughterhouse.

The contrast with the situation in 1992 is equally revealing. Export markets for manufactured meat in the United States provided the financial reserves for licensed slaughterhouses to compete with Mexico City importers. Nevertheless, they won the market only through dramatic government action, essentially outlawing the sale of freshly slaughtered meat. Moreover, the change came so rapidly that traditional importers had no opportunity to adapt, for example, by establishing slaughterhouses outside the Federal District but close enough to allow the transport of fresh meat. Given the new market situation, consumers had the choice of refrigerated meat or none at all, and tastes adjusted accordingly.

But this change came far too late to help DeKay. In 1926, he filed for payment of the Huerta government bonds through the U.S.-Mexico Claims Commission, which adjudicated cases of damage caused by revolutionary fighting. His appeal never came before the commission, having been disallowed by agreement of the U.S. and Mexican representatives in

1934. Despite the ill-fated Mexican venture, or perhaps because of it, he still maintained financial connections in Europe, including a Swiss bank account. DeKay ultimately settled with his wife Dorothy and daughter Callie in Ashburn, Virginia, where he died about 1938. The packinghouse he built in Uruapan had already fallen into ruins, becoming simply another local memory of Porfirian industrialization.[88]

The sausage rebellion represented a great success for meat importers, delaying for nearly a century the transformation of their business. The incipient Porfirian reorganization of industry following U.S. corporate models failed to take root in the meat industry, and made relatively little progress in other sectors of the economy as well. Wholesale merchants also retained their firm control over slaughterhouse workers and tablajeros, making the rebellion considerably less of a victory for tradesmen. As a result, as late as the 1980s, workers at the Ferrería abattoir maintained a Porfirian, if not colonial, tradition of claiming the so-called *boato*—stealing meat from carcasses as a way of compensating for their low pay. By the same token, the slaughterhouse continued to collect the *esquilmos*: hides, hooves, and blood to be used for industrial purposes. Even the coming of refrigeration represented simply another generational change for the importers, although the growth of supermarket chains may yet transform the industry one day.

For consumers, the sausage rebellion had mixed results, ensuring their access to traditional styles of meat, but at higher prices than might otherwise have been the case. The government provisioning program, which subverted the consumer movement into a form of political patronage, represented an equally inefficient method for delivering social services. And by making traditional Mexican cooking dependent on unsustainable supply chains, the system left consumers vulnerable to the forces of globalization at the end of the twentieth century. The 470-year tradition of eating freshly slaughtered beef in Mexico City thus came to an end as an incidental side effect of neoliberal reform.

CONCLUSION

Fajitas on the Zócalo

A t the turn of the Millennium, a new fad swept through the fashionable restaurants of Condesa, Polanco, the Zona Rosa, and Mexico City's historic center: affluent Mexicans acquired a taste for fajitas. Exactly where this trend came from is difficult to determine. Perhaps the demands of U.S. tourists for "familiar" Mexican food finally spread to the local elite, or maybe the latter discovered the Tex-Mex specialty while on vacation north of the Rio Bravo. In any event, restaurateurs not only imported the presentation—complete with sizzling hot grill plates and the whole range of condiments: onions, green peppers, and sour cream—they even imported the skirt steak. With packinghouse workers forbidden to slaughter livestock by the closing of the municipal abattoir, they instead earned their pay by opening cases of frozen meat from the United States and Canada and preparing it portion-ready for the finest local restaurants using the same high-pressure marinade machines pioneered by U.S. mass-market chains such as Chili's. The spectacle of sophisticated Mexicans imitating a Tex-Mex imitation of Mexican food seemed all the more ironic when ordinary consumers could not satisfy their preference for freshly slaughtered meat, or given the economic crisis, obtain any meat at all. The sausage rebellion had finally run its course.[1]

Mexican food stands out as one of the great anachronisms of the modern world, a stubbornly peasant cuisine in the midst of a rapidly modernizing society. Apart from the "nueva cocina mexicana" served in trendy restaurants, the international cuisine that emerged in eighteenth-century France has had little influence on the traditional tastes of Mexico. The national dish, *mole poblano*, still preserves the cooking techniques of Native American societies and of Medieval Europe, before French chefs dictated the transition from robust blends of spices to more subtle herb reductions. Mexican methods of cooking meat likewise emphasize the freshness of flavors while forgoing the tenderizing effects of aging that has become common in the United States. And that quintessential peasant food, the corn tortilla, provides the natural companion for everything from a festive mole or carne asada to an everyday pot of beans. Traditional cooks have not rejected modern technology out of hand; they patronize corn mills to save hours of hand grinding to make tortillas, purchase electric blenders to reduce the work in preparing mole, and even jerry-rig barbecue grills out of discarded Pemex oil drums. Nevertheless, even these updated versions of old-fashioned cooking depend on provisioning systems that have survived the industrial transformations of the twentieth century only with the assistance of state subsidies. As the contemporary Mexico City meat supply demonstrates, the continued viability of these networks has become doubtful under neoliberal administrations.[2]

The sudden closing of the Ferrería slaughterhouse at the end of the twentieth century was only the latest in a long line of political transitions that profoundly influenced the meat provisioning of Mexico City. The Scholastic ideals of moral economy embodied in the colonial abasto de carne gave way during the late nineteenth century to Enlightenment faith in free trade. This privatization process was completed soon after independence when government regulation of the meat supply vanished in the chaos of the early republic. Liberal administrations about midcentury therefore confronted the ironic task of reestablishing municipal oversight on the meat trades, which they accomplished by ignoring their own ideology and trampling the property rights of the meat importers. The city council had no sooner reasserted its authority than positivist científicos attempted to modernize the industry by transforming the municipal slaughterhouse into a private packinghouse. The Revolution of 1910 revisited each of these stages, from collapse and chaos to a welfare state reminiscent of the colonial abasto, before culminating in a neoliberal transition to private packinghouses. While trying to emulate diverse ideologies from Europe and the United States, Mexico thus failed to achieve the institutional stability that provided continuity from one administration to the next and even across revolutionary regimes in countries such as France.[3]

The question of just who would regulate the meat supply remained a source of ongoing contention throughout this process of modernization. During the colonial period, the abasto contractor and tocinero guilds served a dual function of provisioning the city and regulating the supply, subject to the higher authority of the fiel ejecutor. When the colonial courts were abolished with independence, the butcher trades asserted their superior knowledge as a justification for claiming autonomy from municipal regulation. Although Mexican meat guilds never really worked like their European counterparts, the political functionaries appointed to regulate the trade failed to demonstrate superior knowledge until medical professionals took over the job toward the end of the century. Private enterprise remained an important part of the regulatory process, if nothing else to police against clandestine slaughter. One could even view the attempt by the Porfirian government to force the Mexican National to merge with local businessmen as a regulatory attempt to bring local knowledge to a foreign contractor. As the company's sales of adulterated lard demonstrated, however, the market failed to assure the commitment of private enterprise to public health.

The meat supply did improve over the period from 1900 to 1920, as evidenced by a sharp fall in mortality rates from gastro-intestinal disease, and the Porfirian Health Board surely deserves a measure of credit for this improvement. At the turn of the century, out of every 100,000 residents, an average of 1,500 died each year of such causes. This number fell steadily over the following two decades to less than 1,000, although mortality rates from all causes fell at about the same rate.[4] While inspectors removed a great deal of unwholesome food from market stalls, they displayed more zeal against minor offenders than against the Mexican National, which likewise posed dangers to public health. Lucre alone might have motivated Ramón Corral's services to the meatpackers, but even honorable members of the Health Board found their reputations tied to the supposed benefits of imported technology. In the twentieth century, processed foods such as compound lard gained wide and perhaps mistaken acceptance as healthy, while pure pork fat came to be shunned as a menace to the arteries.[5] Yet there was no guarantee that the Popo product was more wholesome than the fat of hogs slaughtered clandestinely, and in an undernourished society like Porfirian Mexico, the loss of calories meant not slimness but anemia.

Commentators have noted the "dual" nature of modern agriculture in Latin America, and municipal slaughterhouses in rural areas, equipped with little more than a concrete slab floor and a pulley, provide a stark contrast with the modern packinghouses that provision affluent urban markets. Nevertheless, as this study has shown, clandestine slaughter has always constituted an alternative to the formal butcher trades. Just as nineteenth-century capoteros operated outside the law to supply meat to popular barrios, the twentieth-century closing of the Mexico City abattoir made every house in the nearby countryside a potential clandestine slaughterhouse. Even today in working class barrios of Mexico City, a majority of the pork sold in carnicerías comes from outside regular supply channels, in the form of hogs raised on kitchen scraps by members of the community and sold to local butchers.[6] Despite the very real health dangers of meat slaughtered without proper inspection, the informal economy remains an essential element in provisioning Mexico City. Moreover, as Fernando Rello and Demetrio Sodi have observed: "Traditional does not signify inefficiency, nor can one affirm with certainty that modern commerce is more effective for distributing food among the great diversity of consumers in the city. For example, the most modern of the supermarkets does not offer better prices nor more variety of vegetables and fruits than a market on wheels or a *tianguis* (temporary market)."[7]

The persistence of these traditional supply channels across the upheavals of the provisioning system points to continuities in the business history of Mexico. A recent anthropological and economic study of the meat supply in Guadalajara by Gabriel Ascencio Franco has found business practices similar to those of the colonial period. The meat importers in particular retain their role of organizing economic activity through personal relationships. Traditional rivalries between wholesale merchants and retail meat cutters naturally exist, and the latter, when asked about importers in general, ascribed to them every form of mischief. Yet when the discussion turned to their personal supplier, tablajeros spoke of long-term relationships based on trust. Similar personal bonds existed between retailers and consumers. DeKay considered such middlemen an antiquated guild that profited from scarcity, and yet they provided value to Mexican consumers by offering fresh meat cut according to their preferences. The labor-intensive methods of preparing meat did entail higher costs, but as Ascencio Franco has revealed, importers who achieved efficiencies often declined to pass those savings on to consumers. Nor are such practices limited to Mexican livestock merchants; job cutting in the contemporary United States is more often aimed at boosting profitability than at benefiting customers. The scandals at Enron and countless other firms demonstrate the shallowness of corporate concern for the public good.[8]

Even if the system of importers served local consumers, the incipient Porfirian corporate business organization might have helped build export markets for Mexican beef. Although manufacturers from developing countries faced great difficulties competing in global markets, refrigerated meats offered unique potential for industrial modernization, as Argentina clearly demonstrated. Unlike such industries as textiles or steel, Mexican meat producers were not at a great technological disadvantage. If revolutionary fighting had not intervened, John DeKay's Mexican National Packing Co. might have succeeded in capturing European markets, but this is far from certain. One potential barrier lay in the generally poor quality of Mexican beef. The Texas longhorn had already been eclipsed on United States ranges by specially bred, grain-fed cattle. Argentine producers likewise improved the quality of the herds on the vast expanses of temperate grassland known as the pampas. In Mexico, ticks and the tropical climate made such a transition far more difficult for all but the northern tier of states, and successful cross-breeds ultimately came not from Aberdeen Angus but from Indian Zebu cattle, which also brought a plague of foot-and-mouth disease in the 1940s. Another significant problem lay in the company's financial management. DeKay was essentially running a shell game with British and United States investors' money, and it had become precarious by 1910, even before he lost the patronage of Vice President Ramón Corral.

The difficulties faced by the packing company also call into question common assumptions about the preference given to foreign investors by the Porfirian government. DeKay could only dream of holding Mexican officials and competitors in a state of dependency. Unlike firms such as International Harvester, which dominated Yucatecan henequen markets through local agent Olegario Molina, the meatpacker had sunk his capital into Mexico and therefore fell firmly under Mexican government control.[9] Just as important for DeKay's ultimate failure was his inability to understand the practices of Mexican political economy. Without an insider's knowledge, he paid an exorbitant price to the Terrazas for Peralvillo, nor could he count on a pliable workforce. DeKay's need for a private detective to counter open rebellion on the shop floor demonstrated the terminal failure of the company's labor relations.

The sociology of the state can also be furthered by close examination of the Mexico City meat supply over a "long" nineteenth century from the late colonial period to the Revolution of 1910. The fundamental question of what the liberal state would regulate and what would be left to the market was subject to constant negotiation between butchers and government officials. Technological change proved more important than ideological beliefs in defining these shifting positions. Thus, classical liberals used medical knowledge to increase the power of the state while the científico Corral supported the Mexican National's property rights to Peralvillo against the demands of meat importers for government regulation.

Simplistic contrasts between U.S. and Mexican attitudes about the market also fail to account for this convoluted dialogue. Consider a recent formulation by legal scholar George Armstrong, who argued that "Mexico has never developed a materialist culture of egoism and autonomy, [and] that the country lacks a market economy. Instead, the culture of the nation reinforces communitarian paternalism. Consequently, freedom of contract, economic competition, and private exploitation of property have generally been held in low esteem by those who make the laws.... The revolution of 1910–1917 was a reaction against a nascent market society that had begun to develop under the Díaz regime and an expression of the desire of many Mexicans to reestablish a communitarian life."[10] Remaining within this classical liberal Anglo-American perspective leads to an important contradiction. By 1910, Mexico City livestock merchants had come to welcome, indeed demand, state intervention. Contrary to Armstrong's perspective, however, they reacted not against a free market but rather against the incipient monopoly of their industry, fomented by the Porfirian government. The meat trades were organized largely according to the principles of communitarian paternalism, but this did not hinder their belief in free markets. Throughout the nineteenth century, they had asserted liberal property rights and insisted on the operation of free markets. Moreover, the existence of a cohesive community is an implicit axiom of Adam Smith's invisible hand theory.[11] Technological change within the United States meat industry prompted a similar crisis, which was resolved through the replacement of free markets with an oligopolistic industrial structure.[12] Yet one hesitates to depict Porfirio Díaz as the head of a dictatorial welfare state oppressing heroic entrepreneurs.

Philip Corrigan has suggested an escape from this theoretical cul-de-sac by considering the cultural practices of state formation in which "governance becomes unified with the 'private' realm; indeed, seen as constitutive of that crucial 'private'/'public' split."[13] The confused dialogue between government officials and livestock importers, in which actors often speak the wrong lines, then begins to acquire a new clarity. These struggles represented an early stage in the rationalization of the capitalist state in Mexico. With the onset of industrialization about the turn of the century, dislocations inevitably emerged pitting innovative businessmen against traditional merchants. The Porfirian regime appeared less interested in creating a market economy as such than in working out mechanisms for accommodating these interest group conflicts and achieving economic modernization within an authoritarian political structure. Officials such as President Díaz and Treasury Secretary Limantour already discreetly negotiated such important decisions as the sale of the Terrazas interests to DeKay. The organization of chambers of commerce by the postrevolutionary state then served to incorporate the petite bourgeoisie into this shadowy realm of Mexican political economy.

Drawing consumers into this corporatist structure proved even more problematic. Enrique Ochoa's study of food policy in the twentieth century showed that attempts at rational government planning invariably fell victim to the immediate needs of crisis management. Efforts to guarantee adequate meat supplies certainly tended to backfire, as the newspaper *El Universal* observed during the years of wartime shortages: "Although it would appear a joke, housewives complain that every time the metropolitan newspapers announce the authorities had dictated energetic measures to lower the price of meat, they awaken the following day [to find] this article more expensive."[14] Patriarchal revolutionary administrations emphasized workers' movements, at least in rhetoric, and therefore did little to develop political mechanisms for responding to consumer needs, which were viewed as domestic and feminine in nature. In 1983, for example, Congress amended article 4 of the Constitution of 1917 to include public health as a fundamental guarantee, yet two decades later the question of how to fulfill that promise to citizens still remained open.[15]

The final closing of the Mexico City slaughterhouse left many residents with strong feelings of nostalgia, just as previous shortages caused people to look back on supposed golden ages of the past. During the Second World War, for example, the conservative newspaper *La Nación* reported, inaccurately, that the slaughter had fallen to less than half that of the Porfiriato. Even in Native American communities, which have generally not had much access to meat since the sixteenth century, people look forward with great anticipation to the few festivals each year when they can eat like Spaniards. In 1992, journalist Isabel Hernández penned a nostalgic tribute to the Ferrería abattoir and its adjacent markets, recalling in particular the power lunches of past decades, deep fried testicles and blood sausages consumed by political bosses Ernesto Uruchurtu and Fidel Velázquez to demonstrate their machismo. Chronicler Manuel Magaña Contreras shared this poetic view of viscera, describing "finger-licking-good tripe, the highest quality liver, brain soup, testicles, mutton, pork, and other species like goat." He also summarized a widespread view among the popular classes that "the frozen product decreases the nutritive properties of the meat in considerable form, reducing the potency of the proteins and other sources of energy, according to expert testimony." The essay concluded sadly: "Fortunate was the city of Mexico when there were slaughterhouses, because then the products arrived naturally to the consumers, fresh and with all their rich nutrients, and lacking, besides, the additives and conservatives that they now inject into the frozen carcasses."[16]

The dramatic and nearly simultaneous transformation of two of Mexico's most important dietary staples, tortillas and meat, may portend a dark future for all peasant cuisines in the age of globalization. The sudden termination of food subsidies by neoliberal administrations in the 1990s forced the closing not only of the Mexico City slaughterhouse but also of an entire industry of small corn mills. These neighborhood businesses had supplied generations of consumers with tortillas made of freshly ground corn, but they were driven out of business when suddenly forced to compete against the multinational giant, Maseca, an industrial producer of dehydrated tortilla flour (masa harina). Journalist Alma Guillermoprieto graphically described the results: "when the privatization program of Mexico's notorious former President Carlos Salinas delivered the future of the tortilla into their hands...[the tortilla magnates] served up to the Mexican people the rounds of grilled cardboard that at present constitute the nation's basic foodstuff."[17] In much the same way, introducing North American meatpacking technology to Mexico led not to the widespread availability of prime sirloin steaks but rather to the consumption of lean Huastecan cattle that had lost its fresh taste without any corresponding gain in tenderness from the time spent under refrigeration.

From the perspective of taste, globalization thus magnified class differences, by allowing the wealthy to import fajitas from the United States to eat with artisanal tortillas made from freshly ground corn.

From a health perspective, the question remained of whether the transition to modern meatpacking would provide the urban poor greater access to animal protein. An editorial in the newspaper *La Jornada* described this basic trade off when the Ferreria slaughterhouse closed: "The population will suffer changes in their customs and will begin to know, on a massive scale, frozen meat. It is possible that with this measure they will succeed in lowering prices and that this will redound to the benefit of hundreds of thousands of inhabitants of Mexico City, who have given up eating meat on a daily basis owing to the high prices of this product."[18] But in attempting to expand production, livestock raisers have resorted to increasingly dubious practices, causing outbreaks of "mad cow" syndrome in Europe, Japan, and North America. Global fisheries have likewise been depleted, but even with unsustainable production methods, the bulk of the world population continues to subsist on a basically vegetarian diet. In the long run, therefore, the traditional Mexican carne asada, made from freshly slaughtered beef and eaten only on festive occasions, may assure a healthier future than a daily diet of Porterhouse steak.

NOTES

INTRODUCTION

1. Catharine Ulmer Stoker, *Concha's Mexican Kitchen Cook Book* (San Antonio: Naylor Company, 1946), 2.

2. Upton Sinclair, *The Jungle* (New York: Doubleday, Page & Co., 1906).

3. Juan de Dios Arias, "El tocinero. Una persona de sustancia," in *Los mexicanos pintados por sus mismos: Obra escrita por una sociedad de literatos* (Mexico City: Símbolo, 1946 [1855]), 285–86.

4. Robert M. Buffington, *Criminal and Citizen in Modern Mexico* (Lincoln: University of Nebraska Press, 2000); Pablo Piccato, *City of Suspects: Crime in Mexico City, 1900–1930* (Durham, NC: Duke University Press, 2001); Katherine Elaine Bliss, *Compromised Positions: Prostitution, Public Health, and Gender Politics in Revolutionary Mexico City* (University Park: Pennsylvania State University Press, 2001); James A. Garza, "Tales from the Mexican Underworld: Sex, Crime, and Vice in Porfirian Mexico City, 1876–1911" (Ph.D. diss., Texas Christian University, 2001).

5. Stephen H. Haber, *Industry and Underdevelopment: The Industrialization of Mexico, 1890–1940* (Stanford, CA: Stanford University Press, 1989).

6. Priscilla Connolly, *El contratista de don Porfirio: Obras públicas, deuda y desarrollo desigual* (Mexico City: Fondo de Cultura Económica, 1997), 70–77; Concepción Lugo and Elsa Malvido, "Las epidemias en la Ciudad de México, 1822–1850," in *La Ciudad de México en la primera mitad del siglo XIX. Economía y estructura urbana*, ed. Regina Hernández Franyuti (Mexico City: Instituto Mora, 1994), 303–64; Glen David Kuecker, "A Desert in the Tropical Wilderness: Limits to the Porfirian Project in Northeastern Veracruz, 1870–1910" (Ph.D. diss., Rutgers University, 1998); Carlos Contreras Cruz, "Ciudad y salud en el Porfiriato: La política urbana y el saneamiento de Puebla (1880–1906)," *Siglo XIX: Cuadernos de Historia* 1, no. 3 (June 1992): 55–76.

7. Margaret R. Somers, "The Privatization of Citizenship: How to Unthink a Knowledge Culture," in *Beyond the Cultural Turn: New Directions in the Study of Society and Culture*, ed. Victoria E. Bonnell and Lynn Hunt (Berkeley: University of California Press, 1999), 121–61.

8. Charles Taylor, "Modes of Civil Society," *Public Culture* 3, no. 1 (Fall 1990): 95–118; William H. Sewell, Jr., *Work and Revolution in France: The Language of Labor from the Old Regime to 1848* (Cambridge: Cambridge University Press, 1980). For the application of this ideology to subsistence issues, see Judith A. Miller, *Mastering the Market: The State and the Grain Trade in Northern France, 1700–1860* (Cambridge: Cambridge University Press, 1999).

9. Jesús Reyes Heroles, *El liberalismo mexicano*, 3 vols. (Mexico City: Fondo de Cultura Económica, 1988), 3:421–93; Charles A. Hale, *Mexican Liberalism in the Age of Mora, 1821–1853* (New Haven, CT: Yale University Press, 1968), chapter 8; Steven Topik, "The Economic Role of the State in Liberal Regimes: Brazil and Mexico Compared, 1888–1910," in *Guiding the Invisible Hand: Economic Liberalism and the State in Latin American History*, ed. Joseph L. Love and Nils Jacobsen (New York: Praeger, 1988), 117–44.

10. E. P. Thompson, "The Moral Economy of the English Crowd in the Eighteenth

Century," *Past and Present* 50 (February 1971): 76–136.

11. William Bullock, *Six Months Residence and Travels in Mexico* (Port Washington, NY: Kennikat Press, 1971 [1824]), 253–556.

12. John Gregory Bourke, "The Folk-Foods of the Rio Grande Valley and of Northern Mexico." *Journal of American Folk-Lore* (1895): 67.

13. On the Mexican national cuisine, see Jeffrey M. Pilcher, *¡Que vivan los tamales! Food and the Making of Mexican Identity* (Albuquerque, NM: University of New Mexico Press, 1998).

14. *Mexican Herald*, April 15, 1908; *El Imparcial*, April 18, 1908.

15. University of California, Berkeley, Bancroft Library, Manuel Gamio Book Notes, Microfilm 2322, reel 2, page 437, Luis Felipe Recinos, "Vida del Sr. José Rocha," April 8, 1927.

16. Harold McGee, *On Food and Cooking: The Science and Lore of the Kitchen* (New York: Scribners, 1984), 98–99; Bruce Aidells and Denis Kelly, *The Complete Meat Cookbook* (New York: Houghton Mifflin Company, 1998), 83, 90–91.

17. Roger Horowitz, Jeffrey M. Pilcher, and Sydney Watts, "Meat for the Multitudes: Market Culture in Paris, New York City, and Mexico City over the 'Long' Nineteenth Century," *American Historical Review* 109, no. 4 (October 2004): 1055–83.

18. Charles Edward Russell, *The Greatest Trust in the World* (New York: Ridgway Thayer Company, 1905); Rudolf Alexander Clemen, *The American Livestock and Meat Industry* (New York: Ronald Press Company, 1923); J. Ogden Armour, *The Packers, the Private Car Lines, and the People* (Philadelphia: Henry Altemus Company, 1906); Louis F. Swift, *The Yankee of the Yards: The Biography of Gustavus Franklin Swift* (Chicago: A. W. Shaw Company, 1927).

19. The best of these early studies is David Brody, *The Butcher Workmen: A Study of Unionization* (Cambridge, MA: Harvard University Press, 1964). See also, Lewis Corey, *Meat and Man: A Study of Monopoly, Unionism, and Food Policy* (New York: Viking Press, 1950); Theodore V. Purcell, *The Worker Speaks His Mind on Company and Union* (Cambridge, MA: Harvard University Press, 1953). More recent works include Rick Halperin, *Down on the Killing Floor: Black and White Workers in Chicago's Packinghouses, 1904–1954* (Urbana, IL: University of Illinois Press, 1997); Roger Horowitz, *"Negro and White, Unite and Fight!" A Social History of Industrial Unionism in Meatpacking, 1930–1990* (Urbana, IL: University of Illinois Press, 1997); Louise Carroll Wade, *Chicago's Pride: The Stockyards, Packingtown, and Environs in the Nineteenth Century* (Urbana, IL: University of Illinois Press, 1987).

20. Mary Yeager, *Competition and Regulation: The Development of Oligopoly in the Meat Packing Industry* (Greenwich, CT: JAI Press, Inc., 1981).

21. Siegfried Giedion, *Mechanization Takes Command: A Contribution to Anonymous History* (New York: Oxford University Press, 1948); Edward Anderson, Jr., *Refrigeration in America: A History of a New Technology and its Impact* (Princeton, NJ: Princeton University Press, 1953); James Harvey Young, *Pure Food: Securing the Food and Drugs Act of 1906* (Princeton, NJ: Princeton University Press, 1989).

22. William Cronon, *Nature's Metropolis: Chicago and the Great West* (New York: Norton, 1991).

23. Roger Horowitz, *Meat in America: Technology, Taste, Transformation* (Baltimore: Johns Hopkins University Press, forthcoming).

24. For the early history of meat in Mexico, see Alfred Crosby, Jr., *The Columbian Exchange: Biological and Cultural Consequences of 1492* (Westport, CT: Greenwood, 1972); François Chevalier, *Land and Society in Colonial Mexico: The Great Hacienda* (Berkeley: University of California Press, 1970); Elinor Melville, *A Plague of Sheep: Environmental Consequences of the Conquest of Mexico* (Cambridge: Cambridge University Press, 1994); Ivonne Mijares, *Mestizo alimentario: El abasto de la ciudad de México en el siglo XVI* (Mexico City: UNAM, 1993). On the late colonial period, see John E. Kicza, "Consumption and Control: The Mexico City Business Community and Commodity Marketing in the Eighteenth Century," *Estudios de Historia Novohispana* 12 (1992): 159–69; Ward Barrett, "The Meat Supply of Colonial Cuernavaca," *Annals of the Association of American Geographers* 64, no. 4 (December 1974): 525–40; Eric Van Young, *Hacienda and Market in Eighteenth-Century Mexico: The Rural Economy of the Guadalajara Region, 1675–1820* (Berkeley: University of California Press, 1981); Guy P. C. Thompson, *Puebla de los Angeles: Industry and Society in a Mexican City, 1700–1850* (Boulder, CO: Westview Press, 1989); Jan Bazant, *Cinco haciendas mexicanas: Tres siglos de vida rural en San Luis Potosí (1600–1910)* (Mexico City: El Colegio de México, 1975); D. A. Brading, *Haciendas and Ranchos in the Mexican Bajío, León, 1700–1860* (Cambridge: Cambridge University Press, 1978); Charles H. Harris, III, *A Mexican Family Empire: The Latifundio of the Sánchez Navarros, 1765–1867* (Austin: University of Texas Press, 1975); Herman Konrad, *A Jesuit Hacienda in Colonial Mexico: Santa Lucía, 1576–1767* (Stanford, CA: Stanford University Press, 1980).

25. A few notable exceptions to the lack of nineteenth-century studies are Jorge Silva Riquer, "El abasto al mercado urbano de la ciudad de México, 1830–1860," in *La ciudad de México en la primera mitad del siglo XIX*, vol. 1, *Economía y estructura urbana*, ed. Regina Hernández Franyuti (Mexico City: Instituto Mora, 1994), 64–115; Francisco Téllez Guerrero, *De reales y granos: Los finanzas y el abasto de Puebla de los Anglees, 1820–1840* (Puebla: Cuadernos de la Casa Fresno, Universidad Autónoma de Puebla, 1986).

26. José Napoleón Guzmán Avila, *Michoacán y la inversión extranjera, 1880–1911* (Morelia: Universidad Michoacana de San Nicolás de Hidalgo, 1982), chapter 5.

CHAPTER ONE

1. Archivo Histórico de la Ciudad de México (hereafter AHCM), vol. 3763, exp. 25, Municipal report, November 1897.

2. Pedro Saucedo Montemayor, *Historia de la ganadería en México*, vol. 1 (Mexico City: UNAM, 1984), 249.

3. Bernal Díaz del Castillo, *The Discovery and Conquest of Mexico, 1517–1521*, trans. A. P. Maudslay (London: George Routledge, 1928), 290–91; Fanny Calderón de la Barca, *Life in Mexico: The Letters of Fanny Calderón de la Barca*, ed. Howard T. Fisher and Marion Hall Fisher (Garden City, NY: Doubleday, 1966), 55, 156.

4. Margaret Park Redfield, "Notes on the Cookery of Tepoztlan, Morelos," *American Journal of Folklore* 42, no. 164 (April-June 1929): 178–80; Charles Julian Bishko, "The Peninsular Background of Latin American Cattle Ranching," *Hispanic American Historical Review* 32, no. 4 (November 1952): 513; Sydney Watts, "Meat Matters: The Butchers of Old Regime Paris" (Ph.D. diss., Cornell University, 1999), 65, 92; Joaquín García Icazbalceta, *Noticias de México, recogidas*

por D. Francisco Sedano vecino de esta ciudad desde el año de 1756 (Mexico City: J. R. Barbedillo, 1880), 67–68; John C. Super, *Food, Conquest, and Colonization in Sixteenth-Century Spanish America* (Albuquerque: University of New Mexico Press, 1988), 85.

5. *Recetario de doña Dominga de Guzmán, siglo XVIII: Tesoro de la cocina mexicana* (Mexico City: Consejo Nacional para la Cultura y las Artes, 1996), 110; Watts, "Meat Matters," 70; William H. Dusenberry, "The Regulation of Meat Supply in Sixteenth-Century Mexico City," *Hispanic American Historical Review* 28, no. 1 (February 1948): 45.

6. Patricia T. Arroyo, *The Science of Philippine Foods* (Quezon City: Abanito Enterprises, 1973); Frans J. Schyer, *Ethnicity and Class Conflict in Rural Mexico* (Princeton, NJ: Princeton University Press, 1990), 82.

7. Juan de Dios Arias, "El tocinero," 287; AHCM, Actas, vol. 629A, May 7, 1527.

8. Fanny Chambers Gooch [Iglehart], *Face to Face with the Mexicans* (New York: Fords, Howard, and Hulbert, 1887), 564.

9. Following the depredations of the Wars of Independence, the sheep supply recovered in the mid-1820s, then turned downward and continued to decline for decades. Politics doubtless contributed to this trend, since the supply peaked in 1826, the year before the expulsion of thousands of peninsular Spaniards, who were among the capital's leading consumers of mutton. The subsequent trough in 1830 likewise coincided with a renewal of Apache wars along the northern frontier, which disrupted supplies, at least temporarily. See Harold D. Sims, *The Expulsion of Mexico City's Spaniards* (Pittsburgh: University of Pittsburgh Press, 1990); William B. Griffen, *The Apaches at War and Peace: The Janos Presidio, 1750–1858* (Albuquerque: University of New Mexico Press, 1988).

10. *Novísimo arte de cocina* (Mexico City: Alejandro Valdés, 1831), 12–24; *El cocinero mexicano*, 3 vols. (Mexico City: Galván, 1831), 2:6–58; *Manual del cocinero y cocinera tomado del periodico literario La Risa* (Puebla: José María Macías, 1849), 84, 90–135. See also *Nuevo y sencillo arte de cocina* (Mexico City: Santiago Pérez, 1836), 50, 164, 217; *Manual del cocinero, dedicado a las señoritas mexicanas* (Mexico City: Murguía, 1856), 27–28.

11. Vicenta Torres de Rubio, *Cocina michoacana* (Zamora: Imprenta Moderna, 1896), 45, 110; Jacinto Anduiza, *El libro del hogar* (Pachuca: Imprenta "La Europea," 1893), 198; *Nuevo cocinero mexicano en forme de diccionario: reproducción facsimilar* (Mexico City: Porrúa, 1986 [1888]), 70.

12. Antonio Garcia Cubas, *El libro de mis recuerdos* (Mexico City: Porrúa, 1986 [1904]), 251.

13. Determining the exact timing of this decline is made difficult by uncertainties about the urban population. Previously accepted figures indicated that the city may have grown from 130,000 inhabitants at the end of the colonial period to nearly 200,000 by mid-century and 330,000 by the census of 1895. This would mean the fall came during the early republic, corresponding to John Coatsworth's calculation that per capita domestic product for the entire nation fell from $73 in 1800 to $49 in 1860. More recent studies of actual censuses suggest, to the contrary, that the city's population remained roughly stable throughout the period, with any increases due to migration being offset by the mortality of disease, particularly cholera. If the city's population was constant,

then consumption actually increased slightly during the early republic, thus supporting a revisionist claim that Mexico experienced a moderate economic improvement in the 1840s. Under this assumption, the decline in living standards occurred during the liberal reform or the Porfiriato. Calculations are based on an average late colonial dressed weight of 115 kilograms and Porfirian weight of 140 kilograms per head of cattle and a flat 10 kilograms per sheep and 80 for hogs. For a summary of traditional population estimates, see Silvia Marina Arrom, *The Women of Mexico City, 1790–1857* (Stanford, CA: Stanford University Press, 1985), 285. The revisionist case is advanced by Sonia Pérez Toledo, *Los hijos del trabajo: Los artesanos de la ciudad de México, 1780–1853* (Mexico City: El Colegio de México, 1996), 39–49. John Coatsworth, "Obstacles to Economic Growth in Nineteenth-Century Mexico," *American Historical Review* 83, no. 1 (Feb. 1978): 80–100; Richard J. Salvucci, "Mexican National Income in the Era of Independence, 1800–1840," in *How Latin America Fell Behind: Essays on the Economic Histories of Brazil and Mexico, 1800–1914*, ed. Stephen Haber (Stanford, CA: Stanford University Press, 1997), 216–42.

14. *El Imparcial,* June 20, 1902.

15. Archivo Histórico de la Secretaría de Salud (hereafter AHSS), Inspección de Alimentos y Bebidas, exp. 20; *El Monitor Republicano,* December 18, 1848. For a modern description of a similar preparation, see Diana Kennedy, *My Mexico* (New York: Clarkson Potter, 1998), 465–71.

16. AGN, Abasto, vol. 8, exp. 16, fo. 266. See also Gabriel Haslip-Viera, *Crime and Punishment in Late Colonial Mexico City, 1692–1810* (Albuquerque: University of New Mexico Press, 1999), 76–77; Perez Toledo, *Los hijos del trabajo,* 229.

17. See, for example, García Cubas, *El libro de mis recuerdos,* 238–39; AHCM, vol. 3768, exp. 27, Carbajal report, November 30, 1849.

18. Quote from Manuel Antonio Carreño, *Manual de urbanidad y buenas maneras* (New York: D. Appleton, 1880), 262. Thanks to Victor Macías for pointing out this source. See also Carol J. Adams, *The Sexual Politics of Meat: A Feminist-Vegetarian Critical Theory* (New York: Continuum, 2000); Nick Fiddes, *Meat: A Natural Symbol* (London: Routledge, 1992); Lynn Stephen, *Zapotec Women* (Austin: University of Texas Press, 1991), 185–87; Chevalier, *Land and Society,* 106; William H. Beezley, "The Porfirian Smart Set Anticipates Thorstein Veblen in Guadalajara," in *Rituals of Rule, Rituals of Resistance: Public Celebrations and Popular Culture in Mexico,* ed. William H. Beezley, Cheryl English Martin, and William E. French (Wilmington, DE: Scholarly Resources, 1994), 180.

19. Hortensia Rendón de García, *Antiguo manual de cocina yucateca; fórmulas para condimentar los platos más usuales en la península,* 7th ed., 3 vols. (Mérida: Librería Burrel, 1938 [1st ed., 1898]), 55.

20. For a description of London meat jobbers, see Richard Perren, *The Meat Trade in Britain, 1840–1914* (London: Routledge & Kegan Paul, 1978), 36–41.

21. Ivonne Mijares, *Mestizo alimentario: El abasto de la ciudad de México en el siglo XVI* (Mexico City: UNAM, 1993); Barrett, "Meat Supply of Cuernavaca," 527; Constantino Bayle, *Los cabildos seculares en la América Española* (Madrid: Sapienta, 1952), 473–79; Dusenberry, "Regulation of Meat Supply," 41; AHCM, Actas, vol. 632A, March 21, 1539, vol. 635A, May 7, 1554, vol. 636A, February 19, 1563. On the European antecedents, see María Antonia Carmona Ruiz, *La ganadería en el*

reino de Sevilla durante la baja edad media (Sevilla: Diputación de Sevilla, 1998), 300–306. A similar system operated in southern France. See Louis Stouff, *La table provençale: Boire et manger en Provence à la fin du Moyen Age* (Avignon: Éditions A. Barthélemy, 1996), 99–103, 110.

22. Barrett, "Meat Supply of Cuernavaca," 526–27; Van Young, *Hacienda and Market*, 49–53; Thompson, *Puebla de los Angeles*, 131–35; Jorge Silva Riquer and María José Garrido Aspero, "Formas de abasto al mercado de Valladolid (1793–1800)," *Siglo XIX: Cuadernos de Historia* 3, no. 8 (January-April 1994): 45–77.

23. This division of retail markets was known as the *reparto de tablas*. For a listing of stockmen, see Doris M. Ladd, *The Mexican Nobility at Independence, 1780–1826* (Austin: University of Texas Press, 1976), 46–50, 94. See also Harris, *A Mexican Family Empire*, 79–85; D. A. Brading, *Miners and Merchants in Bourbon Mexico, 1763–1810* (Cambridge: Cambridge University Press, 1971), 124–28; AHCM, Actas, vol. 667A, November 19, 1714, p. 93, November 28, 1718, p. 143, March 6, 1719, p. 172, March 16, 1719, p. 175; Ignacio González-Polo, ed., *Reflexiones y apuntes sobre la ciudad de México (fines de la colonia)* (Mexico City: Departamento del Distrito Federal, 1981), 26; Hipólito Villarroel, *Efermedades políticas que padece la capital de esta Nueva España* (Mexico City: Conaculta, 1979), 167.

24. Archivo General de la Nación (hereafter AGN), Abasto, vol. 5, exp. 13, fo. 376; AHCM, vol. 8, exp. 256; Jorge González Angulo Aguirre, *Artesanado y ciudad a finales del siglo XVIII* (Mexico City: Fondo de Cultura Económica, 1983), 64.

25. Enrique Florescano, *Precios de maíz y crisis agrícolas* (Mexico City: El Colegio de México, 1969); Virginia García Acosta, "Las catastrophes agrícolas y sus efectos en la alimentación. Escasez y carestía de maíz, trigo, y carne en el México central a fines de la época colonial," in *Sociedad, economía y cultura alimentaria*, ed. Shoko Doode and Emma Paulina Pérez (Mexico City: CIESAS, 1994), 347–65.

26. AGN, Abasto, vol. 5, exp. 12, fo. 359, exp. 13, fo. 387–88, 393; González-Polo, *Reflexiones sobre la ciudad*, 26.

27. Thompson, *Puebla de los Angeles*, 130–35; Barrett, "Meat Supply of Cuernavaca," 538–40. On Enlightenment thought in the Spanish colonies, see more generally, D. A. Brading, *The First America: The Spanish monarchy, Creole patriots, and the Liberal state, 1492–1867* (Cambridge: Cambridge University Press, 1992); Robert J. Shafer, *The Economic Societies in the Spanish World (1763–1821)* (Syracuse, NY: Syracuse University Press, 1958); Dorothy Tanck de Estrada, "La abolición de los gremios," in *El trabajo y los trabajadores en la Historia de México*, ed. Elsa Cecilia Frost, Michael C. Meyer, and Josefina Zoraida Vázquez (Mexico City: El Colegio de México, 1979), 311–31.

28. AGN, Abasto, vol. 8, exp. 10, fo. 186, 191, quote from exp. 16, fo. 280; AHCM, vol. 8, exp. 256, 260, vol. 3768, exp. 7. Guy Thompson examined the effects of free trade in the city of Puebla and concluded: "The abolition of the abasto thus offers perhaps the only example of how a liberal economic reform directly contributed to a marked expansion of production and exchange, to the benefit of local and provincial interests and less privileged social groups." See, *Puebla de los Angeles*, 134–35. The question remains of how successfully Mexico City provisioned itself during the insurgency. By 1814, supplies of mutton had recovered from their earlier slump in 1812 and 1813 at least briefly, although it is impossible to draw similar conclusions about beef because cattle butchers had

largely abandoned the rastro and seldom paid municipal taxes. Certainly after 1815 and the abolition of customs duties on meat, the statistics are too sporadic to draw any firm conclusions. See AHCM, vol. 8, exp. 273, 280.

29. AHCM, vol. 3768, exp. 1, various rent statements, exp. 23, Francisco Carbajal report, August 29, 1849.

30. AHCM, vol. 3768, exp. 23, Carbajal report, January 20, 1849; Harris, *A Mexican Family Empire*, 244, 248.

31. Luis Cossío Silva, "La ganadería," in *El porfiriato: La vida económica*, vol. 7 of *Historia moderna de México*, ed. Daniel Cosío Villegas (Mexico City: Editorial Hermes, 1965), 135–78; Möisés González Navarro, *Estadísticas sociales del porfiriato* (Mexico City: Dirección General de Estadística, 1956), 9–11; *Anuario estadístico de la República Mexicana: 1906* (Mexico City: Secretaría de Fomento, 1910), 37–39.

32. Diego López Rosado, *Historia y pensamiento económico de México*, 6 vols. (Mexico City: UNAM, 1968), 1:116–17; Karl Kraeger, *Agricultura y colonización en México en 1900*, trans. Pedro Lewin and Gudrun Dohrmann (Chapingo: Universidad Autónoma de Chapingo, 1986), 301; Cuauhtémoc Esparza Sánchez, *Historia de la ganadería en Zacatecas, 1531–1911* (Zacatecas: Universidad Autónoma de Zacatecas, 1988), 68.

33. Schyer, *Ethnicity and Class Conflict*, 81–83, 102; Cossío Silva, "La ganadería," 147–49, 152; *Mexican Year Book* (London : McCorquodale & Co., 1910), 397–98. ·

34. The Spanish term "ranchero" differed from its English cognate by referring to freehold farmers generally rather than just stockmen. Ranchero society has been described most famously by Luis González y González, *Pueblo en vilo: Microhistoria de San José de Gracia* (Mexico City: El Colegio de México, 1972). For an analysis of the early growth of smallholders, see D. A. Brading, *Haciendas and Ranchos in the Mexican Bajío León, 1700–1860* (Cambridge: Cambridge University Press, 1978). Margaret Chowning has described the effects of the reform laws, and concluded that there may well have been efficiency gains as a result. See her *Wealth and Power in Provincial Mexico: Michoacán from the Late Colony to the Revolution* (Stanford, CA: Stanford University Press, 1999), 263, 288. On colonization, see Hubert Cochet, Eric Léonard, and Jean Damien de Surgy, *Paisajes agrarios de Michoacán* (Zamora: El Colegio de Michoacán, 1988).

35. Schyer, *Ethnicity and Class Conflict*, 153–54; Cossío Silva, "La ganadería," 147–48; Guy P. C. Thompson with David G. LaFrance, *Patriotism, Politics, and Popular Liberalism in Nineteenth-Century Mexico: Juan Francisco Lucas and the Puebla Sierra* (Wilmington, DE: Scholarly Resources, 1999), 32, 188; AHCM, vol. 3773, exp. 431.

36. Information on importer practices was gained from a Mexico City interview with TIF inspector Laura Varinia Muñoz Huerta, the granddaughter of a Porfirian livestock merchant, on July 19, 2001. For a comparison of merchant practices in New York and Mexico City, see Horowitz, Pilcher, and Watts, "Meat for the Multitudes," 1060–65. On village commons, see Andrés Lira, *Comunidades indígenas frente a la Ciudad de México: Tenochtitlan y Tlatelolco, sus pueblos y barrios, 1812–1919* (Mexico City: El Colegio de México, 1995), 209; Charles Gibson, *The Aztecs Under Spanish Rule: A History of the Indians of the Valley of Mexico, 1519–1810* (Stanford, CA: Stanford University Press, 1964), 369–70.

37. Sandra Kuntz Ficker, *Empresa extanjera y mercado interno: El Ferrocarril Central Mexicano, 1880–1907* (Mexico City: El Colegio de México, 1995), 228–34;

Arthur Schmidt, *The Social and Economic Effect of the Railroad in Puebla and Veracruz, Mexico, 1867–1911* (New York: Garland, 1987), 202; Schyer, *Ethnicity and Class Conflict*, 153; "Successful and Interesting Trial Trip of a New Cattle Car," *American Railroad Journal* 57, no. 3 (June 1883): 98.

38. Ireneo Paz and Manuel Tornel, *Nueva guía de México* (Mexico City: Imprenta de I. Paz, 1882), 811; John W. DeKay, *The Men of Mexico and the Land They Love* (Syracuse, NY: Mason-Henry Press, 1906), 22; Roderic A. Camp, *Mexican Political Biographies, 1884–1935* (Austin: University of Texas Press, 1991), 284–338.

39. Biblioteca Nacional de Antropología e Historia, Fondo Lira, vol. 346, 409–10.

40. AHCM, vol. 3768, exp. 3, Pérez Gálvez proposal, June 20, 1844.

41. Barrett, "Meat Supply of Cuernavaca," 527; AGN, Abasto, vol. 8, exp. 16, fo. 266.

42. John E. Kicza, *Colonial Entrepreneurs: Families and Business in Bourbon Mexico City* (Albuquerque: University of New Mexico Press, 1983), 196–200.

43. AGN, Abasto, vol. 8, exp. 16, fo. 266.

44. Margaret Chowning, "Reassessing the Prospects for Profit in Nineteenth-Century Mexican Agriculture from a Regional Perspective: Michoacán, 1810–60," in *How Latin America Fell Behind: Essays on the Economic Histories of Brazil and Mexico, 1800–1914*, ed. Stephen Haber (Stanford, CA: Stanford University Press, 1997), 201; Bullock, *Six Months in Mexico*, 259; *Guía de forasteros de la ciudad de México* (Mexico City, 1854), 326–17; González Angulo, *Artesanado y ciudad*, 79, 85–87; Kicza, *Colonial Entrepreneurs*, 196–200; Thompson, *Puebla de los Angeles*, 140–46; Archivo General de Notarías del Distrito Federal (hereafter AGNDF), José Qurejazu, vol. 3731, fo. 245–60, August 18, 1854, Miguel Aristegui, vol. 296, fo. 15–22, February 18, 1851.

45. This point has been made recently by Sonia Pérez Toledo, "Artesanos y gremios de la ciudad de México: Una desaparición formal y una continuidad real, 1780–1842," in *Ciudad de México: Instituciones, actores sociales y conflicto político, 1774–1931*, ed. Carlos Illades and Ariel Rodríguez (Zamora: El Colegio de Michoacán, 1996), 223–44. An earlier generation of labor historians argued that the abolition of guilds caused a decline in skilled trades. See, most notably, Felipe Castro Gutiérrez, *La extinción de la artesanía gremial* (Mexico City: UNAM, 1986).

46. Chowning, "Reassessing Profit in Mexican Agriculture," 201.

47. AGN, Gobernación, 2a Series, 870, box 3, exp. 1, petition of Pedro Serrano, et al, to council, May 1870.

48. *El Monitor Republicano*, July 5, 1870; AGN, Gobernación, 2a series, 880, box 1, exp. 3, Montiel to Minister of Gobernación, May 13, 1872.

49. AGNDF, vol. 296, fo. 15, Miguel Aristegui, February 18, 1851; vol. 617, fo. 1024–31, Agustín Roldán, October 1, 1892; AHCM, vol. 3670, exp. 165, Fernández report, February 18, 1882, Aragón report, May 24, 1882.

50. AHCM, vol. 3771, exp. 297, Manuel Navarette, September 8, 1877. See also Emiliano Busto, "Cuaderno estadístico de la industria en el Distrito Federal," annex 3 of *Estadístico de la República Mexicana*, 3 vols. (Mexico City: Ignacio Cumplido, 1880); Ireneo Paz and Manuel Tornel, *Nueva guía de México* (Mexico City: Imprenta de I. Paz, 1882), 850.

51. AHCM vol. 3771, exp. 351, proposal dated May 6, 1879; vol. 1106, exp. 7, 8, various plans.

52. Quoted by Jean Claude Bonnet, "The culinary system in the *Encyclopedie*," in

Food and Drink in History: Selections from the Annales Economies, Sociétés, Civilisations, ed. Robert Forster and Orest Ranum, trans. Elborg Forster and Patricia Ranum (Baltimore: Johns Hopkins University Press, 1979), 165; Maguelonne Toussaint-Samat, *A History of Food*, trans. Anthea Bell (Cambridge, MA: Blackwell, 1992), 111; Emily Gowers, *The Loaded Table: Representations of Food in Roman Literature* (Oxford: Clarendon Press, 1993), 77; Carlo Poni, "Local market rules and practices. Three guilds in the same line of production in early modern Bologna," in *Domestic strategies: Work and family in France and Italy, 1600–1800*, ed. Stuart Woolf (Cambridge: Cambridge University Press, 1991), 88; Stouff, *La table provençale*, 79.

53. Arias, "El tocinero," 286.
54. AGNDF, vol. 2174, fo. 81–89, Tomás Hidalgo de los Reyes, October 23, 1811; González Angulo, *Artesanado y ciudad*, 64; Kicza, *Colonial Entrepreneurs*, 196–99; Gibson, *Aztecs under Spanish Rule*, 346.
55. On France, see Sydney Watts, "Meat Matters," 130–42; Dusenberry, "Regulation of Meat Supply," 43; AGN, Padrones, vols. 54–77, Censo de 1811.
56. Quote from AHCM, vol. 8, exp. 282, común de carniceros petition, May 20, 1813; exp. 52, inventory, February 27, 1759; vol. 1106, exp. 1, Manuel Alvarez statement, March 17, 1751, Gaspar Hurtado de Mendoza statement, March 8, 1752.
57. Quote from AHCM, vol. 8, exp. 282, May 20, 1813. See also González Angulo, *Artesanado y ciudad*, 51, 64.
58. AGN, Gobernación, 2a. series, 870, vol. 3, exp. 1, Robert to Juárez, December 12, 1870; *El Tiempo*, August 25, 1905; *El Imparcial*, August 30, 1897.
59. Quote from *El Siglo XIX*, December 5, 1870. See also AHCM, vol. 3728, exp. 47, Junta de Policia, July 24, 1798; vol. 3732, exp. 363, petitions of Miguel Gómez Flores, November 16, 1861, J. G. Brito, April 4, 1862.
60. *El Economista Mexicano*, May 3, 1902.
61. See, for example, Antonio Garcia Cubas, *El libro de mis recuerdos* (Mexico City: Porrúa, 1986 [1904]), 238–39, AHCM, vol. 3768, exp. 27, Carbajal report, November 30, 1849; Carlos Chanfón Olmos, ed., *Historia de la architectura y el urbanismo mexicanos*, vol. 3, *El México independiente*, tome 2, *Afirmación del nacionalism y la modernidad* (Mexico City: UNAM, 1998), 126.
62. AHCM, vol. 645, exp. 9, Xochimilco sanitary inspector report, September 13, 1904; vol. 3739, various market inspection reports; vol. 3732, exp. 317, Elena Piniano petition, February 19, 1857; AGN, Padrones, vol. 60, fo. 182; Ramo Civil, leg. 84, no. 30, undated but probably late eighteenth century; Sonya Lipsett-Rivera, "*De obra y palabra*: Patterns of Insults in Mexico, 1750–1856," *The Americas* 54, no. 4 (April 1998): 529; Kicza, *Colonial Entrepreneurs*, 197; Thompson, *Puebla de los Angeles*, 86; Van Young, *Hacienda and Market*, 55. Women also worked as tripe makers in the slaughterhouses of Rio de Janeiro. See Mary Karasch, "Suppliers, Sellers, Servants, and Slaves," in *Cities and Society in Colonial Latin America*, ed. Louisa Schell Hoberman and Susan Migden Socolow (Albuquerque: University of New Mexico Press, 1986), 267.
63. AGN, Criminal, vol. 187, exp. 13, fo. 239–49, January 1783; AGN, Inquisición, vol. 458, exp. 20, fo. 234–35, April 1657, vol. 973, exp. 9, fo. 189–90, October 13, 1753.
64. AGN, Inquisición, vol. 458, exp. 20, fo. 234–35, April 1659.

65. *Ordenanza del ramo*, 7–8.
66. Kuecker, "A Desert in the Tropical Wilderness," chapter 3; Contreras Cruz, "Ciudad y salud," 66–70. For comparative perspective, see Barbara Gutmann Rosenkrantz, *Public Health and the State: Changing Views in Massachusetts, 1842–1936* (Cambridge, MA: Harvard University Press, 1972).
67. Quoted in Dusenberry, "Regulation of Meat Supply," 45. See also Mijares, *Mestizo alimentario*, 93; John Super, *Food, Conquest, and Colonization*, 44–49.
68. Quote from González-Polo, *Reflexiones sobre la ciudad*, 27. See also AGN, Abasto, vol. 8, exp. 16, fo. 266; Haslip-Viera, *Crime and Punishment*, 76–77.
69. Villarroel, *Efermedades políticas*, 167; AHCM, Actas, vol. 629A, October 26, 1526; Super, *Food, Conquest, and Colonization*, 46–47; John Preston Moore, *The Cabildo in Peru Under the Habsburgs* (Durham, NC: Duke University Press, 1954), 169–70.
70. AHCM, vol. 3668, exp 21, council decrees of February 9, 1822 and November 4, 1831; vol. 3768, exp. 7, council decree of June 23, 1821; AGN, Gobernación, 2a. series, 870, box 3, exp. 1, Antonio Escandón to Minister of Gobernación, April 27, 1869. See more generally Anne Staples, *"Policia y Buen Gobierno*: Municipal Efforts to Regulate Public Behavior, 1821–1857," in *Rituals of Rule, Rituals of Resistance: Public Celebrations and Popular Culture in Mexico*, ed. William H. Beezley, Cheryl English Martin, and William E. French (Wilmington, DE: Scholarly Resources, 1994), 115–26.
71. AHCM, vol. 3758, exp. 22, Ramón Rayón to council, March 17, 1839.
72. AHCM, vol. 3622, exp. 8, Commission report, May 2, 1844.
73. *El Siglo XIX*, June 15, 1844, supplement; *El Mosquito Mexicano*, June 18, 1844. See also Cheng-chung Lai, ed., *Adam Smith Across Nations: Translations and Receptions of* The Wealth of Nations (Oxford: Oxford University Press, 2000).
74. AHCM, vol. 3768, exp. 5, contract of October 21, 1848, exp. 23, Carbajal report, April 9, 1849.
75. AHCM, vol. 3768, exp. 23, Carbajal report, July 31, 1849, Cárdenas et al. to council, May 22, 1849, Carbajal report, August 29, 1849.
76. The indemnification package consisted of land, water rights, and at least $2,100 in cash, plus the return of all fees and fines paid in the previous year and a half. See AHCM, vol. 3768, exp. 23, Ramírez and Arellano agreement, November 26, 1849. *Ordenanza del ramo de carnes de la municipalidad de México* (Mexico City: Imprenta Vicente García Torres, 1850).
77. AHCM, vol. 3769, exp. 39, Carbajal report, July 3, 1851, vol. 3768, exp. 23, Carbajal report, April 12, 1849, González de Cosío to Carbajal, April 27, 1849.
78. AHCM, vol. 3769, exp. 48, Tosta to council, June 27, 1853, Buenrostro to council, June 28, 1853, District Governor, August 21, 1853.
79. Ignacio Trigueros, *Memoria de los Ramos Municipales* (Mexico City: Imprenta Económica, 1866), 79–80.
80. AGN, Gobernación, 2a series, 870, box 3, exp. 1, petitions of Antonio Escandón et al, to Secretary of Interior, April 12, 27, 1869, petition of Pedro Serrano, et al, to ayuntamiento, May 1870; *El Monitor Republicano*, July 5, 1870.
81. Trigueros, *Memoria de los Ramos Municipales*, 55.
82. AGN, Gobernación, 2a series, 870, box 3, exp. 1, Vélez to Gobernación, December 2, 1870.
83. *El Siglo XIX*, December 4, 1870.

84. AGN, Gobernación, 2a series, 870, box 3, exp. 1, Ocaranza to Juárez, December 7, 18, 1870; Cipriano Robert to Juárez, December 12, 1870.

85. AGN, Governación, 2a series, 870, box 3, exp. 1, Saavedra decree, January 12, 1871; General Francisco Paz report, November 21, 1874.

86. Joanna Swabe, *Animals, Disease and Human Society: Human-Animal Relations and the Rise of Veterinary Medicine* (London: Routledge, 1999), 85–94; Calvin Schwabe, *Cattle, Priests, and Progress in Medicine* (Minneapolis: University of Minnesota Press, 1978), 156–57; Saucedo Montemayor, *Historia de la ganadería*, 240–43; Trigueros, *Memoria de los Ramos Municipales*, 54.

87. AGN, Gobernación, 2a. series, 872, box 8, exp. 8, Fuentes and Gutiérrez to Juárez, April 22, 1872, 880, box 1, exp. 3, Montiel to Minister of Gobernación, May 13, 1872.

88. Glen David Kuecker, "The Consejo Superior de Salubridad Pública in Porfirian Mexico" (unpublished manuscript).

89. Ariel Rodríguez Kuri, *La experiencia olvidada. El Ayuntamiento de México: política y gobierno, 1876–1912* (Mexico City: El Colegio de México, 1996), 62; AHCM, vol. 3772, exp. 420, regulation dated December 28, 1886; vol. 3773, exp. 435, Julian Herrera petition, September 18, 1888.

90. On popular stereotypes, see, for example, *La Patria*, September 8, 1897.

91. José Antonio Aguilar Rivera, *En pos de la quimera: Reflexiones sobre el experimento constitucional atlántico* (Mexico City: Fondo de Cultura Económica, 2000), 34–43. Any comparison between the economic application of liberalism in the United States and Mexico must also consider William Novak's persuasive argument that antebellum municipal governance gave far more concern to the "people's welfare" than to the supposedly preeminent liberal ideal of private property. See, *The People's Welfare: Law and Regulation in Nineteenth-Century America* (Chapel Hill: University of North Carolina Press, 1996).

CHAPTER TWO

1. Alan Knight, *The Mexican Revolution*, 2 vols. (Cambridge: Cambridge University Press, 1986), 1:15.

2. Carlos Marichal, "Las estrategias de la deuda durante el Porfiriato: La conversión del empréstito de 1888 y el papel de Banamex como el banco del gobierno," in *Don Porfirio presidente..., Nunca omnipotente: Hallazgos, reflexiones y debates. 1876–1911*, ed. Romana Falcón and Raymond Buve (Mexico City: Universidad Iberoamericana, 1998), 39–62.

3. This debate is summarized by Oscar Schwartz, *Public Abattoirs and Cattle Markets* (London: "Ice and Cold Storage" Publishing Company, Ltd., 1901), 1–45.

4. *Boletín del Consejo Superior de Salubridad*, September 20, 1880.

5. Ibid; AHCM, vol. 3670, exp. 162, proposal dated 1882; Buffington, *Criminal and Citizen*, 96.

6. Quoted in Giedion, *Mechanization Takes Command*, 213.

7. Ibid, 211–24; Margaret Walsh, *The Rise of the Midwestern Meat Packing Industry* (Lexington: University Press of Kentucky, 1982), 27–29; Yeager, *Competition and Regulation*, 58–63. The exception to this rule came from kosher butchers catering to the Jewish immigrant population.

8. AHCM, vol. 1106, exp. 12, Lewis to council president, October 5, 1890, August

25, 1891; *El Imparcial,* June 15, 1901. Inquiries in the Swift papers at the Newberry Library in Chicago turned up nothing on Mexican ventures.

9. AHCM, vol. 3762, exp. 39, Jesús Galindo y Villa report, September 30, 1900; Piccato, *City of Suspects,* 118–19.

10. AHCM, vol. 3762, exp. 4, commission report, March 6, 1890, vol. 3773, exp. 441, Antonio Torres Torrija report, November 24, 1888.

11. Connolly, *El contratista de don Porfirio,* 52–72; AHCM, vol. 3762, exp. 4, commission report, March 6, 1890.

12. AHCM, vol. 3762, exp. 6, Blanco to council, May 6, August 7, 1890, Blanco to Díaz, October 20, 1890, Torres Torrija commission, October 20, 1890; Piccato, *City of Suspects,* 193.

13. AHCM, vol. 3762, exp. 6, Arozarena to Blanco, July 28, 1891, exp. 5, Blanco to council president, April 20, 1891, Torres Torrija to council president, April 27, 1891.

14. AHCM, vol. 3762, exp. 6, Blanco to council president, August 1, 1891.

15. AHCM, Actas, vol. 702A, October 27, November 17, 30, 1891; Manuel María Contreras, *Memoria del Ayuntamiento de la Ciudad de México de 1892* (Mexico City: Impreso de F. Díaz de León, 1893), 117–32; Camp, *Mexican Political Biographies,* 172–73, 209–10; Rodríguez Kuri, *La experiencia olvidada,* 64.

16. AHCM, vol. 3762, exp. 7, arbitration decree of June 28, 1892, Torres Torrija to council, October 2, 1892.

17. Various proposals and the contract can be found in AHCM, vol. 3762, exp. 9, vol. 3773, exp. 459, 460. A report by city commissioners was printed in *El Municipio Libre,* June 22, 1893.

18. AHCM, vol. 3762, exp. 12, Arozarena to municipal president, June 6, 1894, Hahn to municipal president, July 2, 1894, exp. 13, commission report, September 5, 1893, vol. 3763, exp. 14, Plowes to municipal president, December 10, 1894, exp. 18, inspection report, April 30, 1895.

19. AHCM, vol. 3763, exp. 18, inspection report, April 30, 1895.

20. AHCM, vol. 3763, exp. 18, Hahn to council, July 4, 1895.

21. AHCM, vol. 3763, exp. 25, slaughterhouse commission report, December 17, 1897; Sebastián Camacho, *Memoria del Ayuntamiento de la Ciudad de Mexico de 1895* (Mexico City: Imprenta "La Europea," 1896), 110.

22. AHCM, vol. 3763, exp. 15, commission report, November 18, 1895, exp. 16, Gómez to Health Board, June 15, 1895.

23. The health code is printed in Sebastián Camacho, *Memoria del Ayuntamiento de la Ciudad de México de 1897* (Mexico City: Imprenta "La Europea," 1898), 364–75. See also AHCM, vol. 3670, exp. 201, city council ruling, March 7, 1894. For the published inspection reports, see the issues beginning with *El Municipio Libre,* April 13, 1894.

24. Ariel Rodríguez Kuri, in *La experiencia olvidada,* 152–57, has documented Macedo's role in concentrating the railroad holdings in the Federal District. In 1898, for example, the Mexican lawyer replaced MacLean as president of the railroad company. Macedo's negotiations to establish the Nueva Colonia del Rastro are described in *Boletín del Consejo de Gobierno,* July 30, 1909, p.129. AHCM, vol. 3763, exp. 24, contains the draft agreement, dated June 7, 1897, between Plowes, MacLean, and Macedo. It is unclear whether de Ghest still

retained any interest in the colonia.

25. This description comes from the December 17, 1897, report of commissioner José de la Luz Gómez, AHCM, vol. 3763, exp. 25; *El Mundo*, September 2, 1897.

26. *Mexican Herald*, September 5, 1897; *El Popular*, September 4, 8, 1897; *El Mundo* and the *Mexican Herald* mistakenly reported González had died in the accident.

27. *Diario del Hogar*, September 8, 9, 1897; *El Nacional*, September 6, 1897; AHCM, vol. 3763, exp. 25, Gómez report, December 17, 1897.

28. AHCM, vol. 3774, exp. 493, importers' petition, September 1897; *Diario del Hogar*, September 9, 1897; *El Imparcial*, September 15, 1897.

29. AHCM, vol. 3774, exp. 499, butcher captains to council, September 14, 1897.

30. Gómez response quoted in *El Imparcial*, September 8, 1897; *La Patria*, September 28, 1897; *Diario del Hogar*, September 25, 1897.

31. AHCM, vol. 3763, exp. 25, Manuel G. Aragón to Gómez, September 30, 1897, Gómez report, December 17, 1897; *Diario del Hogar*, September 28, 1897.

32. *El Mundo*, October 5, 1897.

33. Richard Weiner, "Competing Market Discourses in Porfirian Mexico," *Latin American Perspectives* 26, no. 1 (January 1999): 44–64.

34. *El Imparcial*, August 30, September 8, 30, 1897; *El Mundo*, September 2, 1897.

35. *El Imparcial*, September 8, 15, 1897.

36. *Diario del Hogar*, September 7, 9, 25, 28, 1897.

37. *El Popular*, September 4, 11, 1897; *La Patria*, September 7, 8, 28, October 6, 1897.

38. *El Tiempo*, September 7, 22, October 6, 1897.

39. Ibid, September 7, October 3, 14, 1897.

40. *La Patria*, September 8, 1897; *El Popular*, September 11, 1897.

41. *La Patria*, September 12, 1897.

42. Ibid, September 25, 1897.

43. Quote from *El Tiempo*, September 30, 1897; AHCM, vol. 3764, exp. 30, Fernández et al., to González Cosío, April 1899.

44. AHCM, vol. 3774, exp. 499, butcher captains to council, September 14, 1897.

45. On the paternalistic nature of Porfirian labor, and the subsequent revolutionary mobilization of urban workers, see John Lear, *Workers, Neighbors, and Citizens: The Revolution in Mexico City* (Lincoln: University of Nebraska Press, 2001).

46. AHCM, vol. 3763, exp. 25, Gómez report, Dec 17, 1897; exp. 28, Ramírez report, June 8, 1898; vol. 3764, exp. 39, Galindo report, September 30, 1900.

47. AHCM, vol. 3763, exp. 28, Ramírez report, June 8, 1898, vol. 3764, exp. 39, Galindo report, September 30, 1900; Miguel S. Macedo, *Memoria documentada de los trabajos municipales de 1899* (Mexico City: Tip. "La Europea," 1900), 230.

CHAPTER THREE

1. *El Imparcial*, July 8, 1902.

2. Ibid, July 9, 1902; Mark Wasserman, *Capitalists, Caciques, and Revolution: The Native Elite and Foreign Enterprise in Chihuahua, Mexico, 1854–1911* (Chapel Hill: University of North Carolina Press, 1984), 5, 45.

3. Yeager, *Competition and Regulation*, 178–212. See more generally Alfred D. Chandler, Jr., *The Visible Hand: The Managerial Revolution in American Business* (Cambridge: Harvard University Press, 1977).

4. Wasserman, *Capitalists, Caciques, and Revolution*, chapters 2, 3.

5. Centro de Estudios de Historia de México, Condumex, Archivo José Yves Limantour (hereafter, AJYL), roll 4, carp. 14, A. J. Morris to Limantour, August 24, 1900; AGN, Industrias Nuevas, box 6, leg. 11, Joaquín D. Casasus to Secretary of Development, November 17, 1902; Kraeger, *Agricultura y colonización*, 301–3; Wasserman, *Capitalists, Çaciques, and Revolution*, 58–59; *El Economista Mexicano*, September 27, 1902; *El Tiempo*, November 25, 1900; *El Imparcial*, March 5, 1905.

6. *El Economista Mexicano*, September 6, November 8, 1902, April 22, 1911; *Monterey News*, September 15, 1903, May 16, June 30, August 3, 1905; *México Industrial*, November 15, 1905; Cuauhtémoc Esparza Sánchez, *Historia de la ganadería en Zacatecas, 1531–1911* (Zacatecas: Universidad Autónoma de Zacatecas, 1988), 130–34.

7. *El Economista Mexicano*, May 3, 1902. See also *El Imparcial*, February 17, 1902.

8. *El Imparcial*, February 7, June 20, 1902; *El Tiempo*, May 11, 1900; *El Hijo del Ahuizote*, July 16, 1899.

9. *El Mundo*, March 27, 1890; *El Imparcial*, July 28, 1898, February 7, 1902.

10. *La Patria*, September 8, 1897.

11. *El Imparcial*, February 18, 1902. For a fuller discussion of Porfirian nutritional discourse, see Pilcher, *¡Que vivan los tamales!*, Chapter 4.

12. *El Imparcial*, January 9, 10, 1902; *El Mundo*, January 28, February 18, 1902.

13. AHSS, Inspección, box 1, exp. 15, Health Board report, October 5, 1894, R. Mancerola to Secretary of Interior, October 9, 1894; *Gil Blas*, September 28, 1894.

14. *El Imparcial*, August 6, 1898. AHCM, vol. 3774, exp. 522, Manuel Aragón report, June 2, 1898.

15. AHCM, vol. 3775, exp. 560, Rafael Gómez to Municipal President, March 1, 1900, Manuel Aragón report, March 12, 1900, Jesús Galindo y Villa report, March 16, 1900.

16. AGNDF, Agustín Roldán, vol. 4282, fo. 715–19, August 31, 1892; Eduardo Galán, vol. 1940, fo. 778–82, December 26, 1889.

17. AGNDF, Agustín Roldán, vol. 4282, fo. 1632–43, December 3, 1892; Alberto Ferreiro, 1896, 2a. Semester, 1a. Parte, fo. 593–96, August 19, 1896; AHCM, vol. 3774, exp. 528, Rastro Commission, July 1, 1898, Ramírez petition, January 26, 1899.

18. AGNDF, Alberto Ferreiro, 1898, 2a. semestre, 2a. parte, fo. 677–78, October 18, 1898, 1901, 1a. semestre, fo. 4–19, December 22, 1900; AHCM, vol. 3774, exp. 524, Aragón report, May 11, 1898; *El Tiempo*, December 23, 1900; *El Imparcial*, June 15, 1901.

19. AHCM, vol. 3774, exp. 3774, Eduardo Noriega report, October 30, 1898, exp. 528, Ramírez and Zepeda, July 7, 1902; vol. 3775, exp. 559, Manuel Aragón to Regidor de Rastros, April 19, 1900, exp. 585, Aragón, August 24, 1901; quote from vol. 3776, exp. 608, Ramírez and Zepeda to Municipal President, August 1, 1902.

20. AHCM, vol. 3776, exp. 613, Martínez report, January 15, 1903.

21. AHCM, vol. 3776, exp. 610, Municipal Treasury audit, April 17, 1903, exp. 613, Ramírez and Zepeda to Municipal President, May 8, 1903.

22. Quote from *El Tiempo*, January 21, 1903. See also AHCM, vol. 3776, exp. 605, Ramón Corral to Municipal President, April 4, 1902, exp. 612, Rastro report,

April 17, 1903.

23. AHCM, vol. 3776, exp. 600, importers' proposal, June 17, 1902.

24. AHCM, vol. 3776, exp. 603, González brothers to Municipal President, June 20, 1902.

25. Arturo Grunstein, "Surgimiento de los Ferrocarriles Nacionales en México (1900–1913): ¿Era inevitable la consolidación monopólica?" in *Historia de las grandes empresas en México, 1850–1930*, ed. Carlos Marichal and Mario Cerutti (Mexico City: Fondo de Cultura Económica, 1997), 78–82.

26. AHCM, vol. 3764, exp. 45, opinion and contract, August 21, 1903.

27. AHCM, vol. 3776, exp. 600, importers' memoranda, September 2, 16, 1902, exp. 602, memo, September 18, 1902.

28. AHCM, vol. 3764, exp. 46, Ortega to Ayuntamiento, September 8, 1902. Comparative profit yields were calculated by Haber, *Industry and Underdevelopment*, 111–14.

29. AHCM, vol. 3764, exp. 48, contract dated November 14, 1903.

30. *El Tiempo*, January 23, 25, 1900.

31. Rodríguez Kuri, *La experiencia olvidada*, 66, 72–80; *Boletín Oficial del Consejo Superior de Gobierno del Distrito Federal*, July 7, 1903.

32. AHCM, vol. 3764, exp. 48, commission report, November 27, 1903; Wasserman, *Capitalists, Caciques, and Revolution*, 41; *El Tiempo*, April 23, 1903.

33. *Boletín del Consejo de Gobierno*, January 8, 1904.

34. Ibid, March 3, 1905.

35. *El Imparcial*, February 9, 1905; *El Tiempo*, January 26, 1905.

36. Hira de Gortari Rabiela and Regina Hernández Franyuti, ed., *La ciudad de México y el Distrito Federal (1824–1928)*, 4 vols. (Mexico City: Instituto Mora, 1988), 2:265; Dean MacCannell, *The Tourist: A New Theory of the Leisure Class* (New York: Schocken Books, 1976).

37. *Monterey News*, February 27, 1905.

38. *El Tiempo*, February 28, 1905; *Boletín del Consejo de Gobierno*, March 3, 1905; *El Imparcial*, March 5, 1905, December 15, 1907.

39. AHCM, vol. 1279, exp. 5, Luis Padilla and Adolfo Fernández petition, March 20, 1905.

40. *El Tiempo*, March 12, 1905.

41. *El Imparcial*, March 14, 1905.

42. AHCM, vol. 1279, exp. 5, Padilla and Fernández petition, March 20, 1905.

43. AHCM, vol. 1279, exp. 5, Interior Secretary, May 27, 1905; *El Tiempo*, April 15, August 25, 1905.

44. *El Tiempo*, January 22, 28, 31, February 1, 4, 5, 18, 22, 25, 1905.

45. AHCM, vol. 1279, exp. 2, Zepeda to Interior Secretary, May 20, 1905, R. Núñez, June 5, 1905, Guillermo Landa y Escandón, August 15, 1905; *El Imparcial*, June 23, 1905; *El Tiempo*, August 10, 1905.

46. *El Tiempo*, August 25, 26, 27, 31, September 28, October 22, 1905.

47. AHCM, vol. 640, exp. 3, Health Board to Government Council, August 21, September 22, 1903, exp. 5, Health Board to Government Council, July 21, 1905, Tacuba cabildo to Government Council, February 6, 1907, Interior Secretary to Government Council, July 23, 1907. See also Lira, *Comunidades indígenas*.

48. AHSS, Higiene Veterinaria, box 1, exp. 38, report of Francisco Flores, February 11,

1907; Diana Kennedy, *Recipes from the Regional Cooks of Mexico* (New York: Harper & Row, 1978), 127. Kennedy's Oaxacan informant made barbacoa from goat.

49. AHCM, vol. 1278, exp. 1, Luis Espinosa report, July 4, 1904; vol. 640, exp. 20, Hinkle to District Governor, November 19, 1906; exp. 23, Treasury to Escalante, May 31, 1907; AHSS, Inspección, box 1, exp. 24, Dr. Jesús E. Monjarás to Veterinary Inspector Francisco López Vallejo, September 21, 1907.

50. *El Tiempo*, November 9, 1905; *El Imparcial*, July 30, October 2, 1907; Wasserman, *Capitalists, Caciques, and Revolution*, 58.

51. Rodríguez Kuri, *La experiencia olvidada*, 69.

CHAPTER FOUR

1. Washington National Record Center (hereafter WNRC), U.S.-Mexico Claims, RG 76, entry 125, agency 4850, "John W. DeKay Memorial," June 3, 1927, 10. Notice of his arrival appeared in *El Imparcial*, August 15, 1901. On Díaz's personal relationship with foreign investors, see Colin M. MacLachlan and William H. Beezley, *El Gran Pueblo: A History of Greater Mexico*, 2d ed. (Upper Saddle River, NJ: Prentice-Hall, 1999), 168–69.

2. WNRC, Claims, RG 76, entry 125, agency 4850, "DeKay Memorial," 1. His claim of U.S. citizenship was challenged by the Mexican government. See ibid, "Mexican Government Response," 1. See also José Napoleón Guzmán Avila, "Inversiones extranjeras: Origen y desarrollo," in *Historia general de Michoacán*, vol. 3, *El siglo XIX*, ed. Gerardo Sánchez Díaz (Morelia: Gobierno de Michoacán, 1989), 174; Tony Morgan, "Proletarians, Politicos, and Patriarchs: The Use and Abuse of Cultural Customs in the Early Industrialization of Mexico City, 1880–1910," in *Rituals of Rule, Rituals of Resistance: Public Celebrations and Popular Culture in Mexico*, ed. William H. Beezley, Cheryl English Martin, and William E. French (Wilmington, DE: SR Books, 1994), 157. On Lipton, see Jack Goody, *Cooking, Cuisine, and Class: A Study in Comparative Sociology* (Cambridge: Cambridge University Press, 1982), 168–69; L. G. Wickham Legg, ed., *Dictionary of National Biography, 1931–1940* (Oxford: Oxford University Press, 1949), 539–40.

3. Juan E. Richelet, *La ganadería argentina y su comercio de carnes* (Buenos Aires: J. Lajouane & Cía, 1928), 19–21, 47, 169.

4. William Schell, Jr., *Integral Outsiders: The American Colony in Mexico City, 1876–1911* (Wilmington, DE: SR Books, 2001).

5. Edward Beatty, *Institutions and Investment: The Political Basis of Industrialization in Mexico Before 1911* (Stanford, CA: Stanford University Press, 2001).

6. José María Pérez Hernández, *Compendio de la geografía del estado de Michoacán de Ocampo* (Mexico City: Imprenta del comercio de Nabor Chávez, 1872), 88–89.

7. *El Imparcial*, August 15, 1901; *Monterey News*, April 29, 1905.

8. Universidad Iberoamericana, Archivo Porfirio Díaz (hereafter APD), leg. 34, no. 014172, Ortega to Díaz, August 1909; WNRC, Claims, RG 76, entry 125, agency 4850, "Mexican Government Response," Annex 2, contract between Mercado and Cortes Rubio, May 2, 1899; José Napoleón Guzmán Avila, "Uruapan del Progreso," in *Pueblos, villas y ciudades de Michoacán en el Porfiriato*, ed. Gerardo Sánchez Díaz (Morelia: Universidad Michoacana de San Nicolás de Hidalgo, 1991), 178–80.

9.   WNRC, Claims, RG 76, entry 125, agency 4850, "Mexican Government Response," Annex 2, Salvador Cortes Rubio to Macedo, April 6, 1901; *El Imparcial,* August 15, 1901; Guzmán Avila, "Inversiones extranjeras," 180 note 14; *El Economista Mexicano,* March 29, June 7, September 27, 1902; *La Patria,* April 16, 1902; *El Tiempo,* January 22, 1905; AHCM, vol. 3776, exp. 604, Mendez to cabildo, July 4, 1902.

10. WNRC, Claims, RG 76, entry 125, agency 4850, "Mexican Government Response," Annex 1, undated memorandum of Departments of Treasury, Development, Foreign Relations, and Interior; *Monterey News,* January 29, February 9, June 18, 1903.

11. AJYL, roll 55, carp. 24/30, Lafayette Hoyt De Friese to Limantour, July 17, 1908; WNRC, Claims, RG 76, entry 125, agency 4850, "Mexican Government Response," Annex 10, contract between Robert Miller and Henry DeKay, September 14, 1910; Guzmán Avila, "Uruapan del Progreso," 183.

12. WNRC, Claims, RG 76, entry 125, agency 4850, "Mexican Government Response," Annex 1, undated memorandum of Departments of Treasury, Development, Foreign Relations, and Interior; *Monterey News,* February 10, June 18, 1903, April 29, 1905.

13. WNRC, Claims, RG 76, entry 125, agency 4850, "DeKay Memorial," 10, Alfred Bishop Mason affidavit, May 31, 1927; Schell, *Integral Outsiders,* 17.

14. U.S. livestock exports were reversed in any event about 1906 because massive immigration raised domestic demand even as cereal production replaced grazing lands. G. E. Putnam, *Supplying Britain's Meat* (London: Harrap, 1923), 71.

15. AJYL, roll 55, carp. 24/30, DeFriese to Limantour, July 17, 1908; WNRC, Claims, RG 76, entry 125, agency 4850, "DeKay Memorial." DeKay claimed that the bonds sold to the public without discount at 5 percent, but this seems unlikely given that the Bank of England charged a rate of 6 percent.

16. WNRC, Claims, RG 76, entry 125, agency 4850, "Mexican Government Response," Annex 2, "DeKay Memorial," Annex 9.

17. AJYL, roll 55, carp. 24/30, DeFriese to Limantour, July 17, 1908; WNRC, Claims, RG 76, entry 125, agency 4850, "Mexican Government Response," Annex 10, Notary statement of Agustín Silva y Valencia, September 29, 1910; *Mexican Herald,* January 13, 1908.

18. AJYL, roll 55, carp. 24/30, DeFriese to Limantour, July 17, 1908.

19. Camp, *Mexican Political Biographies,* 54; Jesús Luna, "The Public Career of Don Ramón Corral" (Ph.D. diss., North Texas State University, 1973), 24–29, 70–77; Manuel R. Uruchurtu, *Apuntes biográficos del Señor Don Ramón Corral* (Mexico City: Eusebio Gómez de la Puente, 1910), 7, 42ff.

20. Luna, "Public Career," 42, 69, 70–73, 110–111.

21. WNRC, Claims, RG 76, entry 125, agency 4850, "DeKay Memorial," 14.

22. DeKay, *The Men of Mexico,* 27–28.

23. Schell, *Integral Outsiders,* 113–14.

24. APD, leg. 32, no. 16072, DeKay to Díaz, June 2, 1907, no. 16017–16053, DeKay to Díaz, June 3, 1907.

25. APD, leg. 33, no. 6408, DeKay to Díaz, April 22, 1908. For an insightful recent summary of the controversy, see Paul Garner, *Porfirio Díaz* (Harlow, England: Longman, 2001), 212–15.

26. AJYL, roll 55, carp. 24/30, British Mexican Trust Company report, February 27, 1908.

27. Guzmán Avila, *Michoacán y la inversión extranjera*, 151; idem, "Inversiones extranjeras," 174–75; *Mexican Herald*, January 19, 1908.

28. Neither DeKay nor Limantour had any interest in publicizing the incident, and not a word appeared in the press. This account is pieced together from references in WNRC, Claims, RG 76, entry 125, agency 4850, "DeKay Memorial," 15–18; AJYL, roll 55, carp. 24/30, DeKay to Limantour, July 8, 1908, DeFriese to Limantour, July 17, 1908. The appointment of McGinnis was reported by the *Mexican Herald*, January 13, 1908.

29. *Mexican Herald*, January 13, February 23, March 12, 1908.

30. *El Obrero Mexicano*, November 5, 1909, January 14, 28, 1910; Lear, *Workers, Neighbors, and Citizens*, 118–23. See also William E. French, *A Peaceful and Working People: Manners, Morals, and Class Formation in Northern Mexico* (Albuquerque: University of New Mexico Press, 1996); Steven B. Bunker, "'Consumers of Good Taste': Marketing Modernity in Northern Mexico, 1890–1910," *Mexican Studies/Estudios Mexicanos* 13, no. 2 (Summer 1997): 227–69.

31. *Mexican Herald*, February 23, 1908.

32. This importer conservatism continued for decades thereafter. Rockefeller Foundation Archives (hereafter RFA), record group 1.2, series 323, box 2, folder 8, report of Kenneth L. Turk, September 24, 1959. See also John E. Rouse, *The Criollo: Spanish Cattle in the Americas* (Norman: University of Oklahoma Press, 1977).

33. A typewritten copy of the article, dated February 20, 1908, was supplied by DeKay to WNRC, Claims, RG 76, entry 125, agency 4850. An original copy of the obscure *Mexican Daily Record* could not be located.

34. WNRC, Claims, RG 76, entry 125, agency 4850, "DeKay Memorial," 9, 16. On Porfirian business models, see Haber, *Industry and Underdevelopment*, chapter 6.

35. WNRC, Claims, RG 76, entry 125, agency 4850, "DeKay Memorial," 16–17; AJYL, roll 54, carp. 24/30, DeKay to Limantour, March 14, 17, 24, 1908.

36. AJYL, roll 54, carp. 24/30, DeKay memorandum, March 14, 1908.

37. *Mexican Herald*, April 15, 1908; *El Imparcial*, April 18, 1908.

38. *Mexican Herald*, May 24, 1908. AHCM, vol. 1280, exp. 25, Hinkle to Corral, March 26, 1908.

39. APD leg. 33, no. 8039, Wiseman to Díaz, June 17, 1908; AJYL, roll 55, carp. 24/30, memoranda of July 8, 10, 1908; D. A. Holmes to Limantour, August 21, 1908.

40. González's advice was transcribed in WNRC, Claims, RG 76, entry 125, agency 4850, "DeKay Memorial," 19. The Terrazas's skill at extracting money from foreigners was noted by Wasserman, *Capitalists, Caciques, and Revolution*, 90–91.

41. AGNDF, Francisco Díaz de Bonilla, vol. 23, fo. 243–48, September 17, 1908, fo. 260–61, October 23, 1908; AJYL, roll 55, carp. 24/30, DeFriese to Limantour, August 4, 22, 1908; Holmes to Limantour, September 11, 1908.

42. *Mexican Herald*, October 16, 23, 1908; *El Tiempo*, August 1, October 31, 1908.

43. *Financier* (London), January 9, 1909; *Daily Telegraph* (London), January 9, 1909.

44. AHCM, vol. 3773, exp. 448, Serrano et al. petition, June 26, 1890.

45. *El Imparcial*, June 14, 1908; *Boletín Oficial del Consejo Superior de Gobierno del*

Distrito Federal, January 31, 1908.

46. *Mexican Herald,* October 23, 1908. On the size of the American colony, see Schell, *Integral Outsiders,* 51.

47. Jeffrey M. Pilcher, "Empire of the 'Jungle': The Rise of an Atlantic Refrigerated Beef Industry, 1880–1920," *Food, Culture, & Society* 7:1 (Fall 2004): 63–78.

CHAPTER FIVE

1. For a cross-section of the vast revolutionary historiography, mentioning English-language works alone, see Charles Cumberland, *Mexican Revolution: Genesis under Madero* (Austin: University of Texas Press, 1952); Michael C. Meyer, *Mexican Rebel: Pascual Orozco and the Mexican Revolution, 1910–1915* (Lincoln: University of Nebraska Press, 1967); John Womack, Jr., *Zapata and the Mexican Revolution* (New York: Knopf, 1968); David G. LaFrance, *The Mexican Revolution in Puebla, 1908–1913: The Maderista Movement and the Failure of Liberal Reform* (Wilmington, DE: Scholarly Resources, 1989); Allen Wells and Gilbert M. Joseph, *Summer of Discontent, Seasons of Upheaval: Elite Politics and Rural Insurgency in Yucatán, 1876–1915* (Stanford, CA: Stanford University Press, 1996).

2. John Mason Hart, *Empire and Revolution: The Americans in Mexico since the Civil War* (Berkeley, CA: University of California Press, 2001); idem, *Revolutionary Mexico: The Coming and Process of the Mexican Revolution* (Berkeley, CA: University of California Press, 1987); Alan Knight, *The Mexican Revolution,* 2 vols. (Cambridge: Cambridge University Press, 1986); idem, "Peasants into Patriots: Thoughts on the Making of the Mexican Nation," *Mexican Studies/Estudios Mexicanos* 10, no. 1 (Winter 1994): 135–61.

3. Enrique C. Ochoa, *Feeding Mexico: The Political Uses of Food since 1910* (Wilmington, DE: Scholarly Resources, 2000).

4. *Mexican Herald,* October 7, 1909.

5. Rockefeller Foundation Archives (hereafter RFA), group 1.1, series 323, box 5, folder 37, survey report of 1941; WNRC, Claims, RG 76, entry 125, agency 4850, "DeKay Memorial," 20.

6. AHCM, vol. 1279, exp. 10, Hinkle petitions, December 7, 1908, February 11, 1909; vol. 1280, exp. 27, DeKay petition, July 29, 1909; vol. 3773, exp. 448, Serrano et al. petition, June 26, 1890.

7. AHCM, vol. 3774, exp. 526, importers' petition, April 16, 1898; exp. 529, Miranda to cabildo, April 22, 1898, slaughterhouse commission report, September 5, 1902; vol. 3775, exp. 569, Wusterhaus to Municipal President, June 22, 1901; Yeager, *Competition and Regulation,* 68.

8. AHSS, Higiene Veterinario, box 2, exp. 1, Hinkle to Health Board, February 18, 1907; AHCM, vol. 3776, exp. 608, Ramírez and Zepeda to Municipal President, August 1, 1902; vol. 640, exp. 42, Louis DeKay to Government Council President, November 30, 1911.

9. AHCM, vol. 1786, exp. 91, contains the only available employee roster, dating from 1916, but this probably still reflected the organization established by DeKay about 1909. A partial listing of North American workers can be pieced together from *Mexican Herald,* October 23, 1908, October 19, December 15, 1909.

10. AHCM, vol. 640, exp. 31, Puga to Government Council Secretary, March 11, 1909, Monjarás to Government Council Secretary, April 2, 1909.

11. APD, leg. 34, exp. 9146, Mason to Díaz, May 13, 1909; AHCM, vol. 640, exp. 31, Corral to Government Council Secretary, May 31, 1909, September 11, 1909; Government Council to Corral, August 24, 1909.

12. WNRC, Claims, RG 76, entry 125, agency 4850, "Mexican Government Response," Annex 8, notary document, July 13, 1910, *Mexican Herald*, September 12, 1909; *El Economista Mexicano*, January 16, 1909; Emilio Alanis Patiño, "La industria de la carne en México," *Problemas Agrícolas e Industriales de México* 4, no. 3 (Julio-Septiembre 1952): 255.

13. *Mexican Herald*, September 12, 13, 1909.

14. Ibid, September 29, 1909.

15. Ibid, September 12, 1909.

16. Ibid, October 14, November 9, 1909; Schell, *Integral Outsiders*, 165.

17. AHCM, vol. 1280, exp. 29, DeKay to Zakany, October 11, 1909.

18. AHCM, vol. 1282, exp. 55, Chesley notice, August 18, 1909.

19. AHCM, vol. 1280, exp. 29, DeKay to Zakany, October 11, 1909.

20. AHCM, vol. 1280, exp. 27, Landa y Escandón, September 1, 1909; vol. 1282, exp. 55, importers' petition, August 30, 1909.

21. AHCM, vol. 1280, exp. 31, importers' petition, September 23, 1909; vol. 640, exp. 32, Puga to Government Council Secretary, October 1, 1909.

22. AHCM, vol. 1280, exp. 29, DeKay to Zakany, October 11, 1909, exp. 31, H. P. Chesley, November 2, 1909.

23. AHCM, vol. 640, exp. 40, Zakany to Government Council, September 22, 1909.

24. AHCM, vol. 1280, exp. 29, DeKay to Zakany, October 11, 1909.

25. *Mexican Herald*, January 26, 27, 1910; Schell, *Integral Outsiders*, 100, 165–66.

26. AJYL, roll 54, carp. 24, DeFriese to Limantour, July 17, 1908; WNRC, Claims, RG 76, entry 125, agency 4850, "Mexican Government Response," 9, 15–16, Annex 11, Stavert to Civil Court Judge, March 4, 1911; *Mexican Herald*, December 5, 1909.

27. Schell, *Integral Outsiders*, 165–67; *Mexican Herald*, January 26, 1910.

28. WNRC, Claims, RG 76, entry 125, agency 4850, "Mexican Government Response," Annex 4, Francisco Díaz de Bonilla notary statement, February 3, 1910; AHCM, vol. 1283, exp. 60, Corral to Government Council Secretary, February 9, 1910; *Mexican Herald*, February 3, 4, 5, 1910.

29. AHCM, vol. 1281, exp. 43, Importers to Corral, March 19, 1910.

30. AHCM, vol. 1281, exp. 43, Corral to Importers, March 28, 1910, vol. 1283, exp. 60, Robert Miller prospectus, June 30, 1910; WNRC, Claims, RG 76, entry 125, agency 4850, "Mexican Government Response," Annex 10, Contract between Robert Miller and Henry DeKay, September 14, 1910; *El Imparcial*, March 15, 1910; Schell, *Integral Outsiders*, 167–68.

31. AHCM, vol. 60, exp. 39, Montiel to Zakany, September 10–26, 1910.

32. AHCM, vol. 640, exp. 39, Zakany to Government Council Secretary, September 22, 1910, Casas to Government Council Secretary, November 19, 1910.

33. AHCM, vol. 1785, exp. 8, Zakany to Government Council Secretary, March 21, 1911; exp. 7, Zakany to Government Council Secretary, March 11, 1911.

34. AHCM, vol. 1785, exp. 4, Inspector General to District Governor, January 23, 1911; *El Imparcial*, August 30, 1911.

35. WNRC, Claims, RG 76, entry 125, agency 4850, "Mexican Government

Response," Annex 11, Stavert to Civil Court Judge, March 4, 1911, Annex 14, undated Norsworthy memorandum, Annex 20, J. Luis Patiño memorandum, January 5, 1914, "DeKay Memorial," 28.

36. AHCM, vol. 640, exp. 42, Monjarás to Government Council Secretary, July 3, 1911.

37. AHCM, vol. 640, exp. 42, Zakany to Government Council Secretary, August 4, 1911.

38. AHCM, vol. 640, exp. 42, Torres to Government Council President, August 8, 1911; DeKay to Government Council President, November 24, 1911.

39. WNRC, Claims, RG 76, entry 125, agency 4850, "Mexican Government Response," Annex 14, undated Norsworthy memorandum, Annex 15, Norsworthy to Hernández, November 9, 1911; *El Tiempo*, December 13, 1911.

40. Rodríguez Kuri, *La experiencia olvidada*, 243–45; Lear, *Workers, Neighbors, and Citizens*, 151–52.

41. AGN, Suprema Corte, box 715, exp. 2710. On the labor situation, see Lear, *Workers, Neighbors, and Citizens*, 146–50.

42. *Mexican Herald*, January 5, 1912.

43. AHCM, vol. 640, exp. 42, Torres to Government Council, January 20, 1912.

44. AHCM, vol. 641, exp. 50, Interior Secretary to Government Council President, January 30, 1912; Ibáñez to Government Council Secretary, August 3, 1912.

45. AHCM, vol. 640, exp. 42, González report, August 6, 1912.

46. AHCM, vol. 641, exp. 51, González to Government Council President, March 7, 1912; vol. 1785, exp. 11, Antonio González to District Governor, June 20, 1911, exp. 17, Escalante to Government Council Secretary, March 13, 1912; exp. 21, Pedro Pacheco to Government Council Secretary, September 11, 1912; Knight, *Mexican Revolution*, 1:405; Lear, *Workers, Neighbors, and Citizens*, 195–201.

47. AHCM, vol. 646, exp. 35, Juan Bribiesca to Government Council Secretary, February 7, 1912; report of Nicolás Ramírez de Arrellano, February 17, 1912; vol. 3671, exp. 224, Municipal Secretary to Government Council President, March 28, 1912.

48. AHSS, Inspección, box 2, exp. 4, J. L. González to Government Council President, May 17, 1912.

49. AHCM, vol. 3671, exp. 224, Gutiérrez de Lara report, June 4, 1912; AHSS, Inspección, box 2, exp. 4, J. L. González to Government Council President, June 13, 1912.

50. AHCM, vol. 3671, exp. 230, R. González to Municipal President, August 1, 1912; Municipal Secretary to R. González y Hermanos, August 9, 1912.

51. AHCM, vol. 640, exp. 42, Rafael Norma to González Garza, August 26, 1912.

52. AHCM, vol. 646, exp. 36, Alfonso Craviolo to Government Council Secretary, September 4, 1912; D. Orvañanos to Government Council President, September 23, 1912.

53. AHCM, vol. 3671, exp. 224, Gutiérrez de Lara report, October 1, 1912.

54. AHCM, vol. 3671, exp. 224, José Mota report, October 31, 1912; José Gómez report, November 9, 1912; Interior Secretary to Municipal President, December 10, 1912; Gutiérrez report, December 17, 1912.

55. AHSS, Inspección, box 2, exp. 5, Secretaría de Estado y del Despacho de Gobernación, *Reglamento para la venta de comestibles y bebidas en el Distrito Federal* (Mexico City: Imprenta del Gobierno Federal, 1912), 3–5, 9, 20. See also *Boletín*

Oficial del Consejo Superior de Gobierno, November 15, 1912: 627.

56. *El Imparcial*, August 19, 1909.

57. WNRC, Claims, RG 76, entry 192, docket 2871, undated draft prospectus; entry 125, agency 4850, "Mexican Government Response," 18, Annex 19, Antonio Philippe Serrano to Treasury Undersecretary, January 5, 1914; *El Economista Mexicano*, February 1, 1913.

58. Quoted in Friedrich Katz, *The Secret War in Mexico: Europe, the United States, and the Mexican Revolution* (Chicago: University of Chicago Press, 1981), 233.

59. Charles C. Cumberland, *Mexican Revolution: The Constitutionalist Years* (Austin: University of Texas Press, 1972), 63.

60. AHCM, vol. 640, exp. 42, Fernández to Government Council Secretary, July 12, 1913; AGN, Suprema Corte, box 715, exp. 2710, decision of May 29, 1913.

61. AHCM, vol. 640, exp. 42, Licéaga to Government Council President, October 4, 1913.

62. AHCM, vol. 641, exp. 50, Aragón report, May 31, 1913; vol. 1785, exp. 27, Torres to Secretary of Government, May 6, 1913; exp. 35, González brothers to Interior Secretary, August 7, 1913.

63. WNRC, Claims, RG 76, entry 125, agency 4850, "Mexican Government Response," Annex 19, Serrano to Treasury Undersecretary, January 5, 1914.

64. WNRC, Claims, RG 76, entry 125, agency 4850, contracts dated January 10, 1914.

65. AHCM, vol. 3776, exp. 630, supply accounts dated February 3, 1915; vol. 1785, exp. 40, Health Board and police reports January through March, 1914, exp. 43, Ramírez contract, March 23, 1914; vol. 641, exp. 57 Fernández to Government Council Secretary, December 16, 1913; exp. 59, José Guevara to Subsecretary of the Interior, January 9, 1914. See also Michael C. Meyer, "The Militarization of Mexico, 1913–1914," *The Americas* 27 (1971): 293–306.

66. WNRC, Claims, RG 76, entry 125, agency 4850, "DeKay Memorial," 40–42, 58–60, 71; "Mexican Government Response," 35; Annex 22, contact between DeKay, Leroy, and Banque Cantonale de Berne, March 6, 1914. The outbreak of World War I prevented the St. Chamond order from ever being filled.

67. Michael C. Meyer, "The Arms of the Ypiranga," *Hispanic American Historical Review* 50, no. 3 (August 1970): 543–56; Katz, *Secret War in Mexico*, 233–40; Cumberland, *Mexican Revolution: Constitutionalist Years*, 124; John W. DeKay, *Dictators of Mexico: The Land where Hope Marches with Despair* (London: Effingham Wilson, 1914). WNRC, Claims, RG 76, entry 125, agency 4850, correspondence between DeKay and the Hamburg-American Steamship Company, April 1914.

68. WNRC, Claims, RG, 76, entry 125, agency 4850, DeKay affidavit, February 17, 1926; Cumberland, *Mexican Revolution: Constitutionalist Years*, 124.

69. WNRC, Claims, RG 76, entry 125, agency 4850, "DeKay Memorial," 5, "Mexican Government Response," 42; *Financial Times*, August 14, December 5, 1914.

70. AHCM, vol. 1786, exp. 67, Aurelio Esquivel to César López de Lara, October 12, 1915; exp. 72, Slaughterhouse Delegate to López de Lara, September 14, 1916

71. For an insightful analysis of bread riots in Mexico City, and popular mobilization more generally, see Lear, *Workers, Neighbors, and Citizens*, 257, 305–15. See also AHCM, vol. 3760, exp. 35, Lundberg and Östlund to Municipal President, March 21, 1918; vol. 3776, exp. 635, Luis Zubirán y Campo to Ignacio Rodríguez,

January 20, 1915; exp. 639, de la Mora to Rodríguez, February 8, 1916.

72. AHCM, vol. 1786, exp. 62, A. M. de la Mora to Gen. César López de Lara, September 6, 1915; exp. 63, E. Alfaro to López de Lara, September 22, 1915; exp. 72, Delegate to López de Lara, July 12, 1916; exp. 86, inventory dated May 2, 1916; vol. 3776, exp. 632, Secretary of Government, April 9, 1915; exp. 641, Jesús Acuña, April 24, 1916.

73. AHCM, vol. 1786, exp. 50, Slaughterhouse manager to District Governor, May 21, 1917; exp. 55, Rodríguez to Governor, May 22, 1917; *Memoria de la Secretaría de Hacienda y Crédito Público, 1923–1925*, 2 vols. (Mexico City: Talleres de la Editorial "Cvltvra," 1926) 1:163, xxiii-xxx.

74. Archivo Plutarco Elías Calles (hereafter APEC), exp. 72, Rastro de la Ciudad de México, gaveta 64, fo. 2–3, inv. 4757, Agrupaciones to Calles, July 2, 1927.

75. AHSS, Servicio Jurídico, box 10, exp. 4, describes union activism at the slaughterhouse in 1928.

76. APEC, Fototeca, Fondo P.E.C., albums 42–45, "Informe gráfico de la labor administrativo desarrollada en el Rastro General de la Ciudad de México," 4 vols., 1932. See also AHSS, Higiene Veterinaria, box 2, exp. 9, transfer statement September 21, 1927; Secretaría de la Economía Nacional, *La industria de la carne: Abasto de ganado, distribución y consumo* (Mexico City: Talleres Gráficos de la Nación, 1934), 41, 167; Gabriel Ascencio Franco, *Los mercaderes de la carne* (Morelia: El Colegio de Michoacán, 1992), 32, 58.

77. *Resumen*, June 24, 1931, pp.28–31, 47; *Excelsior*, May 8, 1931; Departamento de Salubridad Pública, *Reglamento del Rastro General de la Ciudad* (Mexico City: N.p., 1931), 12–15; APEC, Fototeca, Fondo P.E.C., album 44, "Informe gráfico," 3:1–34.

78. *El Universal*, August 9, 17, 1939, January 30, 1940; Ochoa, *Feeding Mexico*, 77, 91; Niblo, *War, Diplomacy, and Development: The United States and Mexico, 1938–1954* (Wilmington, DE: Scholarly Resources, 1995); *La Nación*, October 30, 1943. Quote from *Excelsior*, July 9, 1945.

79. Niblo, *Mexico in the 1940s*, 124–31; *La Nación*, 10–30–43, *El Universal*, October 27, 1943, July 2, 17, September 13, 1944, July 12, 1945.

80. The dualism of Mexican agriculture was described by Cynthia Hewitt de Alcántara, *Modernizing Mexican Agriculture: Socioeconomic Implications of Technological Change, 1940–1970* (Geneva: United Nations Research Institute for Social Development, 1976); Alain de Janvry, *The Agrarian Question and Reformism in Latin America* (Baltimore: Johns Hopkins University Press, 1981). See also Steven A. Sanderson, *The Transformation of Mexican Agriculture: International Structure and the Politics of Rural Change* (Princeton, NJ: Princeton University Press, 1986), 124–27, 171; *El Universal*, November 22, 1946; Alanis Patiño, "La industria de la carne," 250; *El Nacional*, September 5, 7, 1955; Comisión Económica para América Latina, *La industria de la carne de ganado bovino en México: Análisis y perspectivas* (Mexico City: Fondo de Cultura Económica, 1975), 165; Schyer, *Ethnicity and Class Conflict*, 152–56.

81. *El Financiero*, March 11, 1992; *Uno más uno*, March 11, 1992; *La Jornada*, March 14, 17, 1992; *Excelsior*, March 17, 1992; Comisión Económica, *La industria de la carne*, 165, 188; Fernando Rello and Demetrio Sodi, *Abasto y distribución de alimentos en las grandes metropolis* (Mexico City: Nueva Imagen, 1988), 106–8

82. Quote from *Ultimas Noticias*, March 12, 1992, see also March 13, 1992; *Novedades,*

March 11, 1992; *Metrópoli*, March 11, 1992; *Uno más uno*, March 11, 1992; *Ovaciones*, March 14, 1992; *La Jornada*, March 14, 1992.

83. *Excelsior*, March 12, 1992; see also *Ultimas Noticias de Excelsior* and *La Prensa* for the same day.

84. *Excelsior*, March 10, 1992; *Ovaciones*, March 13, 1992; *La Prensa*, March 14, 1992.

85. Ochoa, *Feeding Mexico*, 214–20.

86. Richelet, *La ganadería argentina*, 165–66.

87. Pilcher, "Empire of the 'Jungle,'" 73–75.

88. WNRC, Claims, RG 76, entry 192, docket 2871, Lora Power to Mrs. James Van Dusen, April 3, 1946. The slaughterhouse ruins were described as a picturesque destination in the tourist guide by Marian Starm, *Enjoying Uruapan* (Mexico City: N.p., 1945), 694.

CONCLUSION

1. A further irony emerges from the specific history of the dish in south Texas, where poor Mexican Americans found an appetizing way of cooking the tough diaphragm muscle of the cow because it was the only meat they could buy. When fajitas finally caught on among mainstream U.S. consumers in the 1980s, the price of skirt steak rose to the point that the original cooks could no longer afford it. See Mario Montaño, "Appropriation and Counterhegemony in South Texas: Food Slurs, Offal Meats, and Blood," in *Usable Pasts: Traditions and Group Expressions in North America*, ed. Tad Tuleja (Logan: Utah State University Press, 1997), 50–67.

2. On the anachronistic nature of mole poblano, see Pilcher, *¡Que vivan los tamales!*, 65.

3. On the importance of institutions for economic development, see Douglass C. North, *Institutions, Institutional Change, and Economic Performance* (Cambridge: Cambridge University Press, 1990).

4. *Boletín del Departamento de Salubridad* 1 (1926), 53–54, 87.

5. Dietary experts have recently begun to question the supposed health benefits of margarine and other polyunsaturated fats, not to mention the dangers of omega-6 fatty acids in oils such as cottonseed. See Susan Allport, "The Skinny on Fat," *Gastronomica* 3, no. 1 (Winter 2003): 28–36.

6. Carol Meyers de Ortiz, *Pequeño comercio de alimentos en colonias populares de Ciudad Nezahuacóyotl: Análisis de su papel en la estructura socioeconómica urbana* (Guadalajara: Editorial Universidad de Guadalajara, 1990), 108 note 9; *Ultimas Noticias*, March 16, 1992.

7. Rello and Sodi, *Abasto y distribución de alimentos*, 75.

8. Ascencio Franco, *Los mercaderes de la carne*, 23, 67, 84.

9. Allen Wells, *Yucatan's Gilded Age: Haciendas, Henequen, and International Harvester* (Albuquerque: University of New Mexico Press, 1985); Gilbert M. Joseph, *Revolution from Without: Yucatán, Mexico, and the United States, 1880–1924* (Durham, NC: Duke University Press, 1982).

10. George Armstrong, *Law and Market Society in Mexico* (New York: Praeger, 1989), x.

11. Martin Carnoy, *The State and Political Theory* (Princeton, NJ: Princeton University Press, 1984), 25.

12. Yeager, *Competition and Regulation*, Chapter 7.

13. Philip Corrigan, "State Formation," in *Everyday Forms of State Formation: Revolution and the Negotiation of Rule in Modern Mexico*, ed. Gilbert M. Joseph and Daniel Nugent (Durham: Duke University Press, 1994), xviii.
14. *El Universal*, September 13, 1944.
15. Guillermo Soberon Acevedo, et al, *Derecho constitucional a la protección de la salud* (Mexico City: Porrúa, 1983).
16. Quote from Manuel Magaña Contreras, *Los años de oro*, vol. 1 of *Ciudad abierta* (Mexico City: Analisis y Evaluación de Prensa, 1996), 295, 300; *La Nación*, October 30, 1943; Isabel Hernández, "Cierra Ferrería: Pecado de la carne," *Ovaciones*, March 13, 1992.
17. Alma Guillermoprieto, "In search of the real tortilla," *The New Yorker*, November 29, 1999.
18. *La Jornada*, March 14, 1992.

Bibliography

ARCHIVES

Archivo General de la Nación (AGN)
    Abasto
    Criminal
    Gobernación
    Industrias Nuevas
    Inquisición
    Padrones
    Ramo Civil
    Suprema Corte de la Nación
Archivo General de Notarías del Distrito Federal (AGNDF)
Archivo Histórico de la Ciudad de México (AHCM).
Archivo Histórico de la Secretaría de Salud (AHSS)
Archivo Plutarco Elías Calles (APEC)
Biblioteca Nacional de Antropología e Historia, Fondo Lira (BNAH)
Centro de Estudios de Historia de México, Condumex, Archivo José Yves
    Limantour (AJYL)
El Colegio de Michoacán, Archivo Ramón Fernández Fernández (ARFF)
Rockefeller Foundation Archives, North Terrytown, New York (RFA)
Universidad Iberoamericana, Archivo Porfirio Díaz (APD)
University of California, Berkeley, Bancroft Library, Manuel Gamio Book Notes
Washington National Record Center, Suitland, Maryland (WNRC)

NEWSPAPERS

Boletín del Consejo Superior de Salubridad.
Boletín del Departamento de Salubridad.
Daily Telegraph (London).
Diario del Hogar.
El Día.
El Economista Mexicano.
El Financiero.
El Globo.
El Hijo del Ahuizote.
El Imparcial.
El Monitor Republicano.
El Mosquito Mexicano.
El Mundo.
El Municipio Libre.
El Nacional.
El Obrero Mexicano.
El Popular.
El Siglo XIX.

El Tiempo.
El Universal.
Excelsior.
Financial Times (London).
Financier (London).
La Jornada.
La Nación.
La Patria.
La Prensa.
Metrópoli.
Mexican Herald.
México Industrial.
Monterey News.
Novedades.
Ovaciones,
Resumen.
Ultimas Noticias.
Uno más uno.

BOOKS AND ARTICLES

Abastecedora de Carnes, S.A. *El abastecimiento de carne en el Distrito Federal.* Mexico City: N.p., 1952.

Adams, Carol J. *The Sexual Politics of Meat: A Feminist-Vegetarian Critical Theory.* New York: Continuum, 2000.

Aguilar Rivera, José Antonio. *En pos de la quimera: Reflexiones sobre el experimento constitucional atlántico.* Mexico City: Fondo de Cultura Económica, 2000.

Alanis Patiño, Emilio. "La industria de la carne en México." *Problemas Agrícolas e Industriales de México* 4, no. 3 (Julio-Septiembre 1952): 233–301.

Allport, Susan. "The Skinny on Fat." Gastronomica 3, no. 1 (Winter 2003): 28–36.

Altamiras, Juan. *Nuevo arte de cocina, sacado de la escuela de la experiencia economica.* Barcelona: Imprenta de María Angela Martí Viuda, 1767.

Anderson, Edward, Jr. *Refrigeration in America: A History of a New Technology and its Impact.* Princeton, NJ: Princeton University Press, 1953.

Anduiza, Jacinto. *El libro del hogar.* Pachuca: Imprenta "La Europea," 1893.

Anuario estadístico de la República Mexicana: 1906. Mexico City: Secretaría de Fomento, 1910.

Arias, Juan de Dios. "El tocinero. Una persona de sustancia." In *Los mexicanos pintados por sus mismos: Obra escrita por una sociedad de literatos.* Mexico City: Símbolo, 1946 [1855].

Armour, J. Ogden. *The Packers, The Private Car Lines, and the People.* Philadelphia: Henry Altemus Company, 1906.

Armstrong, George. *Law and Market Society in Mexico.* New York: Praeger, 1989.

Arrom, Silvia Marina. *The Women of Mexico City, 1790–1857.* Stanford, CA: Stanford University Press, 1985.

Arroyo, Patricia T. *The Science of Philippine Foods.* Quezon City, Philippines: Abanito Enterprises, 1973.

Ascencio Franco, Gabriel. *Los mercaderes de la carne.* Morelia: El Colegio de

Michoacán, 1992.

Barrett, Ward. "The Meat Supply of Colonial Cuernavaca." *Annals of the Association of American Geographers* 64, no. 4 (December 1974): 525–40.

Bauer, Arnold J. *Goods, Power, History: Latin America's Material Culture.* New York: Cambridge University Press, 2001.

Bayle, Constantino. *Los cabildos seculares en la América Española.* Madrid: Sapienta, 1952.

Bazant, Jan. *Cinco haciendas mexicanas: Tres siglos de vida rural en San Luis Potosí (1600–1910).* Mexico City: El Colegio de Mexico, 1975.

Beatty, Edward. *Institutions and Investment: The Political Basis of Industrialization in Mexico Before 1911.* Stanford, CA: Stanford University Press, 2001.

Beezley, William H. "The Porfirian Smart Set Anticipates Thorstein Veblen in Guadalajara." In *Rituals of Rule, Rituals of Resistance: Public Celebrations and Popular Culture in Mexico,* edited by William H. Beezley, Cheryl English Martin, and William E. French. Wilmington, DE: Scholarly Resources, 1994.

Bishko, Charles Julian. "The Peninsular Background of Latin American Cattle Ranching." *Hispanic American Historical Review* 32, no. 4 (November 1952): 491–515.

Bliss, Katherine Elaine. *Compromised Positions: Prostitution, Public Health, and Gender Politics in Revolutionary Mexico City.* University Park: Pennsylvania State University Press, 2001.

Bonnet, Jean Claude. "The culinary system in the *Encyclopedie.*" In *Food and Drink in History: Selections from the* Annales Economies, Sociétés, Civilisations, edited by Robert Forster and Orest Ranum, translated by Elborg Forster and Patricia Ranum. Baltimore: Johns Hopkins University Press, 1979.

Bourke, John Gregory. "The Folk-Foods of the Rio Grande Valley and of Northern Mexico." *Journal of American Folk-Lore* (1895): 41–71.

Brading, D. A. *Haciendas and Ranchos in the Mexican Bajío, León, 1700–1860.* Cambridge: Cambridge University Press, 1978.

_____. *Miners and Merchants in Bourbon Mexico, 1763–1810.* Cambridge: Cambridge University Press, 1971.

_____. *The First America: The Spanish monarchy, Creole patriots, and the Liberal state, 1492–1867.* Cambridge: Cambridge University Press, 1992.

Brody, David. *The Butcher Workmen: A Study of Unionization.* Cambridge, MA: Harvard University Press, 1964.

Buffington, Robert M. *Criminal and Citizen in Modern Mexico.* Lincoln: University of Nebraska Press, 2000.

Bullock, William. *Six Months Residence and Travels in Mexico.* Port Washington, NY: Kennikat Press, 1971 [1824].

Bunker, Steven B. "'Consumers of Good Taste': Marketing Modernity in Northern Mexico, 1890–1910." *Mexican Studies/Estudios Mexicanos* 13, no. 2 (Summer 1997): 227–69.

Busto, Emiliano. "Cuaderno estadístico de la industria en el Distrito Federal." Annex 3 of *Estadístico de la República Mexicana.* 3 vols. Mexico City: Ignacio Cumplido 1880.

Calderón de la Barca, Fanny. *Life in Mexico: The Letters of Fanny Calderón de la Barca,* edited by Howard T. Fisher and Marion Hall Fisher. Garden City, NY: Doubleday, 1966.

Camacho, Sebastián. *Memoria del Ayuntamiento de la Ciudad de Mexico de 1895.* Mexico City: Imprenta "La Europea," 1896.

_____. *Memoria del Ayuntamiento de la Ciudad de México de 1897.* Mexico City: Imprenta "La Europea," 1898.

Camp, Roderic A. *Mexican Political Biographies, 1884–1935.* Austin: University of Texas Press, 1991.

Cardoso, Ciro, ed. *México en el siglo XIX, 1821–1910. Historia económica y de la estructura social.* Mexico City: Nueva Imagen, 1988.

Carmona Ruiz, María Antonia. *La ganadería en el reino de Sevilla durante la baja edad media.* Sevilla, Spain: Diputación de Sevilla, 1998.

Carnoy, Martin. *The State and Political Theory.* Princeton, NJ: Princeton University Press, 1984.

Carreño, Manuel Antonio. *Manual de urbanidad y buenas maneras.* New York: D. Appleton, 1880.

Carrera Stampa, Manuel. *Los gremios mexicanos.* Mexico City: Ediapsa, 1954.

Castro Gutiérrez, Felipe. *La extinción de la artesanía gremial.* Mexico City: UNAM, 1986.

Cerutti, Mario. "Los empresarios del Porfiriato y la investigación regional (1975–1995)." In *Don Porfirio presidente..., Nunca omnipotente: Hallazgos, reflexiones y debates. 1876–1911,* edited by Romana Falcón and Raymond Buve. Mexico City: Universidad Iberoamericana, 1998.

Chandler, Alfred D., Jr. *The Visible Hand: The Managerial Revolution in American Business.* Cambridge, MA: Harvard University Press, 1977.

Chauvet, Michelle. *La ganadería bovina de carne en México: Del auge a la crisis.* Mexico City: Universidad Autónoma Metropolitana—Azcapotzalco, 1999.

Chevalier, François. *Land and Society in Colonial Mexico: The Great Hacienda.* Berkeley: University of California Press, 1970.

Chowning, Margaret. "Reassessing the Prospects for Profit in Nineteenth-Century Mexican Agriculture from a Regional Perspective: Michoacán, 1810–60." In *How Latin America Fell Behind: Essays on the Economic Histories of Brazil and Mexico, 1800–1914,* edited by Stephen Haber. Stanford, CA: Stanford University Press, 1997.

_____. *Wealth and Power in Provincial Mexico: Michoacán from the Late Colony to the Revolution.* Stanford, CA: Stanford University Press, 1999.

Clemen, Rudolf Alexander. *The American Livestock and Meat Industry.* New York: Ronald Press Company, 1923.

Coatsworth, John. *Growth Against Development: The Economic Impact of Railroads in Porfirian Mexico.* DeKalb: Northern Illinois University Press, 1981.

_____. "Obstacles to Economic Growth in Nineteenth-Century Mexico." *American Historical Review* 83, no. 1 (February 1978): 80–100.

Cochet, Hubert, Eric Léonard, and Jean Damien de Surgy. *Paisajes agrarios de Michoacán.* Zamora: El Colegio de Michoacán, 1988.

Coe, Sophie. *America's First Cuisines.* Austin: University of Texas Press, 1994.

Comisión Económica para América Latina. *La industria de la carne de ganado bovino en México: Análisis y perspectivas.* Mexico City: Fondo de Cultura Económica, 1975.

Connolly, Priscilla. *El contratista de don Porfirio: Obras públicas, deuda y desarrollo desigual.* Mexico City: Fondo de Cultura Económica, 1997.

Contreras Cruz, Carlos. "Ciudad y salud en el Porfiriato: La política urbana y el saneamiento de Puebla (1880–1906)." *Siglo XIX: Cuadernos de Historia* 1, no. 3 (June 1992): 55–76.

Contreras, Manuel María. *Memoria del Ayuntamiento de la Ciudad de México de 1892.* Mexico City: Impreso de F. Díaz de León, 1893.

Corey, Lewis. *Meat and Man: A Study of Monopoly, Unionism, and Food Policy.* New York: Viking Press, 1950.

Corrigan, Philip. "State Formation." In *Everyday Forms of State Formation: Revolution and the Negotiation of Rule in Modern Mexico,* edited by Gilbert M. Joseph and Daniel Nugent. Durham, NC: Duke University Press, 1994.

Cossío Silva, Luis. "La ganadería." In *El porfiriato: La vida económica.* Vol. 7 of *Historia moderna de México,* edited by Daniel Cosío Villegas. Mexico City: Editorial Hermes, 1965.

Cronon, William. *Nature's Metropolis: Chicago and the Great West.* New York: Norton, 1991.

Crosby, Alfred W., Jr. *The Columbian Exchange: Biological and Cultural Consequences of 1492.* Westport, CT: Greenwood Press, 1972.

Cumberland, Charles C. *Mexican Revolution: Genesis under Madero.* Austin: University of Texas Press, 1952.

———. *Mexican Revolution: The Constitutionalist Years.* Austin: University of Texas Press, 1972.

DeKay, John W. *Dictators of Mexico: The Land where Hope Marches with Despair.* London: Effingham Wilson, 1914.

———. *The Men of Mexico and the Land They Love.* Syracuse, NY: Mason-Henry Press, 1906.

———. *The People's Money: A Brief Analysis of the Present Position in America, With some Observations on the World-Organisation of Labour.* London: Effingham Wilson, 1913.

Departamento de Salubridad Pública, *Reglamento del Rastro General de la Ciudad.* Mexico City: N.p., 1931.

Díaz del Castillo, Bernal. *The Discovery and Conquest of Mexico, 1517–1521,* translated by A. P. Maudslay. London: George Routledge, 1928.

Dusenberry, William H. "The Regulation of Meat Supply in Sixteenth-Century Mexico City." *Hispanic American Historical Review* 28, no. 1 (February 1948): 38–52.

El cocinero mexicano. 3 vols. Mexico City: Galván, 1831.

Esparza Sánchez, Cuauhtémoc. *Historia de la ganadería en Zacatecas, 1531–1911.* Zacatecas: Universidad Autónoma de Zacatecas, 1988.

Fiddes, Nick. *Meat: A Natural Symbol.* London: Routledge, 1992.

Florescano, Enrique. *Precios del maíz y crisis agrícolas.* Mexico City: El Colegio de México, 1969.

Freeman, Susan Tax. "Mining the Pig Slaughter: An Appreciation of a Culinary Ethnography from Spain." *Petits Propos Culinaires* 48 (November 1994): 47–50.

French, William E. *A Peaceful and Working People: Manners, Morals, and Class Formation in Northern Mexico.* Albuquerque: University of New Mexico Press, 1996.

Frye, David L. *Indians into Mexicans: History and Identity in a Mexican Town.* Austin: University of Texas Press, 1996.

Gamboa Ramírez, Ricardo. "Las finanzas municipales de la ciudad de México, 1800–1850." In *La ciudad de México en la primera mitad del siglo XIX.* Vol. 1. *Economía y estructura urbana,* edited by Regina Hernández Franyuti. Mexico City: Instituto Mora, 1994.

García Acosta, Virginia. "Las catastrophes agrícolas y sus efectos en la alimentación. Escasez y carestía de maíz, trigo, y carne en el México central a fines de la época colonial." In *Sociedad, economía y cultura alimentaria*, edited by Shoko Doode and Emma Paulina Pérez. Mexico City: CIESAS, 1994.

_____. *Las panaderías, sus dueños y trabajadores. Ciudad de México, siglo XVIII*. Mexico City: CIESAS, 1989.

Garcia Cubas, Antonio. *El libro de mis recuerdos*. Mexico City: Porrúa, 1986 [1904].

García Icazbalceta, Joaquín. *Noticias de México, recogidas por D. Francisco Sedano vecino de esta ciudad desde el año de 1756*. Mexico City: J. R. Barbedillo, 1880.

Garner, Paul. *Porfirio Díaz*. Harlow, England: Longman, 2001.

Garner, Richard L., with Spiro E. Stefanou. *Economic Growth and Change in Bourbon Mexico*. Gainesville: University Press of Florida, 1993.

Garza, James A. "Tales from the Mexican Underworld: Sex, Crime, and Vice in Porfirian Mexico City." Ph.D. diss., Texas Chrisitan Univ., 2001.

Gibson, Charles. *The Aztecs Under Spanish Rule: A History of the Indians of the Valley of Mexico, 1519–1810*. Stanford, CA: Stanford University Press, 1964.

Giedion, Siegfried. *Mechanization Takes Command: A Contribution to Anonymous History*. New York: Oxford University Press, 1948.

González Angulo Aguirre, Jorge. *Artesanado y ciudad a finales del siglo XVIII*. Mexico City: Fondo de Cultura Económica, 1983.

González Navarro, Moisés. *Estadísticas sociales del porfiriato*. Mexico City: Dirección General de Estadística, 1956.

_____. *El Porfiriato: La vida social*. Volume 4 of *Historia moderna de México*, edited by Daniel Cosío Villegas. Mexico City: Editorial Hermes, 1957.

González-Polo, Ignacio, ed. *Reflexiones y apuntes sobre la ciudad de México (fines de la colonia)*. Mexico City: Departamento del Distrito Federal, 1981.

González y González, Luis. *Pueblo en vilo: Microhistoria de San José de Gracia*. Mexico City: El Colegio de México, 1972.

Gooch [Iglehart], Fanny Chambers. *Face to Face with the Mexicans*. New York: Fords, Howard, and Hulbert, 1887.

Goody, Jack. *Cooking, Cuisine, and Class: A Study in Comparative Sociology*. Cambridge: Cambridge University Press, 1982.

Gootenberg, Paul. *Imagining Development: Economic Ideas in Peru's "Fictitious Prosperity" of Guano, 1840–1880*. Berkeley: University of California Press, 1993.

Gortari Rabiela, Hira de, and Regina Hernández Franyuti, ed. *La ciudad de México y el Distrito Federal (1824–1928)*. 4 vols. Mexico City: Instituto Mora, 1988.

Gowers, Emily. *The Loaded Table: Representations of Food in Roman Literature*. Oxford: Clarendon Press, 1993.

Griffen, William B. *The Apaches at War and Peace: The Janos Presidio, 1750–1858*. Albuquerque: University of New Mexico Press, 1988.

Grunstein, Arturo. "Surgimiento de los Ferrocarriles Nacionales en México (1900–1913): ¿Era inevitable la consolidación monopólica?" In *Historia de las grandes empresas en México, 1850–1930*, edited by Carlos Marichal and Mario Cerutti. Mexico City: Fondo de Cultura Económica, 1997.

Guillermoprieto, Alma. "In search of the real tortilla." *The New Yorker*, November 29, 1999.

Guzmán Avila, José Napoleón. "Inversiones extranjeras: Origen y desarrollo." In *Historia general de Michoacán*. Vol. 3. *El siglo XIX*, edited by Gerardo Sánchez Díaz. Morelia: Gobierno de Michoacán, 1989.

_____. *Michoacán y la inversión extranjera, 1880–1911.* Morelia: Universidad Michoacana de San Nicolás de Hidalgo, 1982.

_____. "Uruapan del Progreso." In *Pueblos, villas y ciudades de Michoacán en el Porfiriato,* edited by Gerardo Sánchez Díaz. Morelia: Universidad Michoacana de San Nicolás de Hidalgo, 1991.

Haber, Stephen H. *Industry and Underdevelopment: The Industrialization of Mexico, 1890–1940.* Stanford, CA: Stanford University Press, 1989.

Hale, Charles A. *Mexican Liberalism in the Age of Mora, 1821–1853.* New Haven, CT: Yale University Press, 1968.

Halperin, Rick. *Down on the Killing Floor: Black and White Workers in Chicago's Packinghouses, 1904–1954.* Urbana: University of Illinois Press, 1997.

Harris, Charles H., III. *A Mexican Family Empire: The Latifundio of the Sánchez Navarros, 1765–1867.* Austin: University of Texas Press, 1975.

Hart, John M. *Empire and Revolution: The Americans in Mexico since the Civil War.* Berkeley: University of California Press, 2001.

_____. *Revolutionary Mexico: The Coming and Process of the Mexican Revolution.* Berkeley: University of California Press, 1987.

Haslip-Viera, Gabriel. *Crime and Punishment in Late Colonial Mexico City, 1692–1810.* Albuquerque: University of New Mexico Press, 1999.

Hewitt de Alcántara, Cynthia. *Modernizing Mexican Agriculture: Socioeconomic Implications of Technological Change, 1940–1970.* Geneva: United Nations Research Institute for Social Development, 1976.

Horowitz, Roger. *Meat in America: Technology, Taste, Transformation.* Baltimore: Johns Hopkins University Press, forthcoming.

_____. *"Negro and White, Unite and Fight!" A Social History of Industrial Unionism in Meatpacking, 1930–1990.* Urbana: University of Illinois Press, 1997.

Horowitz, Roger, Jeffrey M. Pilcher, and Sydney Watts. "Meat for the Multitudes: Market Culture in Paris, New York City, and Mexico City over the Long Nineteenth Century." *American Historical Review* 109, no. 4 (October 2004): 1055–83.

Humboldt, Alexander von. *Political Essay on the Kingdom of New Spain,* translated by John Black. 4 vols. London: Longman, 1811.

Illades, Carlos. *Hacia la república del trabajo: La organización artesanal en la ciudad de México, 1853–1876.* Mexico City: El Colegio de México, 1996.

Jacobsen, Nils. "Livestock Complexes in Late Colonial Peru and New Spain: An Attempt at Comparison." In *The Economies of Mexico and Peru During the Late Colonial Period, 1760–1810,* edited by Nils Jacobsen and Hans-Jürgen Puhle. Berlin: Colloquium Verlag, 1986.

Janvry, Alain de. *The Agrarian Question and Reformism in Latin America.* Baltimore: Johns Hopkins University Press, 1981.

Joseph, Gilbert M. *Revolution from Without: Yucatán, Mexico, and the United States, 1880–1924.* Durham, NC: Duke University Press, 1982.

Karasch, Mary. "Suppliers, Sellers, Servants, and Slaves." In *Cities and Society in Colonial Latin America,* edited by Louisa Schell Hoberman and Susan Migden Socolow. Albuquerque: University of New Mexico Press, 1986.

Katz, Friedrich. *The Secret War in Mexico: Europe, the United States, and the Mexican Revolution.* Chicago: University of Chicago Press, 1981.

Kennedy, Diana. *My Mexico*. New York: Clarkson Potter, 1998.

_____. *Recipes from the Regional Cooks of Mexico*. New York: Harper & Row, 1978.

Kicza, John E. *Colonial Entrepreneurs: Families and Business in Bourbon Mexico City*. Albuquerque: University of New Mexico Press, 1983.

_____. "Consumption and Control: The Mexico City Business Community and Commodity Marketing in the Eighteenth Century." *Estudios de Historia Novohispana* 12 (1992): 159–69.

Knight, Alan. *The Mexican Revolution*, 2 vols. Cambridge: Cambridge University Press, 1986.

Konrad, Herman. *A Jesuit Hacienda in Colonial Mexico: Santa Lucia, 1576–1767*. Stanford, CA: Stanford University Press, 1980.

Kraeger, Karl. *Agricultura y colonización en México en 1900*, translated by Pedro Lewin and Gudrun Dohrmann. Chapingo: Universidad Autónoma de Chapingo, 1986.

Kuecker, Glen David. "A Desert in the Tropical Wilderness: Limits to the Porfirian Project in Northeastern Veracruz, 1870–1910." Ph.D. diss., Rutgers University, 1998.

Kuntz Ficker, Sandra. *Empresa extanjera y mercado interno: El Ferrocarril Central Mexicano, 1880–1907*. Mexico City: El Colegio de México, 1995.

Ladd, Doris M. *The Mexican Nobility at Independence, 1780–1826*. Austin: University of Texas Press, 1976.

LaFrance, David G. *The Mexican Revolution in Puebla, 1908–1913: The Maderista Movement and the Failure of Liberal Reform*. Wilmington, DE: Scholarly Resources, 1989.

Lai, Cheng-chung, ed. *Adam Smith Across Nations: Translations and Receptions of* The Wealth of Nations. Oxford: Oxford University Press, 2000.

Lear, John. *Workers, Neighbors, and Citizens: The Revolution in Mexico City*. Lincoln: University of Nebraska Press, 2001.

Legg, L. G. Wickham, ed. *Dictionary of National Biography, 1931–1940*. Oxford: Oxford University Press, 1949.

Link, Arthur S. *Woodrow Wilson and the Progressive Era, 1910–1917*. New York: Harper & Brothers, 1954.

Lipsett-Rivera, Sonya. "*De obra y palabra*: Patterns of Insults in Mexico, 1750–1856." *The Americas* 54, no. 4 (April 1998): 511–39.

Lira, Andrés. *Comunidades indígenas frente a la ciudad de México: Tenochtitlan y Tlatelolco, sus pueblos y barrios, 1812–1919*. Mexico City: El Colegio de México, 1983.

López Rosado, Diego. *Historia y pensamiento económico de México*. 6 vols. Mexico City: UNAM, 1968.

Lugo, Concepción, and Elsa Malvido. "Las epidemias en la Ciudad de México, 1822–1850." In *La Ciudad de México en la primera mitad del siglo XIX. Vol. 1: Economía y estructura urbana*, edited by Regina Hernández Franyuti. Mexico City: Instituto Mora, 1994.

Luna, Jesús. "The Public Career of Don Ramón Corral." Ph.D. diss., North Texas State University, 1973.

MacCannell, Dean. *The Tourist: A New Theory of the Leisure Class*. New York: Schocken Books, 1976.

Macedo, Miguel S. *Memoria documentada de los trabajos municipales de 1899*. Mexico City: Tip. "La Europea," 1900.

Machado, Manuel A., Jr. *The North Mexican Cattle Industry, 1910–1975: Ideology, Conflict, and Change.* College Station: Texas A & M University Press, 1981.

MacLachlan, Colin M., and William H. Beezley. *El Gran Pueblo: A History of Greater Mexico.* 2d ed. Upper Saddle River, NJ: Prentice-Hall, 1999.

Magaña Contreras, Manuel. *Los años de oro.* Vol. 1 of *Ciudad abierta.* Mexico City: Analisis y Evaluación de Prensa, 1996.

Manual del cocinero, dedicado a las señoritas mexicanas. Mexico City: Murguía, 1856.

Manual del cocinero y cocinera tomado del periodico literario La Risa. Puebla: José María Macías, 1849.

Marichal, Carlos. "Las estrategias de la deuda durante el Porfiriato: La conversión del empréstito de 1888 y el papel de Banamex como el banco del gobierno." In *Don Porfirio presidente..., Nunca omnipotente: Hallazgos, reflexiones y debates. 1876–1911,* edited by Romana Falcón and Raymond Buve. Mexico City: Universidad Iberoamericana, 1998.

Melville, Elinor. *A Plague of Sheep: Environmental Consequences of the Conquest of Mexico.* Cambridge: Cambridge University Press, 1994.

Memoria de la Secretaría de Hacienda y Crédito Público, 1923–1925. 2 vols. Mexico City: Talleres de la Editorial "Cvltvra," 1926.

Memoria que el Ayuntamiento Constitucional de 1871 presenta a sus comitentes. Mexico City: Imprenta de Ignacio Cumplido, 1872.

Meyer, Michael C. "The Arms of the Ypiranga." *Hispanic American Historical Review* 50, no. 3 (August 1970): 543–56.

_____. *Mexican Rebel: Pascual Orozco and the Mexican Revolution, 1910–1915.* Lincoln: University of Nebraska Press, 1967.

_____. *Huerta: A Political Portrait.* Lincoln: University of Nebraska Press, 1972.

_____. "The Militarization of Mexico, 1913–1914." *The Americas* 27 (1971): 293–306.

Meyers de Ortiz, Carol. *Pequeño comercio de alimentos en colonias populares de Ciudad Nezahuacóyotl: Análisis de su papel en la estructura socioeconómica urbana.* Guadalajara: Editorial Universidad de Guadalajara, 1990.

Mexican Year Book. London: McCorquodale & Co., 1910.

Mijares, Ivonne. *Mestizo alimentario: El abasto de la ciudad de México en el siglo XVI.* Mexico City: UNAM, 1993.

Miller, Judith A. *Mastering the Market: The State and the Grain Trade in Northern France, 1700–1860.* Cambridge: Cambridge University Press, 1999.

Montaño, Mario. "Appropriation and Counterhegemony in South Texas: Food Slurs, Offal Meats, and Blood." In *Usable Pasts: Traditions and Group Expressions in North America,* edited by Tad Tuleja. Logan: Utah State University Press, 1997.

Moore, John Preston. *The Cabildo in Peru Under the Habsburgs.* Durham, NC: Duke University Press, 1954.

Morgan, Tony. "Proletarians, Politicos, and Patriarchs: The Use and Abuse of Cultural Customs in the Early Industrialization of Mexico City, 1880–1910." In *Rituals of Rule, Rituals of Resistance: Public Celebrations and Popular Culture in Mexico,* edited by William H. Beezley, Cheryl English Martin, and William E. French. Wilmington, DE: SR Books, 1994.

Morin, Claude. *Michoacán en la Nueva España del siglo XVIII: Crecimiento y desigualdad en una economía colonial.* Mexico City: Fondo de Cultura Económica, 1979.

Niblo, Stephen R. *Mexico in the 1940s: Modernity, Politics, and Corruption.* Wilmington, DE: Scholarly Resources, 1999.

_____. *War, Diplomacy, and Development: The United States and Mexico, 1938–1954.* Wilmington, DE: Scholarly Resources, 1995.

North, Douglass C. *Institutions, Institutional Change, and Economic Performance.* Cambridge: Cambridge University Press, 1990.

Novak, William J. *The People's Welfare: Law and Regulation in Nineteenth-Century America.* Chapel Hill: University of North Carolina Press, 1996.

Novísimo arte de cocina. Mexico City: Alejandro Valdés, 1831.

Nuevo cocinero mexicano en forme de diccionario: reproducción facsimilar. Mexico City: Porrúa, 1986 [1888].

Nuevo y sencillo arte de cocina. Mexico City: Santiago Pérez, 1836.

Ochoa, Enrique C. *Feeding Mexico: The Political Uses of Food since 1910.* Wilmington, DE: Scholarly Resources, 2000.

Ordenanza del ramo de carnes de la municipalidad de México. Mexico City: Imprenta Vicente García Torres, 1850.

Paz, Ireneo, and Manuel Tornel. *Nueva guía de México.* Mexico City: Imprenta de I. Paz, 1882.

Pérez Hernández, José María. *Compendio de la geografía del estado de Michoacán de Ocampo.* Mexico City: Imprenta del comercio de Nabor Chávez, 1872.

Pérez Toledo, Sonia. "Artesanos y gremios de la ciudad de México: Una desaparición formal y una continuidad real, 1780–1842." In *Ciudad de México: Instituciones, actores sociales y conflicto político, 1774–1931,* edited by Carlos Illades and Ariel Rodríguez. Zamora: El Colegio de Michoacán, 1996.

_____. *Los hijos del trabajo: Los artesanos de la ciudad de México, 1780–1853.* Mexico City: El Colegio de México, 1996.

Perren, Richard. *The Meat Trade in Britain, 1840–1914.* London: Routledge & Kegan Paul, 1978.

Piccato, Pablo. *City of Suspects: Crime in Mexico City, 1900–1930.* Durham, NC: Duke University Press, 2001.

Pilcher, Jeffrey M. "Empire of the 'Jungle': The Rise of an Atlantic Refrigerated Beef Industry, 1880–1920." *Food, Culture, Society* 7.1 (Fall 2004): 63–78.

_____. *¡Que vivan los tamales! Food and the Making of Mexican Identity.* Albuquerque: University of New Mexico Press, 1998.

Poni, Carlo. "Local market rules and practices. Three guilds in the same line of production in early modern Bologna." In *Domestic strategies: Work and family in France and Italy, 1600–1800,* edited by Stuart Woolf. Cambridge: Cambridge University Press, 1991.

Purcell, Theodore V. *The Worker Speaks His Mind on Company and Union.* Cambridge, MA: Harvard University Press, 1953.

Putnam, G E. *Supplying Britain's Meat.* London: Harrap, 1923.

Recetario de doña Dominga de Guzmán, siglo XVIII: Tesoro de la cocina mexicana. Mexico City: Consejo Nacional para la Cultura y las Artes, 1996.

Redfield, Margaret Park. "Notes on the Cookery of Tepoztlan, Morelos." *American Journal of Folklore* 42, no. 164 (April-June 1929): 167–96.

Rello, Fernando, and Dematrio Sodi. *Abasto y distribución de alimentos en las grandes metropolis.* Mexico City: Nueva Imagen, 1988.

Reyes Heroles, Jesús. *El liberalismo mexicano.* 3 vols. Mexico City: Fondo de Cultura Económica, 1988.

Richelet, Juan E. *La ganadería argentina y su comercio de carnes*. Buenos Aires: J. Lajouane & Cía, 1928.

Rodríguez Kuri, Ariel. *La experiencia olvidada. El Ayuntamiento de México: política y gobierno, 1876–1912*. Mexico City: El Colegio de México, 1996.

Rosenkrantz, Barbara Gutmann. *Public Health and the State: Changing Views in Massachusetts, 1842–1936*. Cambridge, MA: Harvard University Press, 1972.

Rothschild, Emma. *Economic Sentiments: Adam Smith, Condorcet, and the Enlightenment*. Cambridge, MA: Harvard University Press, 2001.

Rouse, John E. *The Criollo: Spanish Cattle in the Americas*. Norman: University of Oklahoma Press, 1977.

Russell, Charles Edward. *The Greatest Trust in the World*. New York: Ridgway Thayer Company, 1905.

Salvucci, Richard J. "Mexican National Income in the Era of Independence, 1800–40." In *How Latin America Fell Behind: Essays on the Economic Histories of Brazil and Mexico, 1800–1914*, edited by Stephen Haber. Stanford, CA: Stanford University Press, 1997.

―――. *Textiles and Capitalism in Mexico: An Economic History of the Obrajes, 1539–1840*. Princeton, NJ: Princeton University Press, 1988.

Sánchez García, Alfonso. *Toluca del chorizo*. Toluca: Serie de Arte Popular y Folklore, 1976.

Sanderson, Steven A. *The Transformation of Mexican Agriculture: International Structure and the Politics of Rural Change*. Princeton, NJ: Princeton University Press, 1986.

Saucedo Montemayor, Pedro. *Historia de la ganadería en México*. Mexico City: UNAM, 1984.

Schell, William, Jr. *Integral Outsiders: The American Colony in Mexico City, 1876–1911*. Wilmington, DE: Scholarly Resources, 2001.

Schmidt, Arthur. *The Social and Economic Effect of the Railroad in Puebla and Veracruz, Mexico, 1867–1911*. New York: Garland, 1987.

Schwabe, Calvin. *Cattle, Priests, and Progress in Medicine*. Minneapolis: University of Minnesota Press, 1978.

Schwartz, Oscar. *Public Abattoirs and Cattle Markets*. London: "Ice and Cold Storage" Publishing Company, Ltd., 1901.

Schyer, Frans J. *Ethnicity and Class Conflict in Rural Mexico*. Princeton, NJ: Princeton University Press, 1990.

Secretaría de Agricultura y Ganadería, *Reglamento de la Industrialización Sanitaria de la Carne. Inspeccion Federal*. Mexico City: N.p., 1953.

Secretaría de Estado y del Despacho de Gobernación, *Reglamento para la venta de comestibles y bebidas en el Distrito Federal*. Mexico City: Imprenta del Gobierno Federal, 1912.

Secretaría de la Economía Nacional, *La industria de la carne: Abasto de ganado, distribución y consumo*. Mexico City: Talleres Gráficos de la Nación, 1934.

Sevilla, María José. *Life and Food in the Basque Country*. New York: New Amsterdam Books, 1990.

Sewell, William H., Jr. *Work and Revolution in France: The Language of Labor from the Old Regime to 1848*. Cambridge: Cambridge University Press, 1980.

Shafer, Robert J. *The Economic Societies in the Spanish World (1763–1821)*. Syracuse, NY: Syracuse University Press, 1958.

Shaw, Frederick J. "The Artisan in Mexico City (1824–1853)." In *El trabajo y los traba-jadores en la historia de México*, edited by Elsa Cecilia Frost, Michael C. Meyer, and Josefina Zoraida Vázquez. Mexico City: El Colegio de México, 1979.

Silva Riquer, Jorge. "El abasto al mercado urbano de la ciudad de México, 1830–1860." In *La ciudad de México en la primera mitad del siglo XIX*, vol. 1. *Economía y estructura urbana*, edited by Regina Hernández Franyuti. Mexico City: Instituto Mora, 1994.

Silva Riquer, Jorge, and María José Garrido Aspero. "Formas de abasto al mercado de Valladolid (1793–1800)." *Siglo XIX: Cuadernos de Historia* 3, no. 8 (January-April 1994): 45–77.

Sims, Harold D. *The Expulsion of Mexico City's Spaniards*. Pittsburgh: University of Pittsburgh Press, 1990.

Sinclair, Upton. *The Jungle*. New York: Doubleday, Page & Co., 1906.

Smith, Adam. *An Inquiry into the Nature and Causes of the Wealth of Nations*. 2 vols. Chicago: University of Chicago Press, 1976.

Soberón Acevedo, Guillermo, et al. *Derecho constitucional a la protección de la salud*. Mexico City: Porrúa, 1983.

Somers, Margaret R. "The Privatization of Citizenship: How to Unthink a Knowledge Culture." In *Beyond the Cultural Turn: New Directions in the Study of Society and Culture*, edited by Victoria E. Bonnell and Lynn Hunt. Berkeley: University of California Press, 1999.

Staples, Anne. "*Policia y Buen Gobierno*: Municipal Efforts to Regulate Public Behavior, 1821–1857." In *Rituals of Rule, Rituals of Resistance: Public Celebrations and Popular Culture in Mexico*, edited by William H. Beezley, Cheryl English Martin, and William E. French. Wilmington, DE: Scholarly Resources, 1994.

Starm, Marian. *Enjoying Uruapan*. Mexico City: N.p., 1945.

Stephen, Lynn. *Zapotec Women*. Austin: University of Texas Press, 1991.

Stevens, Donald F. *Origins of Instability in Early Republican Mexico*. Durham, NC: Duke University Press, 1991.

Stoker, Catharine Ulmer. *Concha's Mexican Kitchen Cook Book*. San Antonio: Naylor Company, 1946.

Stouff, Louis. *La table provençale: Boire et manger en Provence à la fin du Moyen Age*. Avignon: Éditions A. Barthélemy, 1996.

Super, John C. *Food, Conquest, and Colonization in Sixteenth-Century Spanish America*. Albuquerque: University of New Mexico Press, 1988.

Swabe, Joanna. *Animals, Disease and Human Society: Human-Animal Relations and the Rise of Veterinary Medicine*. London: Routledge, 1999.

Swift, Louis F. *The Yankee of the Yards: The Biography of Gustavus Franklin Swift*. Chicago: A. W. Shaw Company, 1927.

Tanck de Estrada, Dorothy. "La abolición de los gremios." In *El trabajo y los trabajadores en la historia de México*, edited by Elsa Cecilia Frost, Michael C. Meyer, and Josefina Zoraida Vázquez. Mexico City: El Colegio de México, 1979.

Taylor, Charles. "Modes of Civil Society." *Public Culture* 3, no. 1 (Fall 1990): 95–118.

Téllez Guerrero, Francisco. *De reales y granos: Los finanzas y el abasto de Puebla de los Angeles, 1820–1840*. Puebla: Cuadernos de la Casa Fresno, Universidad Autónoma de Puebla, 1986.

Thompson, E. P. "The Moral Economy of the English Crowd in the Eighteenth Century." *Past and Present* 50 (February 1971): 76–136.

Thompson, Guy P. C. *Puebla de los Angeles: Industry and Society in a Mexican City, 1700–1850.* Boulder, CO: Westview Press, 1989.

Thompson, Guy P. C., with David G. LaFrance. *Patriotism, Politics, and Popular Liberalism in Nineteenth-Century Mexico: Juan Francisco Lucas and the Puebla Sierra.* Wilmington, DE: Scholarly Resources, 1999.

Topik, Steven. "The Economic Role of the State in Liberal Regimes: Brazil and Mexico Compared, 1888–1910." In *Guiding the Invisible Hand: Economic Liberalism and the State in Latin American History,* edited by Joseph L. Love and Nils Jacobsen. New York: Praeger, 1988.

Torres de Rubio, Vicenta. *Cocina michoacana.* Zamora: Imprenta Moderna, 1896.

Toussaint-Samat, Maguelonne. *A History of Food,* translated by Anthea Bell. Cambridge, MA: Blackwell, 1992.

Townsend, Camilla. *Tales of Two Cities: Race and Economic Culture in Early Republican North and South America: Guayaquil, Ecuador, and Baltimore, Maryland.* Austin: University of Texas Press, 2000.

Trigueros, Ignacio. *Memoria de los Ramos Municipales.* Mexico City: Imprenta Económica, 1866.

Uruchurtu, Manuel R. *Apuntes biográficos del Señor Don Ramón Corral.* Mexico City: Eusebio Gómez de la Puente, 1910.

Van Young, Eric. *Hacienda and Market in Eighteenth-Century Mexico: The Rural Economy of the Guadalajara Region, 1675–1820.* Berkeley: University of California Press, 1981.

Vargas Salguera, Ramón, ed. *Historia de la arquitectura y el urbanismo mexicanos.* Volume 3. *El México independiente: Afirmación del nacionalismo y la modernidad.* Mexico City: UNAM, Fondo de Cultura Económica, 1998.

Velázquez, María de la Luz. *Evolución de los mercados en la Ciudad de México hasta 1850.* Mexico City: Consejo de la Crónica de la Ciudad de México, 1997.

Villarroel, Hipólito. *Efermedades políticas que padece la capital de esta Nueva España.* Mexico City: Conaculta, 1979.

Villegas Durán, Gregorio, Arturo Bolaños Medina, and Leonardo Loguín Prado. *La ganadería en México.* Mexico City: Plaza y Valdés, 2001.

Wade, Louise Carroll. *Chicago's Pride: The Stockyards, Packingtown, and Environs in the Nineteenth Century.* Urbana: University of Illinois Press, 1987.

Walsh, Margaret. *The Rise of the Midwestern Meat Packing Industry.* Lexington: University Press of Kentucky, 1982.

Wasserman, Mark. *Capitalists, Caciques, and Revolution: The Native Elite and Foreign Enterprise in Chihuahua, Mexico, 1854–1911.* Chapel Hill: University of North Carolina Press, 1984.

Watts, Sydney Evelyn. "Meat Matters: The Butchers of Old Regime Paris." Ph.D. diss., Cornell University, 1999.

Weiner, Richard. "Competing Market Discourses in Porfirian Mexico." *Latin American Perspectives* 26, no. 1 (January 1999): 44–64.

Wells, Allen. *Yucatan's Gilded Age: Haciendas, Henequen, and International Harvester.* Albuquerque: University of New Mexico Press, 1985.

Wells, Allen, and Gilbert M. Joseph. *Summer of Discontent, Seasons of Upheaval: Elite Politics and Rural Insurgency in Yucatán, 1876–1915.* Stanford, CA: Stanford University Press, 1996.

Womack, John, Jr. *Zapata and the Mexican Revolution.* New York: Knopf, 1968.

Yeager, Mary. *Competition and Regulation: The Development of Oligopoly in the Meat Packing Industry.* Greenwich, CT: JAI Press, Inc., 1981.

Young, James Harvey. *Pure Food: Securing the Federal Food and Drugs Act of 1906.* Princeton, NJ: Princeton University Press, 1989.

Index

130, 131, 134, 140–41, 155–57, 193
Lipton, Thomas, 119, 146, 155
livestock fairs, 32, 132–33
livestock raising, 17, 27, 29–32, 36, 37,
   61, 91–92, 132, 146, 174, 191
Locke, John, 8

Macedo, Miguel S., 79
Macedo, Pablo, 72–73, 86
MacLean, Thomas H., 73
Madero, Francisco I., 143–44, 159, 162,
   163, 167, 170
Mallory, Charles C., 122, 176
markets: capital, 120; culture, 59, 80–81,
   83–84, 192; efficiency, 2; functioning, 46, 96, 106; livestock,
   17; oligopoly, 192; preserved
   meats, 19, 120;
   temporary, 97, 190; unregulated,
   17. See also capitalism; livestock
   fairs; monopoly; supermarkets
Martínez, Domingo, 100–101
Martínez, Palemón, 78, 80, 82, 179
Mason, Alfred Bishop, 122–23, 124
Mata, Filomeno, 82
Maximilian, Emperor, 49, 51
meat: adulteration, 45, 97–98, 164,
   167–68, 189; aging, 10; cuts, 10,
   40–41; freshness, 1, 2, 4, 10, 14,
   19, 25, 147, 185, 195; preserved,
   19, 120; prices, 94, 96, 106,
   110–12, 133, 151, 177, 182; shortages, 5, 16, 17, 27, 79, 94, 96,
   110–11, 177, 179; wholesome-
   ness, 1, 2, 7, 11, 46, 59, 91, 131.
   See also beef; consumption; mutton; pork fat
meatpacking: Chicago, 11, 60–62, 90,
   123, 124, 165, 184; introduction
   to Mexico, 2, 65, 93, 98, 176,
   181; technology, 1, 61–62
meat trades. See butchers; merchants,
   livestock; merchants, retail;
   slaughterhouse workers
medical profession: asserting authority,
   3, 12, 15, 17, 44, 51–52, 189;
   Mexican advances, 18; museum,

69; objectivity, 7; veterinary,
   17–18, 51, 71. See also Board
   of Health
Meenen, Gerard, 168, 177
Méndez, Luis, 122–23, 124, 128, 131, 134
Mercado, Aristeo, 122, 130
merchants, livestock: business practices,
   33–35; cartel, 15, 17, 25, 26, 32,
   34, 54; conflicts with government, 12, 29, 46–47, 166; control of slaughterhouse, 85, 185;
   demand government intervention, 144, 154, 157–58, 192; divisions within cartel, 34, 104, 138,
   172; fear of monopoly, 25, 34,
   47, 89, 104, 108, 111; industrial
   concentration, 37, 38, 54; New
   York, 32; opposition to
   Peralvillo, 77–79, 103; organization, 4; political connections,
   33–35, 103, 153–54; relations
   with retail merchants, 3, 46, 50,
   78, 85, 111, 114, 190; relations
   with slaughterhouse workers, 3,
   50, 58, 85; retreat from liberalism, 103–5, 107, 144, 154,
   157–58, 192; use of liberalism,
   8–9, 25, 46–51, 54, 86
merchants, retail: relations with slaughterhouse workers, 3; competition,
   24, 113, 116; customer relations,
   11, 22, 54, 170, 190; organization, 4, 22–23, 40, 108, 113, 116;
   relations with wholesale merchants, 39, 42, 46, 78, 85, 111,
   114, 190
Mexican Herald, 132, 133, 135, 146,
   150, 155
Mexican National Packing Company:
   alliances with importers, 138;
   bankruptcy, 157–59, 170, 183;
   board of directors, 128; business
   plan, 13, 131, 135, 136–37; conflict
   with butchers, 143; construction
   work, 124, 125, 137–38, 146–48;
   exports, 146, 150, 191; financing,
   123–24, 125, 129, 136, 155, 156,

neoliberalism
is not imperialism
entry of foreign investments.
nation...
global immigration labor...